Intellectual Property Rights

iPOLITICS: Global Challenges in the Information Age

RENÉE MARLIN-BENNETT, SERIES EDITOR

Intellectual Property Rights

A CRITICAL HISTORY

Christopher May
Susan K. Sell

LYNNE
RIENNER
PUBLISHERS

BOULDER
LONDON

Published in the United States of America in 2006 by
Lynne Rienner Publishers, Inc.
1800 30th Street, Boulder, Colorado 80301
www.rienner.com

and in the United Kingdom by
Lynne Rienner Publishers, Inc.
3 Henrietta Street, Covent Garden, London WC2E 8LU

Library of Congress Cataloging-in-Publication Data
May, Christopher, 1960–
   Intellectual property rights : a critical history / Christopher May, Susan K. Sell.
      p. cm.— (iPolitics)
   Includes bibliographical references and index.
   ISBN 1-58826-363-0 (hardcover : alk. paper)
   1. Intellectual property—History. 2. Intellectual property—Political aspects.
   3. Intellectual property—Social aspects. I. Sell, Susan K. II. Title. III. Series.
   K1401.M393   2005
   346.04'8'09—dc22

                                                                              2005011010

British Cataloguing in Publication Data
A Cataloguing in Publication record for this book
is available from the British Library.

Printed and bound in the United States of America

⊗   The paper used in this publication meets the requirements
     of the American National Standard for Permanence of
     Paper for Printed Library Materials Z39.48-1992.

     5   4   3   2   1

Contents

Preface

NOT SO MANY years ago, when you said you were interested in intellectual property rights, other academics and your friends looked at you as if you were speaking a foreign language or, worse, had become involved in a strange secret cult. Thinking about patents, copyrights, trademarks, and other forms of intellectual property branded you as either a specialist lawyer or someone whose interests were too arcane for normal discussion. How things have changed! Nowadays, intellectual property policy makes headline news, and its reach has expanded into areas as widespread as trade, health, education, and agriculture. In short, now it is widely recognized that intellectual property rights affect virtually everyone on the planet in one way or another.

This shift in the perception of intellectual property rights as a political economic question has also been reflected in the steady rise of intellectual property issues toward the top of the advocacy agenda, most notably the question of pharmaceutical patents and access to medicines. Of course, for many of our readers (especially the younger among you) in the United States and Europe, the first major impact of intellectual property on your lives will have been the realization that digitally downloading many music files was actually *illegal!* But the deeper issues that intellectual property rights raise place the topic at the heart of the global political economy.

Back in 1997 when Chris was finishing his doctorate and Susan was starting to carve out her reputation in the academy, we both attended the annual conference of the International Studies Association (ISA) in Toronto. As is often the way at international conferences, the organizers had managed to schedule the only two papers on intellectual property on different panels, but at the same time. Luckily, our mutual friend Geoffrey Underhill was able to arrange for us to meet in a corridor that morning, and so began our deep friendship and intellectual collaboration.

Chris's 1997 ISA paper began by criticizing Susan's work as being mere "problem solving theory." Susan had read Chris's paper before our meeting and was excited finally to meet someone else who was hooked on the politics of intellectual property. She teased Chris about the swipe at her work in his ISA paper. Chris's initial feeling on being introduced was deep embarrassment, tempered by the desire to apologize over an orange juice in the conference hotel bar. From that first meeting and by means of subsequent e-mail contacts and visits to each other's homes (in Washington, D.C., and outside Bristol in the UK), we developed a working relationship that has blossomed into a mutually supportive and very productive partnership. We complement each other's views, we have learned a lot from each other, and we have each shifted our position in response to the other's clear insight into our work.

We can both still recall the wonderful lunch we had in Brown's restaurant in Oxford, in transit to a conference at the University of Warwick, when we spent a number of hours camped out with our work spread over the table. While we stayed not just for the meal but for a series of coffees, the project that would become this book started to emerge. Over the subsequent years, we have worked together and developed our understanding of the history of intellectual property, and we have now gathered all of our material into this wide-ranging history.

In the course of any project that has taken this long to develop, the authors accumulate a lot of debts to colleagues who have helped, offered advice and support, or provided intellectual sustenance. Although there are some we are sure we have missed, we would like to take this opportunity to thank for all their help: Deborah Avant, Kurt Burch, John Braithwaite, Thomas Cotter, Claire Cutler, Robert Denemark, Peter Drahos, Rochelle Dreyfuss, Graham Dutfield, Vera Franz, Randall Germain, Stephen Gill, Jacques Gorlin, Debbie Halbert, Virginia Haufler, Richard Higgott, Ian Inkster, Peter Jaszi, Hannes Lacher, Jamie Love, Christine MacLeod, Fiona Macmillan, Keith Maskus, Duncan Matthews, Jonathan Nitzan, Robert Ostergard, Ronen Palan, Heikki Patomaki, Sol Picciotto, Tony Porter, Aseem Prakash, Jerome Reichman, Anthony Seeger, Greg Shaffer, Eric Smith, Jay Smith, Alan Story, Uma Suthersanen, Brendan Tobin, Ruth Towse, Geoffrey Underhill, Rorden Wilkinson, and Peter Yu.

On a personal note, Chris would like to thank Hilary Jagger-May for her continuing support and understanding at home; without Hilary, the world of academia would be all too serious. Chris's late father remains a major intellectual influence, and his mother continues to offer her support in weekly phone calls and monthly visits. Chris knows that without the support of his parents and Hilary, he would not be able to continue to work as he does. Chris also wants to thank Nicola Phillips, Lloyd Pettiford, Jayne Rodgers, Hazel May, and Andrew Chadwick, all of whom have been good friends over the years and whose advice has been valuable.

Susan would like to thank her parents, Donald Miller Sell and Estelle Quinn Sell; her sister, Ellen Sell; and Doug Abrahms, Nicholas Quinn Abrahms, and Timothy Michael Abrahms for their support, balance, love, and good cheer. Susan also thanks Kazuhiro Obayashi for excellent research assistance. Finally, Susan would like to thank her late mentor Ernie Haas, whose intense intellectual curiosity, relentless search for truth with a small "t," and wonderfully refreshing irreverence continue to inspire and motivate her own journey. She would like to dedicate this book to his memory.

Both of us also want to acknowledge the support and enthusiasm of Lynne Rienner and her staff for this project and the excellent advice we received from two anonymous reviewers during the final drafting process.

1

Why You Need to Know About Intellectual Property

IT IS NOT an exaggeration to state that intellectual property rights are a matter of life or death. This is most obvious in the case of the patent protection of acquired immunodeficiency syndrome (AIDS)–related medicines. Since the late 1990s, pharmaceutical patents have been a lightning rod for criticism of the manner in which intellectual property rights function within the global system. The yearly cost of keeping human immunodeficiency virus (HIV)–positive patients alive on the cocktail of drugs currently available in the developed countries has in the past cost up to a thousand times the typical annual health expenditure per capita for developing countries. Under structural adjustment programs (supported by both the World Bank and the International Monetary Fund), many of these countries have also seen health-sector expenditures decline precipitously. The drugs remain prohibitively expensive, costing the lives of the patients too poor to afford the medicines to keep them living with AIDS.

To deal with this problem, in the 1990s Ghana and Brazil tried to import from Indian manufacturers cheaper generic versions of the AIDS-cocktail's component drugs. This action reflected a long history of nonprotection for foreign pharmaceutical patents in India, where a large generic manufacturing sector had developed since independence. This competition from generics prompted some multinational pharmaceutical companies to offer discounts on their AIDS drug treatments (although large-scale importation remains beyond even Brazil, which is relatively wealthy), and in some cases companies offered free shipments of drugs.

The use of generic substitutes for patented drugs also spurred legal action on behalf of Merck and others by the United States against Brazil at the World Trade Organization (WTO), however. The US Trade Representative (USTR) argued that the production and use of generics were directly in contravention of international law and that there could be no justification for the appropriation of US companies' (intellectual) property.

1

This was theft, and the USTR vigorously protested that it helped no one. Despite being subsequently dropped owing to political pressure, this action reveals much about the overall attitude of the office of the USTR: whatever the human costs, intellectual property rights (IPRs) must be upheld.

Although it seems obvious that the AIDS crisis in Africa is an exceptional public health emergency, it took considerable effort to negotiate the 2001 Doha Declaration on the TRIPs Agreement and Public Health as well as the subsequent agreement on implementing paragraph 6 of this declaration as regards cross-border supplies of generic medicines produced under compulsory license. The Agreement on Trade Related Aspects of Intellectual Property Rights (TRIPs) was negotiated as part of the establishment of the WTO and is the key element in the contemporary global governance of IPRs. Although this agreement contains provision for compulsory licenses in exceptional circumstances, under pressure from the US government and specifically the USTR, the provision has been largely disregarded since 1995. In protecting the interests of its national companies, the USTR has argued that protecting the IPRs of the large pharmaceutical companies that produce many of the AIDS-related drugs used in treatments around the world is imperative. Thus, for instance, despite its severe AIDS problem, at the end of the 1990s when Thailand acceded to the TRIPs agreement, the Thai government specifically undertook not to implement Article 8 (on compulsory licensing) for HIV/AIDS treatments.

Ignoring hostile interventions from the USTR and responding to the continuing difficulty of obtaining sufficient AIDS-related (and other) drugs, however, the South African parliament passed the Medicines and Related Substances Control Amendment Act in November 1997. The act's two most controversial provisions allowed the substitution of generic drugs and provided for the supply of cheaper alternative medicines in certain circumstances. Robert Ostergard has pointed out that,

> Section 15(c) of the Bill gave the Health Minister extraordinary powers for increasing the conditions for the supply of affordable drugs, including abrogating patent rights to pharmaceuticals issued under South Africa's Patents Act of 1978, and the importation of identical pharmaceutical compounds from manufacturers other than the registered owner [of a specific patent]. (Ostergard 1999, 879)

Even before the bill was passed, the US ambassador had been instructed to make strong representations against these measures. The South African parliament saw this as a public health issue, whereas the US government, representing US pharmaceutical corporations, regarded it as theft. Legislators and governments in both countries faced a clear, if politically difficult, choice: whose rights were to be protected, the owners of IPRs or those who could be saved by these drugs?

In March 2001 the South African government was challenged in court by an international alliance of thirty-nine companies who disputed the legality of the amendment to the Medicines Act. After an adjournment for the companies to see documents filed by "friends of the court" for the government side, the plaintiffs withdrew their challenge. These documents revealed that the defense case was likely to be fought on the basis of the profits made on specific drugs relative to the costs of developing them. The alliance decided that whatever the costs in Africa, this sort of information was unlikely to help their case at the global level. As Médecins Sans Frontières had already noted, combination cocktails are made up of drugs that were originally developed largely with the help of public funds in the United States (Boseley 2000). The case the companies were about to make was that without patent protection there would be a dangerous decline in important medical research. The logic of this argument would have been seriously undermined, however, by the revelation of the amount of public money received by these companies for conducting the research from which they were now profiting. In a compromise deal, a joint working party was set up to reexamine the act. Nevertheless, South Africa's legal success prompted the Kenyan government to swiftly pass legislation that, although formally complying with TRIPs, explicitly laid out the terms by which the government could mobilize the agreement's public health provisions.

This very public exploration of the balance between private rights to reward and public welfare (the need to support the health of a country's population) reveals the central problem with the uncritical acceptance of the expansion of an intellectual property dimension to the governance of international trade. The current system governing the trade in patent-protected pharmaceuticals privileges the rights of large companies to continue to make a profit (an industry widely regarded as the most profitable in the world) against the rights of poor people to receive treatment for a fatal disease.

This is the most high-profile argument over the justification and use of IPRs in the global political realm. The current political and legal settlement regarding IPRs affects our and others' well-being in many other ways. From technology transfer and its impact on economic development to biopiracy and the control of developing countries' natural resources, from issues concerning the future of the global music industry in the face of widespread downloading of music files from the Internet to the control of the software we might want to use at home and at work, we have all become increasingly aware of the impact on our lives of IPRs. These problems have become more obvious since 1995 owing to a robust global structure for the governance of IPRs.

Intellectual Property: Global Governance and History

Since 1995, intellectual property rights have been subject to the TRIPs agreement, which is overseen by the WTO. Although this agreement does not determine national legislation, to be TRIPs compliant WTO members' domestic intellectual property law must establish the minimum level of protection for IPRs laid out in TRIPs' seventy-three articles. The agreement not only covers general provisions and basic principles but also provides legal mechanisms for the enforcement of IPRs. It is important to note that the WTO's tough cross-sectoral dispute settlement mechanism encompasses international disputes about IPRs. Prior to 1995, there were long-standing multilateral treaties in place regarding the international recognition and protection of IPRs, overseen by the World Intellectual Property Organization (WIPO). These were widely regarded as toothless, however, in the face of "piracy" and the frequent disregard for the protection of non-nationals' intellectual property outside the most developed countries (and even sometimes between them). In the wake of this globalization of governance, the political economy of IPRs has become much more visible and the stakes have risen.

In his discussion of the various forms of property, Boudewijn Bouckaert noted that the "origin of intellectual property rights has its historical roots in deliberate interventions by political authorities rather than in a spontaneously evolved continental legal tradition" (Bouckaert 1990, 790). We agree, and to reinforce and substantiate this argument, we shall recount the history of intellectual property, exploring how this has been entwined with the political, philosophical, and economic history of modern capitalism. Long before there was a formal legal definition of intellectual property, there were many attempts to control valuable knowledge and information by groups who stood to gain from its exploitation. New technologies influenced the development of legal innovations that eventually coalesced into the recognizable beginning of modern intellectual property law in Venice in the late fifteenth century. Technological developments are not the only factor, however; the idea of the individual as "creator" and the growing appreciation of the worth of information in increasingly complex markets also stimulated the emergence of ideas about the possibility of "owning" knowledge and information.

Our history therefore stresses the multifaceted character of the development of property in knowledge. This history is more extensive than is often appreciated, and our historical project rejects those accounts of various forms of IPRs that present them as universal, or even natural, rights. The story of a slow but steady realization of natural rights, producing an atemporal understanding of intellectual property, wrenches intellectual property out of human history. We emphasize how IPRs have always been historically and politically contingent. The recent interest in the history of IPRs is part of the violent and highly politicized struggle over intellectual property that has been going on for centuries.

Across this history the same problems and disputes recur. Similar tensions between private rights to reward and the public, or social, role of knowledge and information appear repeatedly across the half millennia of the formal history of IPRs. We contend that to think fruitfully about the future of the global governance of IPRs, we must examine their past. This perspective is necessary to counter the arguments about the global regulation of IPRs that present a mythical version of this history. For instance, as Jerome Reichman has pointed out:

> Resistance to proposals that would protect folklore and native arts under rights related to copyright law, for example, is often couched in terms of avoiding unacceptable deviations from Western legal traditions and doctrinal orthodoxy. Such purist foot-dragging infuriates the representatives of the poorer countries, who are well aware that the developed countries recently turned orthodox copyright principles on their head in order to accommodate their own manufacturers of computer programs. (Reichman 2000, 452 [footnotes omitted])

Therefore, the history that we explore is not a history leading inexorably to TRIPs, but rather an international history of the idea of making knowledge and information ownable. This history is contingent, contested, and constantly evolving. We begin by laying out the basics of intellectual property, to ensure that all our readers have a clear, if summary, appreciation of IPRs. Readers already familiar with the various forms of intellectual property may wish to skip to the end of this short chapter.

What Are Intellectual Property Rights?

Intellectual property constructs a scarce resource from knowledge or information that is not formally scarce. Unlike material things, knowledge and information are not necessarily rivalrous, and therefore coincident usage seldom detracts from social utility. Whereas two prospective users must compete to use a material resource (and this competition may be mediated through markets and the setting of a price), two or more users of any particular item of knowledge or information can use it simultaneously without competing.

Take the example of a hammer (as material property); if I own a hammer, and you and I would both like to use it, our utility is compromised by sharing use. I cannot use the hammer while you are; you cannot while I am; our intended use is rival. For you also to use my hammer, you have to accept a compromised utility (relying on my goodwill to allow you to use it when I am not); otherwise you must also buy a hammer. The hammer is scarce. The idea of building something with hammer and nails is not scarce, however. If I instruct you in the art of simple construction, once that knowledge has been imparted, your use of that information has no effect on my own ability to use the knowledge at the same time; there is no compromise to my utility. We may be fighting over whose turn it is to use the hammer, but we do not have to argue over whose turn it is to use the idea of hammering a nail into a joint; our use of the idea of cabinet construction is nonrival. Thus we can say that in general, ideas, knowledge, and information are nonrivalrous.

To be sure, if you and I were both cabinetmakers, then instructing you in cabinet construction might lead you to compete for my customers, possibly reducing my income. Here, the skills and knowledge are to some extent rival, inasmuch as if we both deploy these skills, then the advantage I have gained by being the owner is diminished because now you can also compete in the supply of the fruits of that skill. If I refused to teach you how to make cabinets, we might say that my secrecy regarding these skills was anticompetitive. There are also other cases where knowledge may produce advantages for the holder (often called information asymmetries), by enabling the holder to extract a better price or by allowing the holder to gain a market advantage. In both cases, information and knowledge *are* rivalrous, and wider availability of this knowledge would result in compromised market advantage.

Rivalrousness is not necessarily socially beneficial, however. Competition is often beneficial to customers, whereas information asymmetries produce market choices that are not fully informed and that therefore can be inefficient, or even harmful. Thus, when information is naturally rivalrous, the social good may be best served by ensuring that it is shared, not hoarded. For instance, many problems for buyers in the secondhand car market could be ameliorated if all car dealers were required to reveal *all* they knew about the cars they were selling. Doing so would likely reduce the price they could obtain for much of their stock but would enhance the general satisfaction (and even safety) of those who buy secondhand cars.

Leaving aside special cases like those above, generally speaking it is difficult to extract a price for the use of nonrival (knowledge) goods, so a legal form of scarcity is introduced to ensure that a price can be obtained for use. When knowledge and/or information becomes subject to ownership, IPRs express ownership's legal benefits. The three central elements to these benefits are (1) the ability to charge rent for use, (2) the right to receive compensation for loss, and (3) the right to demand payment for transfer to another party through the market. Although IPRs are subdivided into a number of categories, two generate most discussion: industrial intellectual property (patents) and literary or artistic intellectual property (copyrights). Conventionally, the difference between patents and copyrights is presented as between a patent's protection of an idea and a copyright's protection of the expression of an idea. This idea-expression distinction has in recent years started to become problematic, but until recently it was regarded as reasonably robust in discussions of IPRs.

The argument that there are social benefits to be gained from the development and dissemination of new knowledge and information underpins the legal construction of IPRs. To this end, all IPRs encompass a balance between private rights for reward and public needs for the (unconstrained) availability of important knowledge and information. This balance between private reward and public interest has been traditionally expressed through time limits on IPRs: unlike material property, IPRs are temporary. Once their term has expired, that which had been protected is added to the public realm of freely available knowledge and can no longer be owned as property. Broadly speaking, the more important it is for society that specific knowledge or information should be freely available, the shorter the time that the legal institution of IPRs will protect it. Thus, at one end of this continuum, patents have relatively short terms of protection (limited under TRIPs to twenty years). At the other end, where the unrestricted use of specific informational marks would be contrary to the social interest, protection (with certain conditions) is effective in perpetuity (subject to periodic renewal). For example, the effective social use of trademarks requires that companies identify themselves as the makers, or suppliers, of specific goods or services with their authorized mark, not those of a competitor.

For patents, the knowledge that is to be registered and thus made property should be applicable in industry. To be patentable an idea must be:

- *New:* The idea to be patented should not already be in the public domain or the subject of a previous patent.
- *Nonobvious:* The idea (be it a technique or answer to a specific technical problem) should not be commonsense to any accomplished practitioner in the field who, having been asked to solve a particular practical problem, would see this solution immediately. The idea should not be self-evident using available skills or technologies.
- *Useful, or applicable in industry:* The device for which the patent is requested must have a stated function and could immediately be produced to fulfill this function.

Following the 1995 TRIPs agreement, if these three conditions are fulfilled, then an idea can be patented in any member country of the WTO. Although the minutiae of protection may vary, the TRIPs agreement very clearly lays out the legal outcomes that any national intellectual property law should produce. All members must establish mechanisms that enable the registration of patents and the litigation of infringement. Generally speaking, patents are lodged at a national patent office (or with the European Patent Office), which for an agreed fee will allow others access to the patented knowledge as expressed in the patent document. Perhaps more important, the lodging of the patent document at the office establishes the legal right to punish unauthorized usage of the specified idea, although it is left to the patentee to litigate.

Patents are an institutionalized bargain between the state and inventors. The state agrees to establish the legal mechanisms that ensure that the inventors can extract payment for their idea when others use it (for the lifetime of the patent), and the inventors allow the state to lodge the idea in its public records, where it can be accessed by interested parties. Patents are sometimes referred to as industrial property and are intended to cover technological advances that can be deployed in manufacturing or other commercial operations. This may cover specific machines (or new components of machines), processes, or other aspects of technology. One of the most important areas of debate regarding patents is therefore the scope of what is "patentable." Recent disputes have questioned whether business methods are technologies that can be patented, whether software solutions (of which "one-click" ordering is perhaps the most notorious) are really technologies at all, and whether developments in biotechnology (ranging from aspects of the human genome to compounds developed from developing countries' seed base) can be regarded as fulfilling all three of the above criteria for patentability. On one side is the clear intent that inventors and innovators should receive some benefit for their activity; on the other is the profound difficulty of adjudicating on originality and the characteristics of new technological advances.

Unlike patent, copyright is concerned with the form of knowledge and information that would normally be termed "literary and artistic works." This is usually expressed in words, symbols, music, pictures, three-dimensional objects, or some combination of these different forms. Copyright therefore covers literary works (fiction and nonfiction), musical works (of all sorts), artistic works (of two- *and* three-dimensional form and irrespective of content—from "pure art" and advertising to amateur drawings and your child's doodles), maps, technical drawings, photography, audiovisual works (including cinematic works, video, and forms of multimedia), and audio recordings. Under TRIPs, protection is also accorded to broadcasts and can be extended to typographical arrangements of publications. The underlying idea, the plot, the conjunction of colors does not receive protection; only the specific expression attracts copyright. It is important to note that computer software is also protected by copyright, an approach consolidated in the TRIPs agreement and thus universalized across the members of the WTO.

Copyright is intended to ensure that protected matter should not be reproduced without the express permission of the creator (or the owner of the copyright, which may have been legally transferred to another party). This is often limited to an economic right, by which the creator (or copyright owner) is legally entitled to a share of any return that is earned by the utilization or reproduction of the copyrighted knowledge. In some jurisdictions, however (principally in continental Europe), there is an additional moral right not to have work tampered with or misrepresented. In all cases, failure to agree to terms prior to the act of reproduction or duplication may result in any income being awarded to the original copyright holder by the court if an infringement is deemed to have taken place. Unlike patents, however, copyright resides in the work from the moment of creation. To prove an infringement, the creator, or copyright owner, is required to demonstrate that the disputed item (or portion of an item) is an actual reproduction of the original work in terms of content and that the copying was intentional. If a second person has spontaneously produced the same expression, without knowledge of, or contact with, the original, then no infringement is deemed to have taken place.

Contemporary copyrights also last much longer than patents. The key reason for this is that whereas patents cover information and/or knowledge that may be directly useful for socioeconomic development, those items covered by copyright have been regarded as less vital for society to access. Nowadays copyright is usually protected for the life of the author, plus fifty years (the minimum terms under TRIPs). In its early history, there were periods when perpetual copyrights were claimed, however, and also periods when rights could only be enjoyed for fourteen years. As with patents, copyright scope has been subject to dispute. Recent debates have revolved around the protection of television listings and the protection of collections of publicly available information in the form of directories (for example, phone books). Should such compilations of public material be covered by copyright to reflect the work required for compiling and organizing such collections? Other disputes have involved the limitation of rights that copyright holders have been able to enjoy, to allow fair use or fair dealing (for private use or for research purposes), and whether the rights are exhausted after the first sale. These arguments have been fraught, pitching users against owners in often virulent conflicts.

Although patents and copyrights are the two most obvious forms of IPRs, they are by no means the only IPRs that have been developed over the centuries. Trademarks distinguish the products of one company from another and can be made up of one or more distinctive words, letters, numbers, drawings or pictures, emblems, or other graphic representations. The marking of goods far predates any notion of intellectual property and for millennia has been used to differentiate goods from different makers. Generally, contemporary trademarks need to be registered, and in the act of registration a check is carried out to ensure that there are no other companies currently registering the same word, symbol, or other representation as a trademark in the sector(s) of the economy nominated by the registering company. A history of use of a trademark may establish its viability and support its subsequent legal recognition, and conversely such a history of use by a contending company (even if the mark has not been registered) may undermine a claim to register a specific mark. If a particular trademark is too similar to, or liable to cause confusion with, a trademark already registered by another company, it is unlikely to succeed in being registered. A trademark also cannot be registered if the term or symbol is already in common social use. In some jurisdictions the outward manifestation of packaging, provided that it is not a form necessarily dictated by function, may also be subject to trademark status (for example, the Coca Cola bottle).

Trademarks serve a very clear social purpose, conveying information about the character and reputation of the good or service to which they are attached. Certainly, once reputation and goodwill have been established, the trademark itself may acquire commercial value. Many activists now argue that the brand is one way to make trademark holders accountable. Trademarks may take some time to establish, for the "back story" of quality and reliability to become valuable. Activists can attack such reputations through the media, and thus companies may be made accountable through these actions. Trademark disputes can also revolve around the use by others of similar (or even the same) trademarks, in order to pass off their goods as being similar or identical to the trademark holders's goods. In the realm of the Internet, a series of disputes has concerned the link between trademarks and Web page addresses, with some trademark owners in the past having to buy the Web address from opportunistic individuals who had gotten to the Web registry first. This problem has been partially solved through legal action and the more formalized management of Web addresses.

Other forms of intellectual property also designate information or knowledge as ownable property. Process patents are a specific form of patents but cover processes as opposed to actual machines. These are most often used for chemical processes for which the ingredients may be freely available, but the complex admixture is protected. Industrial design protection is related to copyright. It covers specific appearances of products, those that are not purely functional, and also covers textile designs. Unlike copyright, such designs are only protected for a limited period (ten years under TRIPs). The TRIPs agreement also requires signatories to protect layout designs of integrated circuits ("topographies" or "mask works") for a similar period. In both cases something akin to an expression, because of its industrial use, is protected for a very limited period, more like patent than copyright.

Intellectual property also includes geographical indicators (such as *Champagne*) that distinguish local products from generic or other variants. The main issue here has become the identification of specific processes (most often in food and drink) with one area, even though other manufacturers and producers also use these processes. In these cases, although the process may be similar, protection of geographical indicators restricts the use of the term to those products actually produced in the designated area. Thus, champagne produced elsewhere cannot call itself champagne, or Parma ham produced outside that region of Italy cannot claim to be Parma ham even if it is produced in a comparable manner. In recent years there has been some disquiet at the extra protection provided to wines and spirits in agriculturally related international trade and also questions regarding the identification of processes with specific regions or countries, when the ingredients are imported (such as Swiss chocolate made with imported cocoa).

Finally, it is sometimes also useful to think of trade secrets as intellectual property (and indeed the TRIPs agreement's article 39 covers the protection of "undisclosed information"). Although a form that is not made public, trade secrets allow the control or ownership of knowledge. This protection is frequently enhanced by the utilization of labor or service contract provisions for those who come into contact with the secret. In one way the trade secret is the ultimate private knowledge property. Although in some celebrated cases a trade secret can provide a competitive advantage (and again the example of Coca Cola is apposite, along with Kentucky Fried Chicken's "secret blend of herbs and spices"), in the main, however, those who rely on knowledge as a resource adopt an intellectual property approach to protection (a quid pro quo: protection in exchange for disclosure). Indeed, for the knowledge industries it would be counterproductive, impossible even, to function on the basis of knowledge being secret, given the importance of reproduction and transfer of that knowledge to generate income and profit. Intellectual property constructs a balance between public availability and private benefit that allows wider access to knowledge and information than trade secrecy. But, this availability exists only within specific legal limits constructed by intellectual property.

Setting the Stage

For laws regarding the ownership of knowledge to make sense, social ideas about the possibility of knowledge or information being attached to particular individuals (through ownership) needed to be developed. Before its first formalization in the Venetian statute of 1474, there was little that could be regarded as intellectual property proper, despite some interesting prototypical approximations. Ideas about owning knowledge were not novel in the fifteenth century, however.

Rulers seeking to secure new technologies for the enrichment of the territories that they controlled spurred the development of intellectual property. Initially, patents were grants of privilege that in some cases rulers offered to allow the dissemination of particular technical advances, benefiting ruling groups through wealth creation. Under this rationale, when grants of privilege were not merely sinecures for supporters and favorites, these grants emphasized a "public-regarding" intent to further the encouragement of learning and the development of industry. In these cases, rights to reward were not justified on the basis of "natural rights" or the "moral rights" of the putative author or inventor but rather reflected a perceived social need or future benefit. Justifications based on the author or creator would be mobilized only as intellectual property was formalized, broadened its range (geographically and by the scope of protection), and was developed into the contemporary system. Nevertheless, ideas about owning knowledge crop up again and again in history, not least of all with the focus on the individual as creator and the tension this creates with the social value of the wide availability of knowledge and information. These ideas long predate the legal structures to which they are now applied.

It may be that copyright originally represented the formalization of previously recognized moral or customary rights of authors (Streibich 1975). The condemnation of plagiarism and the acknowledgment of the theft of ideas certainly stretches back to the beginnings of recorded history. Nevertheless, the early recognition of the ownership of ideas is almost entirely concerned with the retention of secret knowledge, rather than the rights to reward that remain with the author/creator once a work or innovation is disseminated. Thus, although it may be that preliterate societies develop something that resembles a crude form of intellectual property, primarily in the way that magical practices (and practitioners' ownership of such methods) are controlled (Suchman 1989), this is something separate. Rules and laws similar to intellectual property rights also may have emerged in circumstances other than the early history of Western capitalism (see, for instance, Alford 1995; Hazan 1970). It is the conceptions of intellectual property rights that emerged from that history, however, that have evolved into the system that we now face. Therefore we concentrate our study on what happened, not what might have happened. Although worthy of further research, the history of intellectual property rights in the East is much less well understood and beyond the scope of this study.

The particular European history and prehistory of contemporary capitalism and its technologies, linking and intersecting with the manner in which societies have governed themselves (through legal mechanisms) and the changing perceptions of how innovation or creativity is linked to individuals (the changing idea of where knowledge actually comes from), lie behind the current global settlement regarding IPRs, encapsulated in TRIPs. In Chapter 2 we discuss the general justifications for intellectual property rights and our perspective on historical development. We then proceed to present the history of IPRs before in the final chapters returning to the more general contemporary issues that stimulated our interest in history in the first place.

2

Ideas and Technology

BEFORE PRESENTING our history of intellectual property, in this chapter we examine how intellectual property has come to be justified in the realm of political philosophy. Contemporary justifications of intellectual property, and the policy implications of these diverse views, are significant. These definitions and justifications do not represent a natural or inevitable development; they are contingent on the history of intellectual property itself and not outside such a history. In the second part of the chapter, we discuss our approach to this history, with a focus on the triangulation among legislation, technology, and ideas. Our method offers a historically grounded appreciation of the contemporary political economy of intellectual property rights (IPRs).

Discussing an upswing in interest in the history of copyright, Kathy Bowrey asked who's writing copyright's history and concluded that what was needed was

> a history that addresses what the social pressures were that led to the development of copyright law. We need a discussion of how the law responded to that challenge, and a discussion of the social ramifications of the legal position. We also need to evaluate the significance of opposition to copyright as it has been expressed in law, and to reflect on whether that opposition has engendered new approaches or whether it has merely made manifest sites of resistance to the existing law. (Bowrey 1996, 327)

Like Bowrey, we seek to examine the social context in which laws have developed and examine the interaction between the political economy and the legal sphere.

Bowrey argued that this history need not be written exclusively by legal scholars; indeed, written from inside, the history of intellectual property represents the maintenance of a disciplinary boundary that presents law as something different, something disconnected and special. Thomas

15

Meshbesher made a similar point about comparative legal studies of patent law and concluded that "too often laymen (and a good many general lawyers as well) tend to view all patent law questions as arcane, technical, legalistic, or even purely linguistic or lexical. . . . Yet the truth is that virtually all patent law questions of practical significance are infused with . . . public policy considerations" (Meshbesher 1996, 614). Similarly, we reject these divisions between the technically legal and the political, between the definitional and the realm of public policy. As political economists, we situate the law of intellectual property in the international political economy.

We resist the depoliticized view that scholars adopting a law and economics approach often promote. For example, even though Richard Posner has recognized the problems of rent seeking and enclosure in the deployment and use of IPRs, he concluded that "striking the right balance, which is to say determining the optimal scope of intellectual property rights, requires a comparison of these benefits and costs—and, really, it seems to me, nothing more. The problems are not conceptual; the concepts are straightforward. The problems are entirely empirical. They are problems of measurement" (Posner 2002, 12). This misses the centrality of how the legal institution of intellectual property is established, developed, and maintained through extensive *political* and *rhetorical* processes and strategies. Rent seeking, monopolies, and anticompetitive use of IPRs are implicated in almost any account of IPRs, but Posner's normalization of IPRs themselves misses their fundamentally *political* nature.

A decade ago Paul David also noted that various accounts of IPRs failed to make analytical links among economic arguments, legal scholarship, and the complex history of protection (David 1993, 23). He stressed the importance of the historical context for any study of IPRs, saying that

> although the history of intellectual property rights in the West is replete with instances of redefinitions and reinterpretation in response to pressures to accommodate or advance the economic interests of those most affected by the laws, many of the structure's gross features continue to reflect the remote historical circumstances in which they originated. These legacies from the past should not be ignored, nor should their problematic aspects in contemporary contexts be minimized. (David 1993, 44)

Furthermore, he concluded that the

> protections accorded to intellectual property by nation-states have not manifested any great consistency in adhering to pure principle. Rather, they have pragmatically altered over time in response to changing perceptions of the way the creation and dissemination of information and information products affect "national interests." (David 1993, 56)

Additionally, legal structures shifted and changed as a political response to the challenge of new technologies and new social deployments of technologies. We believe that a political economic approach is well placed to apprehend this complexity in the development and evolution of intellectual property rights.

The study of intellectual property has been marked by sharp disciplinary divisions that are just now giving way to a broader range of perspectives. Nonlawyers are increasingly analyzing intellectual property from a variety of disciplinary and interdisciplinary perspectives. Given the importance of intellectual property for everything from access to textbooks and medicines, to the protection of folklore and germplasm, this is a welcome trend. Disputes over access to pharmaceuticals, and other important social resources, have highlighted the role of intellectual property rights in contemporary capitalism. Equally, these disputes have demonstrated significant differences over the legitimacy of arguments that seek to justify intellectual property's legal existence.

Justifying Intellectual Property

Law reflects social norms and at times is explicitly intended to (re)shape such norms. Law does not exist in a vacuum; it is affected by shifts in social understandings of legitimate interests or justice. Although laws may appear set, judges are able to interpret law's scope and definitions to shadow shifts in social mores (prior to legislative reformulation).[1] Laws require constant and explicit justification in order to function without the continual application of force or threat of sanction, and such justification often takes place through appeals to nonlegal ideas about the role or purpose of legal control. Therefore, when knowledge or information is to be the subject of legal rules that construct scarcity, nonlegal justifications are deployed, often taking the form of ideas about reward for effort or the "efficient" use of knowledge resources.

Property itself is hardly natural: as Walter Hamilton stressed many years ago, it has always been "incorrect to say that the judiciary protected property; rather they called that property to which they accorded protection" (quoted in Cribbet 1986, 4). Property in a legal sense can only be what the law says it is; it does not exist waiting to be recognized as such. Property is the codification of particular social relations, those between owner and nonowner, reproduced as the owners' rights. Karl Polanyi suggested that the idea that labor, land, and money might be commodities required a "commodity fiction" to be developed during the transformation from feudalism to capitalism (Polanyi [1944] 1957, 72ff.). The rendering of things not originally produced for sale as commodities required a story to be told about these resources that was not necessarily linked to their real historical existence or processes of production but rather narrated a propensity to be organized through markets. Similarly, to have a market in knowledge, another commodity fiction is crucial, although the stories that are told about intellectual property are hardly uncontested.

The term *intellectual property* itself is a recent rhetorical construct. Although the term itself was likely in use by the mid-nineteenth century (Hesse 2002, 39), in the first half of the twentieth century the term *industrial property* more often held sway and was only finally superseded in the second half of the twentieth century (David 2000). Lysander Spooner, an American librarian who apparently first used the term *intellectual property* in print in 1855, argued that scientists and inventors should enjoy permanent property rights in their ideas (Dutfield 2003, 53). *Intellectual property* appears only once in US federal court reports prior to 1900, however, and is absent in reports between 1900 and 1930. Then the upswing in use (at least in US courts) gets under way: the term is used twice in the 1930s, 6 times in the 1940s, 10 in the 1950s, 9 times in the 1960s, 41 times in the 1970s, 287 in the 1980s, and over 800 times in the 1990s (Fisher 1999, n105). Reflecting on the introduction of the term *intellectual* into this overall depiction of a set of laws, Paul David speculated that the "obvious objective of giving 'intellectual' spin to such items of property is to try to induce some greater resonance with the more culturally valued and hence 'protection-worthy' expressions of literary and artistic creativity. But, the main rhetorical coup is achieved by designating the whole incoherent collection 'property'" (David 2000, 14). The notion of ownership is also sometimes presented as the duty of parenthood. In the realm of copyright, for instance, Mark Rose pointed out that advocates of highly protective regimes assert the rhetoric of "paternity" over intellectual creations and include arguments alluding to property (as metaphorically linked with real property/real estate) (Rose 2002). Owners of ideas and knowledge have deftly employed commodity fictions to their advantage.

Fictionalization is also central to the Agreement on Trade Related Aspects of Intellectual Property Rights (TRIPs). This agreement encapsulates a forceful invocation of the argument that knowledge can be usefully rendered as property. The agreement is a powerful instrument to construct a metaphorical link between property in knowledge and the legal mechanisms that have been widely developed to protect material property rights. It is the first truly global intellectual property agreement (with robust enforcement mechanisms through the World Trade Organization [WTO]), and the first to cover all forms of IPRs under the same set of legal mechanisms. Soon after it came into force, Kurt Burch argued that the agreement was "a remarkable symbolic document" promoting a specific view of property and market relations as part of a (neo) liberal agenda of global governance (Burch 1995, 216). The agreement, in itself substantially drafted by lawyers and economists representing a group of twelve US multinational corporations (Sell 2003, chap. 2), is an overwhelmingly Anglo-Saxon legal discourse, presenting a specific view of the justification of IPRs and the efficiency benefits from making knowledge and information property.

Much of the legal discussion of intellectual property assumes that there is a clear metaphorical continuity between property in things and property in knowledge. But one of the central functions of the institution of property in knowledge is to construct a scarcity where none necessarily exists. Scarcity needs to be constructed because knowledge, unlike physical property, generally is not rivalrous. In a capitalist economy the construction of rivalrousness is the central role of intellectual property. Although contemporaneous usage detracts little from overall social utility, without imposed rivalry the ability to profit from the use or sale of socially useful information or knowledge would be constrained or impossible. Indeed, as the costs (and technological limitations) of copying/duplication decline, some argue that IPRs must become stronger to continue to construct this scarcity.[2] The imposition of scarcity in knowledge through the use of IPRs is not some accident or by-product of their legal constitution; it is exactly what IPRs are intended to accomplish.

Donald Black suggested that law inversely varies with other forms of social control (Black 1976, 107–111). Therefore it should not be surprising that in an age when the control of knowledge can be quite lucrative, but the social norms for making information or knowledge scarce are unstable, the recourse to law is increasingly important (and the punishments for infringement increasingly harsh). As Tom Tyler's discussion of the psychology of compliance with the law set out (specifically in relation to copyright), however, given the essentially private character of the activity of copying (infringing copyrights), the threat of punishment is discounted owing to the continuing problems of enforcement (Tyler 1997, 224). On one hand, this has led to the development of digital rights management technologies. On the other, the problems of enforcement reveal the reliance of copyright (and IPRs more generally) on compliance underpinned by social norms. Like Jessica Litman (1991), Tyler suggested that there is a serious discrepancy between what the law (and IPR owners) understand the legal limitations on use to be and how consumers often perceive these limitations. Hence, Tyler argued that "the public's awareness of the reasons underlying intellectual property rules needs to be developed more effectively, so that the basis for a positive moral climate can be created" (Tyler 1997, 229). The very campaign that Tyler wants to develop has a long history, however, linked to and working through the narratives of justification that we explore in the next section.

As we have noted, for prices to be established (and market relations supported), the law must construct scarcity (or rivalrousness) if none already exists. The bifurcation of rival/nonrival is not as simple as it might seem; it may be better seen as a continuum with rival goods shading into nonrival across a spectrum (Picciotto and Campbell 2003). Specific forms (or items) of knowledge or information may move across this spectrum on the basis of new or changing technologies that may allow extensions of nonrival use or conversely may enhance the advantages to be gained from (imposed) rivalrousness. The common use of information and knowledge across society is one of the key elements of a shared social existence. The recognition that the legal construction of (information) scarcity may constrain this social utility has prompted the frequent utilization of other reasons to justify a regime of property in knowledge.

Conventionally, there are two philosophical approaches to justifying property and one more pragmatic justification, all of which are used to legitimize and support intellectual property in varying combinations (May 2000, 22–29 and passim). Commentators, legal documents, and judgments all employ these material property-related narratives to justify the recognition of property in knowledge. These justifications underlie the TRIPs agreement and have been mobilized in the cases brought to the WTO's dispute settlement mechanism. They play a profound and important role in the way the global regime of protection of IPRs is governed (and developed through legal precedent).

The first set of justifications argues for labor's desert: the effort that is put into the improvement of nature should be rewarded. In John Locke's still influential formulation, this was modeled on the improvement of land. The application of effort to produce crops and/or improved resource yields justified the ownership of specific tracts of land by whoever worked to produce such improvement. Starting from this initial position, Locke then argued that there was also a right in disposal, mediated by money. Thus, all property, even after its initial sale or transfer, could be justified on the basis that it had originally been produced through the labor of an individual. More important, property was also justified because it encouraged the improvement of nature through the reward of effort. The Lockean argument supports property by suggesting that property encourages individual effort through the reward of ownership of the fruits of work (Locke 1988, second treatise, chap. 4). Locke never explicitly discussed patents in any of his published work.[3] In contemporary debates around intellectual property, the argument that patents and other intellectual properties reward the effort that has been put into their development (the research investment made to develop a patented innovation; the marketing expense in establishing a trademark) is a commonplace.[4]

Sometimes this argument is supported through the mobilization of a second set of justifications, however: the notion of property's links with the self as originally proposed by Georg Hegel. Here the control and ownership of property relate to the establishment of individual social existence. Property rights are how individuals protect themselves from the invasions and attacks of others. For Hegel, the state legislates for property as part of its bargain with civil society. Individuals allow the state to operate in certain areas but protect their individuality (and sovereignty) through the limitations that property rights put upon the state vis-à-vis the individual's own life and possessions (Hegel 1967, 40ff.). In intellectual property law on the European continent, this supports the inalienable moral rights that creators retain over their copyrights even after the formal transfer of title to new owners. In Anglo-Saxon law, this mode of justification has been less widely deployed owing to its implications for the final alienability of intellectual property. Nonetheless, especially in the passing off of trademarks (the unauthorized use of logos and brand names, often on substandard goods) and the pirating of copyrighted material (sampling of music, for instance), this justification can sometimes be noted in the calls for redress based on the diminution of reputation or the ownership of (self-) expression.

There is a third set of additional and important justifications that often underpins the role of intellectual property in the contemporary political economy. In this pragmatic or economic argument, the emergence of property rights is presented as a response to the needs of individuals wishing to allocate resources among themselves (May 2000, 18–21). Douglass North has argued that the enjoyment of benefits (and the assumption of costs) takes place in social relations through the mobilization of useful resources and that the institution of property arose to ensure that such resources have attached to them the benefits (and the costs) that accrue to their use, which increases "efficiency" (North 1990, 34–35). In this influential story, property rights took the place of social (trust) relations and allowed complex trade relations to form over distance. This suggests that efficient resource allocation is established through the use of markets by which property is exchanged and transferred to those who can make best use of it. The development of modern economies is predicated, therefore, on the institution of property and its ability to ensure the efficient use of limited resources. In this justification, it is this efficiency requirement that drives the historical development of property rights and now underpins the commodification of knowledge.

This history presents property's emergence as essentially functional, *not* political. Property rights are presented as the most efficient method of allocation available, even though they often produce a less than perfect solution to resource distribution. In the interests of efficiency, property as an institution is reproduced (and improved) through its legal and social use. This narrative is then brought to bear on the allocation and use of knowledge by knowledge-based industrial sectors and individual commercial entities. If we are to ensure the efficient commercial use of important knowledge and information, then market mechanisms are required. And for there to be a market, we must render knowledge and information as property.

Another common argument utilized to substantiate IPRs is the need to support innovation, and this is a subset of this third justification (but also linked to the first). Drawing from Locke the notion of reward for effort in improvement, and from the third justification the idea of social efficiency, it is then asserted that without IPRs there would be little stimulus for innovation. Why would anyone work toward a new invention who would be unable to profit from its social deployment? Therefore, not only does intellectual property reward intellectual effort, it actually stimulates activities that have a social value, and most important, it serves to support the social good of progress. Underlying this argument is a clear perception of what drives human endeavor: individual reward. Only by encouraging and rewarding the individual creator or inventor (with property, and therefore market-related benefits) can any society ensure that it will continue to develop important and socially valuable innovations, which will serve to make society as a whole more efficient. Donald Richards (2002) linked this third set of justifications back to Jeremy Bentham and utilitarianism, although we see a much less clear line of development than the explicit philosophical foundations of the first two narratives, which in itself may be a comment on the ubiquity of utilitarianism in contemporary political discourse.

One of the central purposes of IPRs therefore is to construct a scarcity (or rivalrousness) that allows a price to be taken and knowledge to be exchanged in market mechanisms to further social efficiency. In a clear statement of this requirement (utilizing the labor desert argument), Kenneth Arrow noted that if "information is not property, the incentives to create it will be lacking. Patents and copyrights are social innovations designed to create artificial scarcities where none exist naturally. . . . These scarcities are intended to create the needed incentives for acquiring information" (Arrow 1996, 125). The construction of scarcity by transforming knowledge into a commodity plays a vital role in the operation of modern capitalism. That the normative foundations of IPRs need constant attention flows from an important difference between property in knowledge or information and material property. As Arnold Plant stressed many years ago, unlike real property rights, patents (and other IPRs)

> are not a *consequence* of scarcity. They are the deliberate creation of statute law; and, whereas in general the institution of private property makes for the preservation of scarce goods, tending (as we might some-

what loosely say) to lead us "to make the most of them," property rights in patents and copyright make possible the *creation* of scarcity of the products appropriated which could not otherwise be maintained. Whereas we might expect the public action concerning private property would normally be directed at the prevention of the raising of prices, in these cases the object of the legislation is to confer the power of raising prices by enabling the creation of scarcity. (Plant 1934, 31)

Knowledge and information, unlike material things, are not necessarily rivalrous; coincident usage does not detract from utility. In this sense, most of the time knowledge (before it is made property) does not exhibit the characteristics of material things, and thus the ability to extract a price is dependent on its legal (re)constitution as property.

As Jeremy Waldron has pointed out, all this talk of property "sounds a lot less pleasant if . . . we turn the matter around and say we are imposing *duties*, restricting *freedom* and inflicting *burdens* on certain individuals for the sake of the greater social good" (Waldron 1993, 862). This is to say that IPRs limit the actions of others regarding knowledge vis-à-vis the owners of intellectual property, and nonowners thus are being forced to sacrifice their particular wants or needs on the altar of social necessity. This has led Howard Anawalt to argue that IPRs represent a particularly forceful form of social power. They "grant control over valuable processes or expressions and deny others the capacity to use them unless the owner's consent is obtained, or unless some legal privilege of use is established that grants access" (Anawalt 2003, 393). Nonowners' rights are constrained because these rights are regarded as less important in law than the support of the social good of innovation by IPRs.

This balance is not natural or self-evident but rather is a manifestation of government intervention in social relations. Taking some account of what Sol Picciotto (2002) has termed a "public welfare criteria," government authorities in the last 500 years have striven to assemble (however imperfectly) some sort of legalized bargain between the public interest and the rights of individuals. This led Robert Merges to argue that

> the key advantage of these rights, from the government's point of view, is that they are "off budget." That is, they do not involve a direct expenditure of government funds. Thus intellectual property represents something of a free lunch in the eyes of the government: a valuable benefit for which business constituents will be grateful, but which also has zero impact on the [government's] budget deficit. (Merges 1995, 111)

Thus, a valued social good can be delivered with little expense, as most patent offices are also self-funding through fee income. Furthermore, given the central role of government in the constitution of IPRs, it is ironic that the restrictions on their scope or duration are often presented as distorting the free play of the market, whereas it is the creation of legal monopoly rights over information and knowledge that more accurately distort "free" market competition (Picciotto and Campbell 2003). Indeed, when we turn to competition, the underlying political economy of IPRs becomes clearer.

Neil Fligstein has argued at some length that the social structures and institutions that have been constructed to govern economic relations are subject to political pressure by market actors wishing to constrain competition. In parallel to the arguments for IPRs that we make in this book, Fligstein noted that the "constitution of property rights is a continuous and contestable political process" and not merely the search for efficient organization (Fligstein 1996, 658). This led him to focus on the control aspect of property and to identify a clear role for the state, inasmuch as governments (and legislators) contribute to the balance of control (and the interests served by such control) through their interventions in, and constitution of, markets. Fligstein emphasized that there are "political contests over the content of laws, their applicability to govern firms and markets . . . [s]uch laws are never neutral" (Fligstein 1996, 660). Most important, "new" markets are profoundly affected by those market actors strong enough to shape new institutional structures in their interests. After an initial period of upheaval, a dominant perception of control is settled on and presented as that which is required to (re)produce an ordered market. Indeed, "a new market is not random, but is shaped by existing conceptions of control, legal conceptions of property and competition, and the existing organization of related markets" (Fligstein 1996, 665). Markets are constructed through politics, and nowhere is this more evident than in the market for intellectual property.

Considerable effort is required to support the argument that scarcity in knowledge or information, and therefore IPRs, is socially beneficial, rather than serving the interests of specific groups of powerful interests. As such, the recourse to various expressions of the justifications we laid out above is frequent and well rehearsed. Certainly, there is some level of social intuition that recognizes that the unauthorized appropriation of others' original ideas or creative expressions may be problematic. Because intellectual property law is at least partly indeterminate (being based on the vague notion of "incentives"), however, it has been captured by commercial interests; owners are always pressing for *more* protection, while at the same time—given other sociotechnological changes—a certain social cynicism has set in regarding the distribution of rewards from the enforcement of IPRs (Sykes 2003, 37–38). One clear attempt to sidestep this problem is to present the justifications of IPRs as outside politics. These modes of justification, these stories about knowledge as property, are by no means, however, the only stories that can be told about the recourse to a property mechanism for the products of the intellect.

One of the key purposes of this book is to integrate into the history of IPRs the development of ideas about how innovations might be owned. Any approach that is based on the (just) rewards to individual endeavor in knowledge creation aims to deny or at least downplay the social context and common heritage on which all new knowledge must be built. Sir Isaac Newton famously remarked in a letter to Robert Hooke: "If I have seen further it is by standing on the shoulders of giants."[5] From the basics of language to the development of complex ideas, we need to learn much before we can innovate, and thus access to what has gone before is crucial to intellectual endeavors. As Waldron pointed out in the realm of copyright, the limitation on activities (such as copying or plagiarism) is hardly life threatening; but what might be the reaction if we look at areas where intellectual property limits the use of less-ephemeral knowledge? The very real consequences of the distribution and control of IPRs lead to a more critical conclusion regarding the social good served by their general protection.

Triangulating the History of Intellectual Property

Having briefly laid out the terrain of contemporary intellectual property, we now present our analytical approach to the history of intellectual property rights. In the last twenty years, intellectual property has become one of the most obvious areas of conflict in the global political economy. Intellectual property rights are one of the key economic resources of the future, if not *the* key resource, but their definition, scope, and legitimacy remain uncertain. This is hardly surprising: there has been a recurrent tension throughout the history of intellectual property between protection/exclusion and dissemination/competition. Although TRIPs appears to be the final triumph of the protection/exclusion position, replete with attendant private rent seeking and monopoly implications, the history we present in subsequent chapters suggests that contestation of the current settlement could lead to a move back from this extreme position. We believe that IPRs are a supremely political issue and must be rescued from the realm of the technical; too often these debates are regarded as arcane, specialized technical issues outside the political process.

We argue that the history of intellectual property has been a competition between two different characterizations of the legitimate ownership of knowledge. On one hand is the belief that individuals should benefit from their intellectual endeavors, but on the other is an understanding that these endeavors have such extensive public worth that there is a clear social interest in their relatively free dissemination. In simple terms, then, this history has been a contest between monopoly power or private rights (limiting public access) and the public-regarding intent to free the flow of information (at the cost of the rights of the individual creator).

Throughout these debates an important third perspective emphasizes the public interest in having incentives for innovation and creativity, as a way of mediating between private rewards and public benefits. In this sense, the creation of knowledge is itself a public good, and property rights in knowledge help to bring that forth. Such property rights may help stimulate innovation and help small innovative enterprises attract investment capital to commercialize their innovations. This perspective also recognizes, however, that an incentive system only works to serve that public good when there are checks in place to prevent abuses of the monopoly property rights. Too many property rights and/or abuses of monopoly power can undermine this purpose by stifling innovation. Indeed, some of the historical examples that follow (particularly the cases of James Watt and Thomas Edison) demonstrate this problem. Although we are not *anti*–intellectual property, we are concerned that as in times past, and certainly in the contemporary climate, the balance has shifted too far in favor of private monopoly at the expense of the public goods of diffusion *and* innovation.

Among the contemporary problems that implicate the intellectual property rights regime are so-called patent thickets, constraining effects on follow-on innovations, and the increasing property rights for research tools that are central to basic science. Patent thickets refer to multiple and overlapping patent rights that require those seeking to commercialize new technology to obtain licenses from multiple patent holders (Carrier 2003, 1090–1091). For example, more than 100 parties have claimed property rights in the genetically modified (vitamin-enriched) germplasm "golden rice." Such claims not only increase transaction costs (not least through threats of litigation) but also threaten to hinder research itself owing to the broad coverage of these claimed rights. As Maskus and Reichman pointed out, "a growing thicket of rights surrounds gene fragments, research tools, and other upstream inputs of scientific research, and the resulting transaction costs impede and delay research and development undertaken in both the public and private sectors" (Maskus and Reichman 2004, 297). Increasingly, even research tools have become patent protected, so that there has been a dramatic reduction of open access to research tools (Rai and Eisenberg 2003, 290–291, 294). This threatens to hinder "open science" (Rai and Eisenberg 2003, 305). Maskus and Reichman feared that this expansion of intellectual property rights "could raise fundamental roadblocks for the national and global provision of numerous . . . public goods, including scientific research, education, health care, biodiversity, and environmental protection" (Maskus and Reichman 2004, 283). Furthermore, contemporary trends threaten to "undermine the national system of innovation" (Reichman and Uhlir 2003, 367) because local parallel research in any specific area may be constrained by patents already awarded in those countries where the most advanced research is taking place.

Reducing these dangers requires explicit measures to prevent abuses of monopoly power and negative effects on innovation. In the past, as indicated in our history, antitrust (or competition) policy has been a useful check on certain types of abuses. Patent and copyright misuse doctrines have also helped to reduce abuse. Maintaining high thresholds for patentability is also a helpful check on offering too many and overly broad property rights. Incorporating well-specified distinctions between upstream and downstream research when devising intellectual property protection systems can also help to contain the erosion of the public domain of "open science" (Rai and Eisenberg 2003, 290–291; 303). As we will address later, these issues have severe international ramifications.

Our account of the rise of intellectual property is informed by an analytical triangulation, linking the development of IPRs to material, institutional, and ideational changes in the international political economy. The significant material capabilities we focus on are those controlled through informational resources (including information-related technologies and innovations defined as intellectual property). The institution at the center of our treatment is the legal construction of intellectual property, and the ideas that influence and shape these developments are those that identify what is considered to be intellectual property and—most important—who has the right to claim ownership of intellectual goods (and why this might be legitimate).

The development of intellectual property law has been a contested political process producing successive phases of settlement or institutionalization. Each settlement has altered the rules of the game, constituted new actors, changed the opportunities for others, and thereby redefined the winners and losers. Each settlement (national, international, or global) has resulted in a new focal point for debate and dispute. This history continues to evolve, and the TRIPs agreement is merely the latest in a long line of moments of settlement, open to subsequent contestation and change. Neither, we would stress, is this a history that develops only along one trajectory: not only could the dominant history of IPRs have taken a different route, differing jurisdictions have developed in varying ways, drawing on differing sets of political arguments and settlements. The history of intellectual property rights is complex and multifaceted. The key issue we take from this pluralized historical context, however, is that any particular settlement can never be *the* final political economic settlement for intellectual property, its protection, and enforcement.

The shifting conceptions of intellectual property and the pressures of technological change drive this continuing historical process. Furthermore, given the distributional consequences of the ability to own (and control, even temporarily) technological innovations, intellectual property frequently has been an instrument of power and, once captured, the basis of further accumulation of power. But, unlike the power that comes from the control of scarce material resources, the holders of intellectual property have had to construct the scarcity of this property through legal instruments. The very process of defining what constitutes intellectual property, rendering some things as property while others remain freely available, effectively benefits some at the expense of others' interests. Indeed, asymmetrical economic power goes a long way toward explaining why semiconductor chips are identified as intellectual property whereas indigenous folklore is not (Drahos 1997b). Political power shapes the agenda of IPRs, not neutral and technical assessments of social well-being.

The governance of intellectual property, first at the national and then at the international level, has been subject to the continued mobilization of interest to establish and reinforce positions of advantage. Our concern with this issue is rooted in our previous recognition of the TRIPs agreement's mobilization of interest to produce a particular contemporary globalized settlement.[6] We regard this settlement as neither inevitable nor without alternatives. Thus, our intention is to begin to identify the grounds on which alternatives can be established. Indeed, restricting one's analysis to the past twenty years or so suggests an inexorable expansion of property rights in intellectual goods, and a singular focus on the TRIPs agreement (and its future) reinforces such a conclusion. The historical picture is much more nuanced, however, and reveals a recurrent tension that has not always been resolved in favor of property holders. Even in the United States, the most aggressive champion of expanded IPRs today, the public-regarding conception held sway in patent law for most of the twentieth century. We explore this tension through history by examining the swings of the pendulum between public-regarding approaches and private protection. Such an examination reveals the fundamentally political nature of the evolution of intellectual property regulation and ultimately seeks to provoke some historically based reflection on alternative possibilities for the future.

Perspectives on Intellectual Property

We locate our approach to the history of intellectual property within a critical framework, distinguishing it from what Robert Cox has referred to as problem-solving approaches. In particular, we present our account as an alternative to possible functionalist and realist perspectives on the international history of intellectual property. Realism in international political economy emphasizes state power and its distribution across the international system as primary explanatory variables. Realism takes power seriously, but it suffers from its statist orientation, treating the state as a unitary actor with well-defined interests. Realism too narrowly focuses on the state as legislator and provides limited leverage in the intellectual property context, as private actors, rather than states, have frequently prompted changes in intellectual property protection.[7] Intellectual property as an institution, although legally dependent on the state for its formal enactment, has been developed through considerable nonstate activity. An approach based in realism would allow sufficient space neither for the recognition of emergent groups (empowered through new technologies) who have pushed for new legal arrangements nor for technological shifts that have undermined specific settlements in the past. We seek to demonstrate the utility of a critical perspective: unlike realism (in international political economy), we are agnostic about the primary actors and stress the links between the micro and macro levels.

Functionalist histories of property suggest that property rights are established to promote efficiency in socioeconomic relations. Many functional histories are based on the supposition that the institution of property emerged to respond to the need for clear signaling in market relations.[8] Thus, as conflicts arose over scarce resources, the costs of such conflicts outweighed the cost of establishing (and policing) some sort of property regime. With shared rules of property, social actors may dispense with the duplication of effort required to constantly renegotiate bilateral coordination. In such accounts, therefore, the emergence of property serves a particular function: the efficient coordination of economic activities. Property rights are institutionalized to provide predictability in economic relations carried out at a distance, where community norms of trust cannot be relied on and where protection by force is impracticable (owing to its costs or the multiplicity of transactions that might need to be enforced at any one time by any particular transactor).

Functionalism assumes that the forces and interests that play out in contests over intellectual property have produced a series of "rational" settlements or "improvements" that reflected the political economic context of the time or fulfilled the needs of a particular stage of industrial development. As William Fisher suggested: "Viewed from this angle, law seems to be superstructural—its development driven by changes in the underlying mode of production and associated relations of production. But this is not the end of the story. To account fully for the development of intellectual property law, one must also take into account some cultural and ideological factors" (Fisher 1999, 6). Indeed, although at first glance functionalism offers a plausible approach to the evolution of intellectual property, functionalist analyses beg the question of what constitutes efficiency and ignore the issue of who defines it—efficiency for what, for whom?

Functionalism does not recognize that emergent settlements represent the ability of powerful actors and groups to enhance their interest at the expense of others. History is not linear but driven by contestation. Indeed, functionalism often lapses into teleology. Histories of intellectual property can often become a reading back of contemporary forms of intellectual property into the past, measuring previous legal settlements against the gauge of the current set of protections. David Saunders has criticized such approaches in the realm of copyright history (Saunders 1994). We wish to avoid the assumption that the history we present leads us to the current settlement as a form of progressive improvement of the legal forms and structures that make property from knowledge and information.

The history of intellectual property protection reveals a process that has vacillated between dissemination and exclusion with neither obviously representing an improvement of functionality at the clear expense of the other. Settlements along this spectrum at any given point have resulted from the complex interplay of ideational, institutional, and material forces, not merely from the state as legislative authority, not from some singular fulfillment of social functionality. No settlement is final, including the current settlement encapsulated in TRIPs. Not only does intellectual property remain contested, but contemporary pressures toward a re-inscription of public-regarding dissemination in intellectual property law are not bound to fail.

Since all activities have costs and benefits attached to them, an important issue for a functionalist approach to property rights is the internalization of external costs and benefits. Property seeks to attach those costs and benefits to the owner of the property that produces them, relative to the nonowner (Demsetz 1967, 348–350). Part of the continuing fluidity in the legal constitution of property rights, however, has been the widespread attempt by owners to secure benefits while keeping costs externalized. Social efficiency might best be served by costs accruing to the property that delivers the benefit, but for individual owners it is more efficient to have the costs met by others. An additional problem here is that social dynamics are more ambiguous than serving a single end (such as social efficiency) that can be achieved in a specific manner. Power manifests itself by constituting whose definition of efficiency is the guiding one and whose benefits are guarded or even expanded. For example, is it the book "pirate" who promotes the efficient distribution of printed matter, or is it the well-protected romantic author or "Yankee genius" for whom the promise of the security of her endeavor provides incentives to create and/or preserve?

Although efficiency may be valued in economic transactions, it is only one, and not necessarily the most important, aspect to the emergence of property as a social institution. In abstract terms we may explain property rights in terms of gains from coordination and cooperation. In the actual history of social relations, however, particular property institutions emerged from much more diverse circumstances, including the exercise of economic power, the impact of technological change, and shifts in ideas about who could own what. Adopting either a realist or functionalist perspective on the history of IPRs would lead to an undifferentiated macro-analysis obscuring significant variations; such explanations would be indeterminate regarding *particular* settlements.

Triangulation and the History of Intellectual Property

Having briefly sketched in general terms our differences with two well-known perspectives that we could have utilized, we now turn to a more substantive discussion of our triangulation approach. Our initial inspiration comes from the triangular interactions that Robert Cox identified among material capabilities, institutions, and ideas (Cox 1996, 98). The history of intellectual property law is a product of the interaction among the political (and social) conception of the role of the knowledge creator (ideas), the character of technologies using intellectual property or subject to its protection (material capabilities), and the legal construction of intellectual property (institutions). Cox's three ideal typical forces are a heuristic device for the examination of more specific complex realities (Cox 1996, 100). Our use of a similar triangulation allows us to develop a historical account of the institutionalization of intellectual property that disputes its emergence as a "rational" solution to a problem of economic organization. Rather, it is but one manifestation of the current hegemony of a systemic logic, reflecting the triumph (or ascendance) of the idea of capitalist markets as the only workable solution to political economic problems.

International political economy is frequently concerned with hegemony in the global system but has often related such hegemony directly to state power, reflecting the continuing influence of realist conceptions of the global system (Cox 1996, 104). Following Cox and others,[9] we regard such hegemony as enacted through the "rules of the game" rather than only (or even primarily) by force. These rules need to be examined in terms of their content and their emergence, alongside their potential for political contestation. It is here that Cox's notion of social forces is especially useful for studying intellectual property. It allows institutions to be located in relation to their own history *and* the material capabilities they are linked with as well as an account of the ideational developments they represent. A crucial point is that such an approach locates these social forces in the workings of the (historically specific) capitalist system (Cox 1996, 101). Recognizing the work of social forces in establishing the rules firmly locates the institution of intellectual property within the contemporary political economy, not in some idealized world of legal relations, separate from the working of the global system.

We are interested in the power that stems from the ownership and control of particular innovations and technologies, established through the institutions of intellectual property, and how that power is able to govern the structures of intellectual property law to reinforce and reproduce advantage (May 2000; Sell 2003). Certain agents maximize their influence through the control of specific resources, but these preferred actors also mobilize (and reproduce) their advantages by the legitimization of their interest through law. These actors bring political resources to bear to defend and extend their rights in intellectual property law, by utilizing and defending the stories (ideas) of labor desert, the expression of self and economic efficiency to justify the rendering knowledge as property. These stories, identifying owners, justifying the protection of their rights, and arguing for the efficiency gains from treating knowledge as property, inform legal arguments that have produced successive moments of settlement in the law of IPRs.

Cox has highlighted the relationship between discourses and institutions insofar as institutions are perceived as legitimated. The weak will acquiesce when the strong, seeing their mission as hegemonic, are willing to make concessions to secure acquiescence and—a crucial point—if the strong can "express this leadership in terms of universal or general interests, rather than just as serving their own particular interests" (Cox 1996, 99). The ability to represent the hegemonic conception of intellectual property as serving the general interest, highlighted by the "settlement" between the protection of private rights of owners and availability in the public domain, is a recurrent motif in the history of intellectual property. Formally, the monopoly rights accorded by intellectual property are balanced with the public interest in disclosure through the time-limited character of intellectual property protection. The duration of protection is not natural and unlike a functionalist perspective, a critical approach helps us to highlight contingency and historical circumstances that lead to these constructions of scarcity.

The question of why certain outcomes have come to pass is a central concern for a "critical theory." In Cox's formulation, such critical theory

> does not take institutions and social power relations for granted but calls them into question by concerning itself with their origins and how and whether they might be in the process of change. . . . Critical theory allows for a normative choice in favor of a social and political order different from the prevailing order, but it limits the range of choice to alternative orders which are feasible transformations of the existing world. (Cox 1996, 88–90)

This is much more than merely the need to "add history and stir," however. What is required is a sensitivity to the interaction of structures and agents within a continuing history of hegemony (and its reproduction). Thus, within the institution of intellectual property (in the same manner that Cox noted for all hegemonic institutions), there

> is always tension between a widely held conception of the world and the realities of existence for particular groups of historical people. Gaps develop between changing material conditions and old intellectual schemata. Such gaps suggest latent conflict, the actualizing of which depends upon a change of consciousness on the part of the potential challengers and their adoption of a contrast image of society. (Cox 1996, 66)

Taking our inspiration from Robert Cox's work, we have sought to develop a specific mode of triangulation that enables us to depict a history of intellectual property as well as engage in a normative project of establishing the routes toward plausible alternatives to the current (disputed) settlement.

The gaps between ideas and material conditions hold the key to understanding change. But this in itself is not sufficient; as Michael Gorges pointed out (in his critique of the "new institutionalism"),

> ideas themselves do not cause outcomes. It is therefore one thing to claim that ideas (and institutions) matter. It is another to explain how those ideas that are "out there" take a particular institutional form at a particular time, or to specify explicitly how ideas matter given the overdetermined nature of dependent variables and the importance of other independent variables. Moreover, these ideas themselves arise out of social, economic and historical factors that may themselves be important explanatory variables. (Gorges 2001, 141)

Gorges also warned against the importation of variables into analysis in an ad hoc fashion, arguing that institutionalism's "utility seems limited if it cannot successfully explain institutional change and institutionalism without employing a miscellaneous collection of variables" (Gorges 2001, 142). Thus, there is a clear need to demonstrate, through analysis and historical/empirical work, how our set of variables produces institutional change but also an imperative to offer a discrete and limited number of key variables. As we have already noted, we utilize three variables in this regard—technological change, ideas (about knowledge), and the institution of intellectual property—that also shape the interactions between changes in ideas and technology.

Margaret Archer offered an excellent way of conceptualizing the relationship among these variables, not least of all because she refused the temptation to identify either structure or agency as the final determining factor in social relations. We understand changes in the intellectual property regime as overdetermined; no single set of forces or structures can produce change alone, nor any finally resist change alone. Archer argued that focusing on agency alone and offering a "bottom-up" causal explanation would make "no allowances for inherited structures, their resistance to change, the influence they exert on attitudes to change, and crucially . . . , the delineation of agents capable of seeking change" (Archer 1995, 250). At the beginning of any particular sequence of history there are structures carried forward, reflecting previous political economic settlements regarding the rules that govern (in our case) intellectual property. But at the same time there are agents who are disadvantaged as well as those who manage to capture the benefits of the system.

This is not to argue that agents have a completely free rein; they are constrained to some degree by the structures in which they find themselves, but equally their actions are not determined by the structures. In other words, as Archer pointed out, "voluntarism has an important place . . . but is ever trammeled by past structural and cultural constraints and by the current politics of the possible" (Archer 1982, 470). Historically extant structures are themselves the products of previous clashes of social forces, previous interactions of ideas, material capabilities, and institutions. Agents' actions may be the immediate cause of specific moments of settlement, but they also remain embedded in larger structures, including material causes, state institutions, and the structure of global capitalism, that both constrain and empower. Indeed, structural change itself can alter agents' interests if such change renders existing institutions less useful and agents begin to be harmed by a continuation of the status quo. Archer stresses that "*all* structural influences . . . *are mediated to people by shaping the situation in which they find themselves*" (Archer 1995, 196; emphasis in original). The key issue is the difference between the inherited structures (playing out in institutionalized settlements) and the continuing (or changing) interests of specific agents.

Put simply, structure conditions but does not determine agency. The power of agency lies in its "capacities for articulating shared interests, organizing for collective action, generating social movements and exercising corporate influence in decision-making" (Archer 1995, 259–260). This led Archer to identify two types of agency: primary and corporate. Primary agents have neither organized nor articulated their interests and do not participate strategically in shaping or reshaping structure. By contrast, corporate agents are "those who are aware of what they want, can articulate it to themselves and others, and have organized in order to get it; [only they] can engage in concerted action to re-shape or retain the structural or cultural features in question" (Archer 1995, 258). In this sense, affected primary agents must develop collective, corporate forms, to engage effectively in the political process of structural change or defense. Corporate agents "pack more punch in defining and re-defining structural forms, and are key links in delimiting whether systemic fault lines (incompatibilities) will be split open . . . or will be contained" (Archer 1995, 191). In order to be successful, agents need some form of organization and the ability to articulate their interests. They need technical expertise, political power, and access to resources, including the very institutions they may wish to change. Agents may become dissatisfied with the status quo, recognizing that the structural incongruities threaten to reduce benefits and power, but unless they are able to organize a collective response, they will be unable effectively to challenge more formalized groupings.

Much of this tension is located in the institutions that work in conjunction with our ideas about the world and the technologies that enable actions. James March and Johan Olsen have argued at some length that political institutions are usually governed by a "logic of appropriateness" rather than a "logic of consequentiality" (March and Olsen 1989). Law is a supremely political institution, and certainly when we look at intellectual property law the rubric of appropriateness is evident. It is the appropriateness of reward and private rights, rather than the immediate consequences that are appealed to. March and Olsen suggested that

> when individuals enter an institution, they try to discover, and are taught, the rules. When they encounter a new situation, they try to associate it with a situation for which rules already exist. Through rules and a logic of appropriateness, political institutions realize both order, stability and predictability, on the one hand, and flexibility and adaptiveness, on the other. (March and Olsen 1989, 160)

Noting that there is often a need to produce post hoc rationalizations for appropriate behavior, March and Olsen stressed that the consequential logic may be mobilized once a decision has been enacted. There is a tension between these two logics: what is appropriate for the governing elite may have consequences that do not garner full social support. But March and Olsen did not ignore the issue of the ideological construction of "appropriateness," noting that political effort is required to maintain the specific identification of appropriate behavior. As we have noted, significant effort is deployed in the realm of intellectual property to maintain a political position that IPRs are an appropriate way of dealing with knowledge. In a similar fashion, however, critics often focus on the logic of consequentiality; are the consequences too large a price to pay to support what is deemed appropriate?

Following Archer: where there is a mismatch between the structurally available benefits and the politicized interests of marginalized agents, this may be translated into tensions and strains in the system,

> experienced as practical exigencies by agents whose interests are vested in the impeded institutions. . . . Their situations are molded in critical

respects by operational obstructions which translate into practical problems, frustrating those upon whose day-to-day situations they impinge, and confronting them with a series of exigencies which hinder the achievement or satisfaction of their vested institutional interests. (Archer 1995, 215)

In these confrontations, the shift in ideas about the structural settlement starts to become more apparent. Although the beneficiaries will attempt to maintain the universality of the systems of justification of the status quo, the challengers will seek to identify the emerging gaps in the institutional reflection of the dominant ideas of the current settlement.

In our triangulation, this process may be spurred by changes in technology, alerting the disadvantaged to new possibilities; by shifts in the ideas of the knowledge creator, emerging in society more generally; or by developments in the institutions (of intellectual property) that are regarded as attempts to further advance the benefits of the dominant group. These structural incongruities present distinctive "situational logics which predispose agents towards specific courses of action for the promotion of their interests" (Archer 1995, 216). Archer called this a "contingent incompatibility" in which reproduction, or a continuation of the status quo, hinders the achievement of specific agents' aims. To claim that structural incongruity "conditions oppositional action is merely to argue that such corporate agents are in a situation whose logic is to *eliminate* practices which are hostile to achieving their vested interests" (Archer 1995, 331; emphasis in original). The aggrieved seek to eliminate hostile practices.

In this perspective on change in the global system, structural incongruities may spur action, but discursive strategies can help solidify it, render it coherent, and legitimate it. Therefore, although structural disparities created incentives to alter rules governing intellectual property protection across its history, important (structurally privileged) interest groups developed new arguments to justify the desired changes or conversely to hamper institutional shifts. But these powerful groups have been unable to forever obscure or hide the inequalities that the structures have rendered normal. As Archer put it:

> The interaction of a variety of material interest groups, each of which has become articulate in its own defense and capable of detecting self-interest in the claims of others, is enough to preclude any drift back to unquestioned structural [settlements]. The groups have mobilized, ideas have helped them to do it, and assertion will not fade away because the material interests it seeks to advance do not evaporate. (Archer 1995, 322)

This indicates why the justifications and arguments for the status quo, or even its further structural strengthening, need to be constantly rearticulated and defended in the political arena. As disparities between perceived reality (both technological and political) and the narrative of the previous (institutionalized) settlement become wider, so the pressure for change grows and the defense becomes more fervent.

Contestation and Change
in the History of Intellectual Property

Over its history, property has moved from a common understanding as physical things held for the owner's use to the more modern conception of property as assets that can be used or otherwise sold to another potential user. As John Commons stressed, however, even though this

> transition was hardly noticeable as long as the merchant, the master, the laborer, were combined under small units of ownership, [it] becomes distinct when all opportunities are occupied and business is conducted by corporations on a credit system which consolidates property under the control of absentee owners. Then the power of property per se, distinguished from the power residing in personal faculties or special grants of sovereignty, comes into prominence. . . . When to this is added the pressure of population and the increasing demand for limited supplies of mineral and metal resources, of water-powers, of lands situated at centers of population, then the mere holding of property becomes a power to withhold, far beyond that which either the laborer has over his labor or the investor has over his savings, and beyond anything known when this power was being perfected by the early common law or early business law. (Commons [1924] 1959, 53)

This move from holding to withholding, the ability to restrict use, is crucially important for our history of intellectual property. When the resources required for social existence are scarce, then the *distribution* of the rights to their use (property rights) becomes a central, if not *the* central, issue of political economy.

The ability to withhold is a crucial mechanism to control resources and has a major impact on others, especially where such ownership has been carved out of resources that otherwise might have been constructed as a form of social wealth (or public resource). As David Lametti recently argued:

> Distributing ultimate control of some item of social wealth to one individual must have an impact on others. Private property confers power in the property-holder over others . . . [and this] allows us to see that the use of resources or social wealth, even the exclusive use by an individual, is necessarily social. Any act on an object of property—even its consumption— changes the normative status of another object. That is, a person can unilaterally eliminate or change the duties owed to a particular object. (Lametti 2004, 48, 61)

The private control of scarce goods includes an outward-facing impact on other members of society because the resources concerned are scarce and their control rival. For intellectual property when the legalized scarcity is neither uncontested nor self-evident, however, the potential effects are more clearly *politicized*. The role of intellectual property is to construct the scarcity that control requires in the realm of knowledge and to make it legitimate whatever the social consequences.

To take one example from our narrative; the history of steam-driven industrialization might have been very different without Britain's early form of intellectual property in the eighteenth century. When James Watt, innovator and creator of the steam engine, was awarded a patent for his invention in 1769, this did not encourage its widespread and immediate dissemination. Six years later the British Parliament renewed his patent for an additional twenty-five years, during which time Watt continued to refuse to license his invention. By doing so he may have "held back the development of the metalworking industry for over a generation" (Renouard [1844] 1987). Had his monopoly expired in 1783, England might have had an extensive railway system much sooner (Renouard [1844] 1987). The imposed scarcity of this particular innovation halted its dissemination and ossified its development until others could build upon Watt's original insights.

The public benefit may have been served by "encouraging" Watt's innovation in the first place (although it is difficult to argue that Watt would not have invented the steam engine had he been unable to patent it). Yet the social benefit of swift use/deployment of such an innovation was certainly not served. This is at odds with North's assessment that sustained innovation only began in earnest after the establishment of intellectual property rights raised the private rate of return for innovation. He attributed the delay in the dissemination and fuller exploitation of Watt's invention to the inadequate development of companion technologies rather than to the power of withholding property and the social inefficiencies generated by such withholding (North 1981, 162–166). The development of companion technologies was itself stifled, however, by the relatively limited diffusion of engines utilizing Watt's patented technology.

Our history of the institution of intellectual property aims to illuminate the persistent tension between those who seek to privately appropriate property in intellectual goods and those who seek its dissemination. Although we focus on the legal construction of intellectual property, we reject the notion of law having an existence separate from its political, social, and economic context. Law both constitutes and is constituted by social, political, and economic struggles (Hunt 1993). Furthermore, as Pierre Bourdieu contended: "Law is the quintessential form of the symbolic power of naming that creates the things named . . . it confers upon the reality which arises from its classificatory operations the maximum permanence that any social entity has the power to confer upon another, the permanence which we attribute to objects" (Bourdieu 1987, 838). Although Bourdieu here was discussing the role of law more generally, this seem to us to particularly exemplify the role of intellectual property law.

Bourdieu went on to stress that "the law can exercise its specific power only to the extent that it attains recognition, that is, to the extent that the element of arbitrariness at the heart of its functioning (which may vary from case to case) remains unrecognized" (Bourdieu 1987, 844). Of all laws, or at least of all laws of property, intellectual property is likely the most arbitrary (in regard to the nonrivalrousness of knowledge and information). Thus, it is no surprise that extensive extralegal political power is mobilized to ensure that such arbitrariness goes (relatively) underrecognized. Conversely, the recognition of this problem and the organization of political resistance around this position repeatedly have prompted the reformation of intellectual property law. Historicizing intellectual property reveals its contingent construction and explicitly denies that it is a transhistorical concept.[10]

Given that law is written, we should not ignore the importance of the manner in which TRIPs itself (as the most recent "settlement") is written. Discussing the "coming global legal order," Lawrence Friedman suggested that the "dominance of English [in the global system] means that US ways of writing contracts and thinking about the law are likely to have more influence than they otherwise would" (Friedman 2001, 355). This is exemplified by the TRIPs agreement, which reflects very specifically US "ways of thinking about the law." Friedman himself suggested that much of the US influence in regard to global legal structures reflects that the United States, "for various reasons, is ahead of the game in devising institutions that fit modern legal needs" (Friedman 2001, 355). This ability to set the initial structures reflects (and reproduces) US legal hegemony over IPRs. The current structures of law in intellectual property reflect the needs (and wants) of a very specific set of agents (Sell 2003). The replacement of the previous, pluralistic structure of international IPR law was an important response to its perceived shortcomings.

We argue that the progression of intellectual property from one structure of law to another, from one settlement to another, has been patterned by periods of contestation reflected in the tensions between private rights of ownership and public circulation of knowledge. These tensions signaled to the contending parties the potential for remaking intellectual property law at particular moments. As Cox has pointed out, this

> developmental potential signifies a possible change of structure. It can be grasped by understanding the contradictions and sources of conflict within

existing structures; and this task may be aided by an understanding of how structural transformations have come about in the past. Thus the determination of breaking points between successive structures—those points at which transformations take place—becomes a major problem of method. (Cox 1996: 54)

This has led us to identify the developments within the institution of intellectual property as our central problem and to regard these "breaking points" as moments when the historical trajectory of intellectual property was underdetermined by its past.

The potential for restructuring the institution of intellectual property is foregrounded by technological change and shifts in the usage of law. Furthermore, any settlement itself may put other aspects of intellectual property into play, either by allowing scope for contestation of previous settled practices or by its necessary privileging of one set of interests over others. Institutional settlements that emerge can be compromised quickly through the complexities of use and the contested character of intellectual property itself. Shifts in the idea of knowledge creation may lead to a disparity between the world of innovation described by the institutions of intellectual property and that world as perceived by users and innovators. Technological changes may enhance the benefits that were previously regarded as reasonable in law and therefore lead to pressure for change by those disadvantaged.

These breaking points may reveal thresholds of technological and political change, but any particular moment may be complex and multitemporal. The recognition of this continued dialectical move from institutional settlement to contestation and dispute, and the re-imposition of settlement, underlies the continuing fragmentation from relatively undifferentiated (intellectual) property laws to the complex of complementary laws we see today, globalized in the form of TRIPs. Indeed "refinement" of the law of intellectual property has led to a complex and variable set of institutional elements, ensuring that in the contemporary global political economy of intellectual property there is no single realm of uncontested and firm rules.

In the following historical account, we provide a critique, therefore, that following Cox "does not take institutions and social power relations for granted but calls them into question by concerning itself with their origins and how and whether they might be in the process of change" (Cox 1996, 88–90). Our explicit intention is to problematize the functionalist and teleological assumptions that underlie much that has been written regarding the current settlement as encapsulated in TRIPs. The current settlement is neither fixed nor final, and our history demonstrates that alternative approaches are both available and plausible.

The TRIPs agreement did not spring fully formed onto the global stage. Indeed, one can conclude that TRIPs can be only be understood as the latest stage in the long *political* process of the expansion of intellectual property protection. Our approach to intellectual property illuminates the conjunction of the present pressures for change with historical continuities (and adaptations). Each phase of intellectual property law represents both a legacy from a previous phase and an accommodation with current technological developments and conceptual shifts. But this is more than path dependency; it also reflects the contested character of intellectual property and the extralegal influences on legal structures and practice.

The disputes between the positions of public-regarding dissemination and monopolized private ownership, the conflicts over the scope of intellectual property in light of emerging technologies, and the volatile legal relationship between private rights and the public domain all feed into the current settlement as encapsulated in TRIPs. These disputes underline the history of intellectual property, and different perspectives "win" at different times. Indeed, despite contemporary justifications built on the role of the author's or inventor's just desert or the need to protect the self, these justifications postdate the emergence of intellectual property as a legal institution during the prenational phase of its development.[11] Often justifications of intellectual property are presented as outside time, as transhistorical; they are not.

Foregrounding the triangulation of social forces that has continually (re)produced the history of intellectual property, we offer a critical perspective. In doing so we suggest the continuing possibility for remaking intellectual property. This history belies any linear conception of the "march" of IPRs in a more proprietary and exclusionary direction. As David Vaver has pointed out: "It is fashionable in some quarters to try and trace the origin of the miscellany of intellectual property rights back to time immemorial, presumably to pretend these devices are natural and inevitable; but the attempt is hopeless and foolish" (Vaver 2001, 128). Certainly to argue that IPRs are somehow "natural and inevitable" so distorts the historical record that we must agree with Vaver. Our project is diametrically opposed to the notion that IPRs are natural and inevitable. Thus, we suggest that the reforming project of scholars such as Vaver can find sustenance in our approach by recognizing that this is not the first time that intellectual property's settlement has been subjected to (political economic) critique.

The protection of intellectual property as codified and formalized in the TRIPs agreement is the result of a long struggle between various groups over the control of economically significant knowledge resources. This struggle need not have necessarily brought us to this juncture, and the fact that it did suggests to us that we need to examine carefully the history of intellectual property and accord appropriate weight to the nonlegal variables that we have identified. To understand intellectual property today, we need to understand its historical roots, and to understand these roots we need to do more than (re)produce the convenient teleological account that seems to have such wide currency in policy-oriented circles today. This complex history is the one we will now relate.

Notes

1. Judges' rulings may either forecast or trail such shifts.

2. James Boyle has criticized this argument at some length (see Boyle 2001, 9 and passim).

3. Adam Mossoff explored the influence of Locke's philosophy on patent law at some length and concluded that, especially in the eighteenth century, it had a significant impact on the consolidation of patents as being (in part) natural rights. Given the totemic position of much judicial opinion as regards patents during this period, Locke's influence on contemporary debates remains significant (Mossof 2001). In addition, Ronald Bettig noted: "Locke did not earn a living from the publication of his books . . . so he probably did not see the need to make a case for authors' rights. Additionally, *the Two Treatises* was published anonymously, suggesting Locke did not prioritize claims to ownership over political expediency" (Bettig 1992, 141–142).

4. It is interesting to note that Seana Valentine Shiffrin's close reading of Locke undermined this common depiction of the Lockean justification for intellectual property (Shiffrin 2001). Although she presented a well-argued critique, however, currently (at least) the perception of a Lockean emphasis on individual reward for effort remains well used in discussions of IPRs.

5 The letter was dated 5 February 1675. We are grateful to Nick Bowen, who advised us (in private correspondence) that this aphorism may have older roots; Robert Burton (1577–1640) and George Herbert (1593–1632) may also be sources, and the phrase "Pigmies placed on the shoulders of giants see more than the giants themselves" is attributed to Didacus Stella by the Roman historian Lucan.

6. See our earlier work (May 2000, 2002b; Sell 1998, 2003).

7. Here realist approaches refer to international political economy and not to legal realism. Prominent examples include Kenneth Waltz (1979), John Mearsheimer (2002), and Stephen Krasner (1985).

8. See North (1990) for the classic telling of this story.

9. Not least of all Susan Strange; see Tooze and May (2002).

10. One of the best historical accounts of evolving philosophical perspectives on intellectual property is Drahos (1996). His book offers considerable discussion of the history of the development of the concept of intellectual property but leaves its connection with the world of material social relations largely undeveloped.

11. Though this is broadly the case, Frank Prager suggested that were it not for the decline of Venice in the sixteenth century, there might have been a swifter move to the justification of intellectual property on the basis of the author or creator (Prager 1944, 719).

3 ———

The Emergence of
Intellectual Property Rights

BEFORE THERE was any formal legal definition of intellectual property, there were many attempts to control valuable knowledge and information. New technologies spurred the development of social and early legal innovations that eventually coalesced into the beginning of a recognizable body of intellectual property rights in Venice in the late fifteenth century. The first part of this chapter is concerned with the prehistory of intellectual property: this reveals the long gestation of the notion of property in the products of intellectual activity. Ideas about owning knowledge were not novel in the fifteenth century. The second part of the chapter focuses on the "Venetian moment" as a pivotal point in the history of intellectual property.

Patents emerged initially as grants of privilege and in some cases were clearly intended to allow the dissemination of particular technical advances that would benefit ruling groups through wealth creation. When this was the underlying rationale for awarding the grant, these grants emphasized a public-regarding intent to further the encouragement of learning and the development of industry, even if the notional "public" was rather limited. These grants were not justified on the basis of natural rights or moral rights but rather reflected a perceived political or social need or future benefit. Below we explore some of the antecedents to intellectual property and some of the early ideas about owning knowledge that repeatedly resurface in our history.

The condemnation of plagiarism and the acknowledgment of the theft of ideas stretches back to the beginnings of recorded history. Much of the early recognition of ownership of ideas was more concerned with the retention of secret knowledge, however, than with the rights to reward that remain with the author once a work is being disseminated. Preliterate societies may develop a form of ownership of ideas, often in the way that magical practices are controlled. In Native American groups, for instance, the limitations are on the owner of magical and traditionally beneficial practices, who within tribal custom might only be able to pass on certain secrets to nominated receivers (Okediji 1995, 133), rather than on the buyers in relation to the originators (as in copyright). Rules constructing some form of scarcity of use suggest that these control mechanisms are distantly related to the prehistory of intellectual property.

Early Antecedents of Intellectual Property

Perhaps the first practice that separated out an information element was the marking of goods. Marks could indicate reliability and the reputation of the craftsman/maker as well as origin. Marking to establish ownership long precedes formalized laws to adjudicate disputes regarding ownership. Marking by owners is likely to have started with the practice of branding animals, the earliest form of proprietary marking. Although such beginnings predate written history, there is widespread evidence from cave paintings of ear-cut branding and other techniques. Indeed, the cutting of animals' ears to produce an individualized sign of ownership, using a specific owner's mark, is still widespread in agrarian cultures, and in modern farming ear tags (and branding) continue to serve a similar function. For more than 6,000 years (perhaps since animals were first domesticated), humans across the globe have marked objects they made, found, or obtained, and as Gerald Ruston noted, although some of these marks were "undoubtedly trademarks in the modern sense . . . marks denoting origin; others were clearly marks identifying the goods with their possessor" (Ruston 1955, 127). Marks were used to identify the owner and, where relevant, the maker (two separate marks are often found on early goods).

Three types of mark were common: a family mark identifying the property of a certain clan or group (if they became merchants this mark might also belong to the next category); the adopted (trade)mark, which in times of mass illiteracy (or prior to formal writing systems themselves) was an important way of identifying specific wares; and the compulsory mark that carried the authority of the state or ruler, usually to establish either legitimacy or confirm that taxes had been paid. This third category also includes the later practice of hallmarking (authorized by specific guilds and often under royal charter) to govern the quality of metals being used to fashion particular commodities (Ruston 1955, 136ff.). With the emergence of formal regimes of law, such practices were codified and given a legitimacy further afield than the local community in which they already had an immediate social significance.

There is considerable evidence from ownership stamps on pottery and other household items excavated from prehistoric sites in Europe and Asia indicating that such practices were widespread and common. By the time of the Egyptian and Mesopotamian empires, brick makers marked their products, alongside the name of the ruling king and the owner of the building where the bricks were used. Stonecutters recorded either the name of the contractor or the individual stonecutter on masonry used for building during this and subsequent periods, possibly to calculate wages for their teams of workmen based on output (Azmi, Maniatis, and Sodipo 1997, 133). In the Greek city-states, this recognition that particular goods might be valued more highly by virtue of the identity of the maker started to spread from material goods to the cultural (and intellectual) realm as well. Until then, scientific and technological knowledge had been protected and controlled through secrecy. In ancient civilizations, the knowledge from which political or religious power flowed was more akin to the contemporary trade secret, with severe punishments for its revelation outside the priesthood. Greek philosophical speculations encouraged the notion of knowledge as valuable in its own right, however, paving the way for its eventual commodification.

Greek Ideas About Owning Ideas

Intellectual property did not emerge (in any form) in the Greek society of Simonides and other poets, but they seem to be the first "creatives" to become intellectual entrepreneurs in a sense that we might now recognize. Prior to the Greek civilization of the sixth century B.C., patrons "kept" artists, poets, or singers, as well as intellectuals, who were expected to perform on demand. In the Greek city-states, direct support by patronage began to be supplemented by prizes for recitations in public as well as paid performances (similar to recitals).

The Sophists are reputed to be the first group to earn significant rewards through their freelance teaching activities. They do not seem to have regarded the content of their teaching as subject to any form of ownership, despite the appearance of manuals in many things they taught (from wrestling to household management). Mostly these were produced by the audiences and then copied by others; there was no technology of publication as such (Masterson 1940, 621). Critics of the Sophists often argued that by allowing their ideas to be set down in writing they lost control over who could read and benefit from their knowledge (Blank 1985, 18–19), implying that the Sophists did not regard knowledge or information itself as an ownable commodity. Rather they may have regarded these manuals and other texts as publicity for their teaching activities (by expanding their reputation). The Sophists were teachers of thinking and doing, rather than providers of defined intellectual commodities.

Poets, on the other hand, produced a clearly defined product: the poem. Simonides is often depicted as the first poet to have demanded a fee for poems. He is therefore at the center of many anecdotes from Greek writers on the greediness of poets (Genteli 1988, 161; Woodbury 1968, 536), although this may be because he was eminent enough to become at least partly exemplary of all poets. Nevertheless, it is not unlikely that Simonides was the first to professionalize poetry because the first social circulation of money coincided with his lifetime. Anne Carson also noted, however, that "Simonidean greed was more resented in its essence than in its particulars. Its essence was the commodification of previously reciprocal and ritual activity, the exchange of gifts [of poetry] between friends" (Carson 1999, 16–17). Simonides was not alone in successfully demanding fees for specific works. His contemporary, Pindar, also received significant monetary rewards for the delivery of poetical works (Genteli 1988, 162). The circulation of money may have been a necessary condition for commodification, but it was not sufficient; ideas about the origin of poetry and creativity also had to be changing.

It was not uncommon to find in Greek culture from the sixth century B.C. onward poets who claimed to be authors of specific works and artists who signed their paintings or illustrations (Ploman and Hamilton 1980, 5). Mladen Vukmir took the appearance of makers' marks (and signatures) on works of art as "reliable evidence of a recognition of the proprietary nature of artistic activity" being both a "recognition of personal achievement and a warning of ownership" of the creative content (Vukmir 1992, 129). Certainly, as Bruno Genteli suggested, the "consciousness of the high quality of one's own work and technical achievements at a level that would be hard to surpass" were already part of the mental universe of the poets of the second half of the fifth century B.C. (Genteli 1988, 165). But, even though there was a contractual relationship between the poet and the purchaser, and although this relationship included the provision of poems, the notion that the poem itself was intellectual property, in a modern sense, is absent. Nevertheless, Simonides is reputed to have believed "poetry is an art that sells its products in the market-place" (Woodbury 1968, 536). In Greek society during the sixth and fifth centuries B.C. we can see the emergence of the idea of creativity that subsequently would underpin the wider ownership of knowledge. The Romantic view of the author as individual genius that emerged in the seventeenth and eighteenth centuries, therefore, finds its distant origins in Greece.

The combination of a means of exchange (and a putative market) alongside the emergence of an individualized notion of creativity prompted a rudimentary form of market in poetry to develop. Indeed, more generally, during this period the organization of some form of market joined the previous models of gift exchange in Greek protoeconomic relations (Morris 1986). The slow development of a new mode of interchange between producer of goods and user was no less likely to have influenced the intellectual arts than the mechanical. Poetry may have been the first creative activity to be (partially) commodified, but it was by no means the last. The emergence of the notion of the individual as creator of art, which might have some value beyond its immediate content linked to the identity of its maker, is a crucial and foundational moment. But only with the Roman Empire did more market-oriented activities and problems associated with contemporary intellectual property more clearly start to emerge.

Roman Developments

In the industrial arts, Roman use of craftsmen's marks continued earlier Greek practice. When inscriptions were not satisfying personal sentiment, they again concerned the payment of tax or the notification of state monopolies and often were a method for contractors and employers to notify the settlement of accounts (Ladas 1975, 1:4). The mark represented the honesty or integrity of each manufacturer, but as it had no legal status, the mark's originator had no recourse against an infringement of a mark. Roman law may have allowed a purchaser to bring an action against the vendor of goods with a fraudulent mark, however, for deceit and the intent to defraud. Additionally, under the Lex Cornelia de iniuriis c. 81 B.C., taking another's name for profit was prohibited, but there is no evidence that a link was made between such illegality and the infringement of (trade)marks (Vukmir 1992, 130). Thus, an early prohibition of passing off might be said to have existed, even if the mark's originator was not accorded any special rights over the mark itself.

Perhaps it is not surprising, with the lack of formal legal recourse, that counterfeiting of specific trademarks was a problem. Roman oil lamps were traded throughout the empire, and those of the most famous maker, Fortis, were especially valued. The lamps and the maker's mark were extensively counterfeited across Europe by local makers, however. Finally, Fortis became the term for a certain sort of lamp, rather than an indication of its manufacturer (Azmi, Maniatis, and Sodipo 1997, 134). Likewise, in the first century A.D., imitation Roman pottery was produced in Belgium. Although, owing to their ignorance of Latin, infringers' marks were often simply meaningless collections of letters, they deceived the still more ignorant Britons who imported the pots (Ruston 1955, 133).

The Roman publishing industry, or more accurately the organized production of multiple copied scribal texts, emerged and expanded in the first century B.C., originally in Alexandria, then moving to Rome in the fifty years before A.D. 100. As had happened previously in Greece, authors were frequently supported by patrons and did not directly receive money from the "publication" of their works. A new model of authorship slowly emerged, however, with a direct link between author and the sale of specific works, and before long, a rudimentary concept of literary property was developed. Salathiel Masterson suggested that "Cicero apparently had a direct business interest in the sale of his books, that is, his publishing arrangements were on a royalty basis" and that on his demise "there is evidence that his works and the right to their continued publication were bought from Atticus by the bookseller Dorus" (Masterson 1940, 622). Therefore, despite the formal lack of any approximation to modern copyright, it is plausible that the well-developed Roman publishing (scribal copying) industry did recognize something similar to intellectual property, at least in prototypical terms. Authors contracted with publishers to reproduce and distribute their work, suggesting that there was some recognition that authors had legitimate rights over these works.

Furthermore, the Romans seemed to distinguish between authorial rights to protect the integrity of the work and the right of reproduction (Ploman and Hamilton 1980, 7). Due to the slow process of copying manuscripts, the literary world of Rome circulated books rather than sold them. This process was sometimes speeded up by the use of slaves, and where authors were popular they might through a "courtesy of trade" assign exclusive distribution rights of their works to a specific bookseller (Vukmir 1992, 133). Nevertheless, the rights accorded to authors were limited to their right to be recognized as an author (a guard against plagiarism) and did not usually extend to the recognition of commercial property in their forms of expression. Additionally, both Vitruvius (author of a widely read series of Roman books on architecture, in the first century B.C.) and then Pliny the Elder (some 150 years later) took trouble to recognize previous authors they cited and also (perhaps more tellingly) were hostile to plagiarism (Long 1991, 854–856). "Theft" of authors' work was starting to seem unacceptable, which in itself implies the early development of individualized ideas of creativity.

We might infer that some prototypical forms of intellectual property existed, but there are no known reported or recorded cases under Roman law (Vukmir 1992, 130). Hence, any discussion of intellectual property in Roman law is at best conjecture. Some other forms of intangible property were recognized (such as services of slaves, which could be temporarily transferred to other owners, or the transfer of inheritances), and although this did not affect trade in knowledge-derived items, Russ VerSteeg argued that this recognition of intangibles would be picked up later to underpin early modern (Roman law–influenced) copyright laws (VerSteeg 2000, 532). Many Roman goods that were traded throughout the empire (and beyond), however, were marked with a form of trademark, or makers' mark. Although this does not indicate a formalized law of intellectual property, the recognition of the ownership of aspects of knowledge may have existed as a form of acceptable practice. Furthermore, Roman law was less an instrument for the social control of commerce and more a resource that citizens could use to solve disputes in their relations with each other (Harries 1999, 80). Given the risks of entering the costly (and sometimes arbitrary) Roman legal system, alongside the rudimentary and partial protection accorded to information (and trade secrets), it is hardly surprising that no body of private Roman case law has been discovered in this area.

After the decline of the Roman Empire, these early (and essentially unformalized) ideas of ownership rights in knowledge or intellectual creations did not entirely disappear. One dispute in sixth-century Ireland has sometimes been identified as the first relatively formal copyright dispute (Birrell [1899] 1971, 42; Gerulaitis 1976, 32; Masterson 1940, 624; Ploman and Hamilton 1980, 8; Stearns 1992, 535n118).[1] As no such thing as copyright existed at this time, such claims are exaggerated, but nevertheless the case has some totemic resonance. It concerns

> Saint Columbia, who in the year 567 surreptitiously copied a psalm book belonging to his teacher, Finnian of Moville. When Finnian objected, the dispute went before King Diarmed. The king concluded that both the original and the copy belonged to Finnian saying, "To every cow her calf, and accordingly to every book its copy." Diarmed saw the book as Finnian's property, the ownership of which entitled Finnian to its product, the copy. (Stearns 1992, 535)

There is considerable doubt as to whether the reported story ever took place (see Scott 2001, 2nn9, 10), but its mythical quality does not detract from its importance as a signal of the continuing appeal of the ownership of knowledge. Legends may exist not so much as accounts of reality, but rather as the way in which attractive and useful ideas can remain in circulation. The legal hiatus after the fall of the Roman Empire did not extinguish the desire to own ideas and knowledge. In the following centuries, newly constituted guilds continued to develop the notion of knowledge as valuable and sought to establish rights of control (and exploitation) to protect their specialized knowledge (on behalf of their members, and against those outside the guild).

The Middle Ages, Guild Knowledge, and the Transition to Intellectual Property

During what used to be termed the Dark Ages, monasteries were the main repositories of knowledge resources in the form of manuscripts and the monks' learning. Although manuscripts were certainly highly valued, no one accorded particular significance to any particular manuscript in addition to a recognition of the hours spent in its copying (often amounting to

serial reproduction) and the physical material. With the rise of the universities after the twelfth century, these intellectual resources were transferred to
the new institutions. The regulations constituting universities often served
to ensure, however, that no one could establish proprietary rights over the
written word. Masterson argued that these regulations "were of such a character as to destroy the author's rights in an original work, it being generally
provided that manuscript dealers could not refuse to loan a copy for hire to
a member of the university even though the purpose of the member was the
producing of copies" (Masterson 1940, 624–625). Thus, any budding
notion of literary property that had survived from Roman practice was
largely rendered ineffective until the grants of patent monopoly in publications in the late fifteenth century.

During the Middles Ages, however, a propriety form of (trade)mark
continued to develop from Greek and Roman practices. Guilds required a
method of differentiating guild-sanctioned goods from others and of
enforcing their chartered monopolies. Ancient guilds do not seem to have
regarded craft-knowledge and its manifestation in goods as proprietary
(Long 1991, 864), but during the thirteenth century, guild attitudes were
changing. For instance, on 28 August 1282, during the tenth session, the
City Council of Parma enacted a statute

> for the protection of guilds and artisans in this state, and to prevent many
> frauds which are or may be committed upon them;—that no persons in the
> trade or guild shall use the mark of any other person in such trade or
> guild, nor place such mark, or similar one, upon knives or swords; and if
> any person in such guild has continuously used a mark upon knives,
> swords or other steel or iron articles for ten years, and any other person is
> found to have used, within one or two years the same mark or an imitation
> thereof, . . . whether stamped or formed in any other way, the latter shall
> not in future be allowed to use such a mark upon knives, swords, or other
> steel or iron articles, under penalty of ten pounds of Parma for each and
> every offence, and that regardless of any compromise or award of arbitra-
> tors, which may have been made. (Quoted in Paster 1969, 560)

Authorities across Europe passed similar statutes covering the products of
different guilds during this period. By the fourteenth century, such perceptions of guild knowledge were becoming relatively common. The weavers,
closely followed by the goldsmiths (both groups received charters from
Henry II in the 1320s), explicitly intended to control their craft knowledge
for their own profit. Over the next century a number of other trades also
established guilds with a similar rationale (Williston 1909, 199). As guilds
were organizations convened to control trade through monopoly, they
sought to develop a way to avoid ruinous competition by limiting the number of practitioners in any particular local market.

Although the guilds never referred to the craft knowledge and practices of their occupation as intellectual property, the assertion that they owned such knowledge, collectively as guild members, exhibits the recognition of value to be gained from establishing scarcity of use of knowledge (through guild membership). Guilds established two separate uses of marks: merchants' marks and production marks. Merchants' marks covered goods consigned for shipment, as proof of ownership when stolen or when shipwrecked goods were recovered. Production marks were more like modern trademarks that the guild system rigidly controlled: guild members were *required* to use marks. As a mode of regulation, marks enabled the tracing of defective goods to help the guild identify and punish the offending craftsman for the collective good of the guild. Marks also helped to prevent non–guild members from selling their products within the area of the guild monopoly (McClure 1979, 310–311). Trademarks were not yet assets representing the earned goodwill of a particular merchant or company, but they did already represent a key aspect of the proprietary knowledge of the guild. Guilds owned their symbols, and none outside the guild could legitimately use them. Marks indicated the guild origin and certified that the appropriate authorities had inspected and approved the goods.

Trademark protection was therefore perhaps the first form of intellectual property to find an expression that resembled current patterns of law. Guild marks established who had the right to produce certain goods. These marks constructed a form of scarcity in the production of goods (and the delivery of services), to maintain prices and protect the welfare of guild members. The guilds already recognized that their marks added competitive value to their products by differentiating them from nonguild goods that might not be produced to the same standards, might not have been authorized, and even might have been illegally imported. The relative scarcity of guild goods also ensured that the guilds could secure a premium.

Guilds also began to recognize that individual members might have an exclusive right to certain knowledge. Thus in 1432 the Genoese silk manufacturers adopted a number of general articles for the governance of their practices. One clearly stated that: "if anyone of said guild has had some pattern or figure designed, no one else shall have such figure or pattern worked" (quoted in Prager 1952, 126). In 1474 the Florentine Woollen Guild adopted a more specific article that stated that it "has been noted that certain fabricators of figured serge, by their own efforts have invented designs and patterns for figured serge, and that many other fabricators of such material are trying by means of fraud and deceit to steal such patterns from said fabricators" (quoted in Prager 1952, 127). The use of the word *steal* clearly signifies that people regarded such knowledge (patterns and designs) as property. The focus on members' "own efforts" exhibits the individualized understanding of innovation that lies at the center of contemporary intellectual property law.

As craft knowledge became more clearly valuable, it also became subject to envious appropriation. The false marking of competing goods, not produced by guild members, was recognized as theft. By the thirteenth century, the problem of unauthorized copying of valuable guild marks was significant enough to cause infringement to be deemed a serious crime with harsh penalties (Rogers 1910, 33). Guild members forcefully resisted cheaper nonguild goods and demanded a halt to their production. By the reign of Charles V in the sixteenth century, for instance, unauthorized producers of tapestries were punished by having a hand cut off. Hence, although monopoly producers may have appealed to arguments about quality and reliability, one can also recognize them as suppressing competition.

Individuals who broke from their guilds and took guild knowledge with them in many cases arrived in a new jurisdiction claiming that their knowledge was innovative and therefore amenable to protection through the introduction of some form of marking law. Where such legislative moves were successful, the protection of knowledge as a form of quasi property right was established and knowledge itself was individualized. What had previously been communal knowledge was now rendered as belonging to the importing individuals. Furthermore, protecting property as belonging to the individual knowledge creator (the genius or inventor) set the scene for the typical patent dispute: arguments over priority. It is hardly surprising that during the sixteenth century, disputes between contemporaries over precedence in invention or discovery became much more frequent (Long 1991, 883). Such individualization struck at the heart of guild knowledge ownership. Individual members themselves, not the guild in general, became the possible owners of novel practices they developed, setting the stage for the further development of the notion of intellectual *property*.

Early Patents

Prior to the legal formalization of intellectual property laws in Europe, rulers often utilized grants for the exclusive exploitation of new or previously unknown practices (David 1993, 46). At the end of the so-called Dark Ages, sovereigns offered patentlike privileges to introduce new processes or practices into their territory. In 1326 the British king encouraged the importation of "new arts." P. J. Federico claimed that this policy produced the "earliest known instance of a royal grant to foreigners," the letters of protection that King Edward III gave to John Kempe and his company, Flemish weavers, in 1331. Similarly, "letters patent [were] granted in 1440 to John Shiedame to introduce into England a newly-invented process of manufacturing salt" (Federico 1929, 293). Again, in 1449, John of Utynam returned from Flanders bringing with him a new method of producing colored glass for which he gained a monopoly grant (or patent) (although he is unlikely to have invented the process). He did promise to instruct others, however, so that once his grant expired the process would be readily available for others in the trade (Klitzke 1959, 627). Technology transfer was at the heart of this desire to establish patents, driven by the desire to reduce imports and expand exports (Prager 1944, 720ff.). At this time England was lagging behind some of the continental economies, and the king was interested in how craftsmen and merchants could "borrow" more advanced industrial practices.

Early patents were a method for encouraging the migration of skilled artisans into the territory concerned. Indeed, as Paul David pointed out, rulers hoped that the

> foreign master craftsmen would introduce English apprentices to the "mysterie" of their respective arts; but because they were not likely to remain in control of the newly skilled workers once they had passed into journeyman's status, a cohort of potential domestic competitors would thereby be created from whom the foreign master obviously wished to be protected. (David 1994, 134)

Thus, the award of monopoly rights over the trade (for a period of fourteen years; twice the period of apprenticeship) would ensure not only technological transfer but also a cohort of accomplished practitioners once the monopoly expired. Similar grants of monopolies were reasonably widespread throughout Europe during the Middle Ages. Owing to increasing international competition in certain economic sectors (woolens being perhaps the most important), many rulers had begun to make the development of national industrial capacity a priority.

These developments led Frank Prager to identify certain grants of privilege during the Middle Ages as "quasi-patents," covering mining operations, various water systems, and other commercial activities. But even though these were exclusive grants, they were not limited to new inventions, and they were often a form of building permit or in many cases a license to hold a monopoly. These privilege systems were not necessarily similar to modern patents, although a number of letters of patent that resemble protointellectual property have been found in archives, with one of the most developed sets preserved in the archives of Venice (Prager 1952, 125). The Duke of Saxony in 1398 granted one such quasi patent for papermaking, although the practice of papermaking had been known in Toledo by 1000 A.D. and in Nuremberg by 1390 (Prager 1952, 123). The grant was enforced through the duke's control of the power needed for production (the water in the river) and its denial to other papermakers under the grant.

These legal innovations reflected medieval urban economic policies to capture important craft knowledge for the benefit of the city and in some cases explicitly to encourage innovation (Long 1991, 875). These ideas then spread more widely when those who broke away from guilds set up in new industries and wished to claim possession of craft knowledge but had no organized guild to protect them from copying and competition (Long 1991, 881). Furthermore, the revival of Roman law after the twelfth century may also have stimulated the development of a prototypical notion of intellectual property, by stressing individual rights and a contract-based legal system (Bugbee 1967, 17). But the idea of a grant of patent also finds elements of its origins in the grant of privileges over mining in the late Middle Ages.

Marcus Popplow argued that the juridical practice of patent grants developed from the custom of granting privileges to mining entrepreneurs *as well as* to merchants (and others) for the introduction of new "arts" or skills to towns. These privileges were intended to defray mining's high costs by awarding a monopoly privilege. The "granting of privileges for inventions developed north of the Alps from the practice of granting the right to exploit mines to the 'first finder' and from the regulations concerning compensation for expenditure in digging drainage channels" (Popplow 1998, 107). Popplow suggested that later, when new water-lifting devices were developed to drain mines, this precedent was followed to protect mine owners from unauthorized copying of their devices. Not all grants included clauses forbidding the copying of devices being used, and during the fifteenth century it became increasingly common that privileges replaced the prohibition of copying with the possibility of licensed construction, thus freeing the privilege holder from actually building the device concerned. This practice was further developed in Venice to allow professional engineers to utilize their protection against unauthorized copying to secure the finance for particular projects, *prior* to the construction of the machines or devices covered by the patent.

If one had to nominate the moment when a prototypical patent first appeared most explicitly, then Filippo Brunelleschi's is as good a candidate as any. Some fifty years prior to the Venetian statute of 1474, the Florentine authorities awarded a patentlike grant to Brunelleschi for a new design of vessel to move loads more cheaply along the Arno River. In the petition for award, the bargain was made explicit: "[The petitioner] refuses to make such machine available to the public in order that the fruit of his genius and skill may not be reaped by another without his will and consent, and that, if he enjoyed some prerogative concerning this, he would open up what he is hiding and would disclose to all" (quoted in David 1993, 46). Thus the authorities rewarded the innovator in exchange for the public disclosure of the innovation. This patent combined a very wide scope, forbidding anyone to operate *any* new means of water transportation in Florentine territory without Brunelleschi's consent, with a limited term of protection; the grant was only for three years. In this it represented the two extremes of future patent provision: scope and temporality; it is crucial that, unlike previous grants of monopolies, it clearly asserted its reliance of the recognition of novelty (Bugbee 1967, 18). The monopoly was somewhat compromised when the vessel apparently sank on its maiden voyage carrying marble on the Arno.

Although Brunelleschi's grant was in one sense the first patent for innovation, the Florentine authorities did not issue a further similar grant in the following fifty years, nor did they make it general law through a legal statute. Bruce Bugbee suggested that this lack of continuity, leading to a "stillborn" system of patents for invention, can be attributed to guild rivalries, the limitation by decree to rewards by tax incentive only (in 1447), and the ascendancy of the Medici family, who preferred patronage as their system of rule (Bugbee 1967, 19). Nonetheless, although the first formal legislation was enacted in Venice, the nascent idea of intellectual property (and specifically grants of patent) was more widespread than just the environs of the lagoon.

Early Copyrights

Whereas the early or prelegislative history of patents was concerned with individual practitioners (who could be, though were not necessarily, the innovators), the early history of copyright is largely concerned with material artifacts. After the fall of Rome, any consideration regarding the rights of authors lapsed, along with Roman law. Little that might be regarded as similar to copyright was recognized until the Renaissance, when the innovation of the printing press stimulated the accelerated distribution of written knowledge. Until then the Middle Ages had remained predominantly an oral culture, and for the popular troubadours to retain "literary rights" in their works would have required them to keep their stories to themselves. One way around this was to seek patronage, as had happened in Roman times, or to offer to sell copies of their songs and stories to other performers (or offer to teach them the words for a fee) (Thomas 1976, 23). Either way, the writer's ability to retain rights over the product was problematic. Nevertheless, Rudolf Hirsch claimed that by the fourteenth century Petrarch "insisted in his letters that it was his sole right to permit or prevent the copying of his texts, until he himself had given it to the public (i.e., had it published) and that he alone controlled the authenticity of the text" (Hirsch 1967, 8). Only his reputation and relatively well known work made such a prohibition even partially possible, however.

Following the fifteenth-century invention of mechanical printing, publishing and bookselling emerged as major industries. The book trade developed very swiftly and reached an international scope in only a couple of years. Printing in Latin meant that trade was not limited to national markets, and despite sporadic localized literacy, an early market had already been developed through the circulation of scribal texts and the activities of monasteries across Europe. Once printers were producing books for sale, they sought some right to restrict copying to ensure that other printers did not copy their books, prompting the development of a form of legislated copyright. This closely parallels the guilds' need to ensure that their products were not reproduced outside the membership. For this emerging copyright the locus of protection was no longer the group, however, but the *individual* producer.

Indeed, only eighteen years after Gutenberg printed the first book using movable type, in 1469 John de Spira was granted the exclusive right to print the epistles of Cicero and Pliny in Venice (Robinson 1991, 56). Originally this monopoly grant had been intended to cover the technique of printing in its entirety (not limited to particular titles). On the death of de Spira a few months after the grant, the Venetian authorities refused, however, to transfer such a wide patent to his heirs. This cleared the way for the development of the Venetian printing industry (Gerulaitis 1976, 35; Hirsch 1967, 79). Attempts to retain control of the industry therefore moved to grants of patent (or *privilegi*) for certain forms of printing. Perhaps the most significant was the grant over the right to print Greek and Latin texts using italics, awarded to Aldus Manutius of the Aldine Press in 1502 by the Venetian authorities (a grant almost immediately subject to severe challenge).

Even before the arrival of printing, illuminators of manuscripts had developed a rudimentary method of taking multiple copies from a single illustration using a kind of tracing paper, and Marcel Thomas noted that during the fourteenth century there were "frequent cases of quarrels and even brawls between illuminators accusing each other of stealing the original cartoon, a priceless resource" (Thomas 1976, 27). An illustration depicting an event in an expensive manuscript was valuable on the basis of the value it added to the book (with better illustrations making manuscripts worth more, there was a clear temptation to appropriate them by "theft"). Furthermore, according to guild documents from the thirteenth century, not only did the stationers and booksellers operate a monopoly in general terms regarding their trade, in some cases they awarded monopolies over the multiple reproduction of any work to the master who obtained an order for it (Prager 1952, 134). The grounds on which property in printed works could be developed were therefore in place before the advent of printing itself started to make their development a serious issue for those involved in the book trade.

The development of rudimentary printing technology removed a bottle-neck in book production. Copying was a laborious and time-consuming task, limiting the supply of texts to retailers. Although printing may have removed the livelihood from many scribal producers, the stationers and retailers themselves merely moved into the wholesale and resale of the new printed texts (Pollard 1937, 19–20). As printing became an emergent indus-try with a stream of new entrants (often workers from established presses who set up on their own in rivalry with their erstwhile masters), competi-tion to produce valued and salable texts grew, and Elizabeth Eisenstein sug-gested that this spurred heated debates concerning monopoly and piracy. She went on to argue that printing "forced the legal definition of what belonged in the public domain," leading to the "enclosure" of a previous literary "common" as "possessive individualism began to characterize the attitude of writers to their work" (Eisenstein 1980, 120–121). Many of the legal innovations that laid the foundations for later copyright laws were first developed in the late fifteenth and early sixteenth century as the exten-sive Venetian publishing industry oscillated between boom and bust.[2]

Despite these precursors to the development of copyright, however, the artist or author as individual creative genius did not fully emerge much before the eighteenth century (Woodmansee 1984). If Alan Macfarlane is correct to argue that individualism first emerged in England owing to the specific circumstances of feudal and peasant society (Macfarlane 1978), then it might also be expected that intellectual property would have emerged first in English law. And indeed, such a claim could be made on the basis of the Statute of Monopolies (1624) and the Act of Anne (1710), both of which represented significant legal innovations (representing the formal origins of *modern* patent law and copyright law respectively), but—as is indicated by the above account—this is not the whole story.

Jacob Burckhardt ([1860] 1944, 81–103) famously made the claim that the notion of individualism, most specifically in the realm of the arts, can be traced back to Renaissance Italy. In this period the individual's "supreme worth was openly proclaimed" (Lukes 1973, 47), but only as the products of intellectual endeavor began to enjoy an economic value over and above their material manifestation would intellectual property develop as an institution. Nevertheless, the Venetian authorities took the crucial step in developing intellectual property more than 100 years before the English legislated for its protection. Subsequently, as the center of economic devel-opment in Europe moved toward England and London, the growing demands for the protection of intellectual property moved with it. Thus, despite making a crucial innovation with their treatment of intellectual property, the Venetians were not to develop it institutionally as far as did the legislators in London. Before we examine the political economy of the

institutionalization of intellectual property in English law, however, there is
the Venetian moment.

The Venetian Moment: Intellectual Property Is Born

Despite the widespread development of ideas about owning knowledge, the
first formalized patent system was only developed in the fifteenth century
in Venice. For the first time a legal and institutional form of intellectual
property rights established the ownership of knowledge and was explicitly
utilized to promote innovation. In one of the few extensive studies of
Venice's legal innovation in this area, Giulio Mandich suggested that
"Venice was the first to have continuously and constantly applied certain
rules to patents of invention, instead of granting an occasional isolated
monopoly" (Mandich 1948, 206). The rules were remarkably prescient,
given subsequent developments. Grants were not recognized where there
was prior knowledge within the territory of the republic of the supposed
innovation or invention (newness); there was a requirement for utility (or
usefulness); the term of the grant was limited (time limits for protection);
rights were transferable (alienability); there was a rudimentary working
requirement, in that patent grants were forfeited by failure to use them
within a certain term, and the state retained a right to compulsory license
(Mandich 1948, 207). Thus, although intellectual property did not emerge
fully formed in Venice at this time, the subsequent history of legal refinement has had much less substantive effect on its central tenets than the
Venetian statute's departure from previous practice.

The Venetian government was not a state in the sense that became
widespread in the following centuries. There was no formal constitution
and no clear separation of authority among legislative, administrative, and
judicial bodies. Instead, custom and precedent guided government behavior, with the overlapping authority of various councils verifying that rule
was essentially impartial (Greif 1995, 735). Venice enacted its first patent
statute in 1474. The new statute-derived patents were not universally adopted by Venetian innovators or entrepreneurial merchants in the next twenty-
five years, however, although this may have been owing to the absence of a
single political authority to enforce the new practice. Nevertheless, the
statute confirms that the Venetian authorities were concerned with the management of the city's economy and recognized the importance of technological innovation to its success.

During the fourteenth and fifteenth centuries the granting of patents for
monopolies as opposed to innovations was broadly similar across the continent of Europe and Britain. Indeed, specific grants of monopolies (in
Venice termed *privilegi*) were far from unknown and survive in the legal

archives of many states. But on 19 March 1474 Venice made its practices unique, when the senate passed the following decree:

> There are in this city and its neighborhood, attracted by its excellence and greatness, many men of diverse origins, having most subtle minds and able to devise and discover various ingenious artifices. And, if it should be provided that no-one else might make or take to himself to increase his own honour the works and devices discovered by such men, those same men would exercise their ingenuity, and would discover and make things which would be of no little utility and advantage to our state.
>
> Therefore it is enacted by the authority of this body that whoever makes in this city any new and ingenious device, not previously made within our jurisdiction, is bound to register it at the office of the *Provveditori di Comun* as soon as it has been perfected, so that it will be possible to use and apply it. It will be prohibited to anyone else within any of our territories to make any other device in the form or likeness of that one without the author's consent or licence, for the term of ten years. But if anyone should act thus, the aforesaid author and inventor would be free to cite him before every office of this city, by which office the aforesaid infringer would be prepared to pay one hundred ducats and his artifice would be immediately destroyed. But our Government will be free, at its total pleasure, to take for its own use and needs any of the said devices or instruments, on this condition, that others than the authors may not employ them. (Quoted in Phillips 1982, 75–76)[3]

For the first time, patents were subject to a generalized law, rather than a process of individual petition and grant.

Previously some grants had awarded monopolies in innovations, but there was no necessary requirement for absolute innovation for the award of monopolies (or other quasi patents) prior to this decree (Long 1991, 877–878). Neither was the petitioner required to be the innovator or originator of the practice for which a monopoly was requested. It remains unclear whether the statute merely codified existing practice as represented by previous individual grants (Bugbee 1967, 23) or represented a legislative departure. Even if it was mainly the formal recognition of customary Venetian practice with regard to innovation, the lack of a previous *generalized* law makes this statute important.

Grants now were based not on the relationship between the petitioner and the authorities but rather on the applicants' ability to fulfill certain fixed criteria. Nevertheless, as David pointed out, "it appears that between 1474 and 1490, very few patents actually were issued under the Venetian code, despite the fact that right through to the middle of the sixteenth century many patent *privilegi* continued to be granted, conferring exclusive production rights for terms varying between 5 and 80 years as well as monopolistic trade privileges" (David 1993, 47). The *privilegi* were not displaced by formal patents for innovation, retaining their utility by virtue of their relationship with the guild-controlled sectors of the economy. When an invention or a new technological improvement was proposed that was likely to impact on an existing guild monopoly, *privilegi* allowed for the city-government sanctioned monopoly to be breached on the grounds of socioeconomic utility.

Privilegi had not been of unlimited duration, nor necessarily exclusive (they diluted monopoly rights previously held), but were subject to the governing authorities' assessment of social (or municipal) utility (Prager 1944, 714). This form of rewarding innovation (as opposed to a formalized law of patent) was around 150 years old when the new statute was enacted.[4] From the twelfth to fifteenth centuries many *privilegi* were granted by the Venetian authorities, sometimes in the face of established guild monopolies. There was often more reward from breaking an existing monopoly than developing a new one (with a new technology or product), although new monopolies could still be very profitable.

The Venetian legislators explicitly forbade some monopolies; having prohibited the glassmakers' guild from the manufacture of "glasses for the eyes, for reading," the *privilegi* was thrown open to the public to allow for maximum distribution. Within this emerging realm of intellectual property, the Venetians already had developed a practical view regarding the balance between public and private benefits from the ownership of knowledge, allied to the need to support innovation (although only for practices that actually worked; the *privilegi* for windmills included a revocation clause if the specific device failed). Thus, the social utility of the wide distribution of reading glasses, especially in a culture where printing and dissemination of knowledge through books were becoming key elements of social life, far outstripped the need to reward (or favor) guild members.

Once the statute had been adopted, a formal distinction emerged between prototypical patents, which encompassed a bargain between private reward and public availability of knowledge, and the notion of privileged private reward encoded through *privilegi*. Even so, for some time potential patent applicants were able to choose *privilegi* over the mechanism of the 1474 statute. Although some applicants utilized the wording of the statute, others continued to relate their applications to customary law, especially in the period immediately after its adoption by the senate (Mandich 1948, 184). The novelty of the statute, and the existence of competing monopoly grants, ensured there was less of a "big bang" and more of a gradual expansion of coverage for the nascent idea of intellectual property. Nonetheless, the statute remains historically important as the first formal institutionalization of intellectual property.

As noted above, the outlines of the modern patent system are discernible within the text of the 1474 Venetian decree. Key components of the statute included a balance of knowledge available through a state-sanctioned public realm, the rights of the innovators to benefit from their intellectual endeavor, and the notion of reward for effort. The last, which is one of the key justifications mobilized to legitimize (intellectual) property, is expressed in general terms here, perhaps for the first time. Within the text labor's desert is made explicit: "if it should be provided that no-one else might make or take to himself to increase his own honour the works and devices discovered by such men, those same men would exercise their ingenuity, and would discover and make things which would be of no little utility and advantage. . . ." Provided these "men of ingenuity" can have their new ideas protected by the Senate (acting on behalf of the Venetian commune), they will continue to develop new ideas. Even though the Senate would act to ensure that any infringer was punished, however, it reserved the right to use such innovations for its own strategic ends. If the Senate can be said in a general sense to represent the interests of its public, then this provision is a first recognition that the (nascent) state itself has a developed interest in securing advances for the economic development of its economy.[5] As Fernand Braudel noted: "Nine times out of ten the patents of invention, serious or not, recorded on the pages of registers and dossiers in the Venetian Senate corresponded to the particular problems of the city. . . . Social considerations were the uppermost" (Braudel 1981, 433–434). Although as yet not a fully fledged public interest in innovation, a preliminary version of the central balance between public benefits of dissemination (as well as wide use) and the private rewards "required" to encourage intellectual activity is evident.

The Venetian authorities had historically tried to use the guilds as one way of balancing public and private interests in the everyday economic life of the city (Mackenney 1987, 14). Thus, this approach was hardly alien to the legislators who drafted the statute. Indeed, at this time the political and social structure of Venice was overwhelmingly corporatist in character (Mackenney 1992). The individualization of knowledge was starting to cause problems for the guilds, however, and therefore the move to a more formalized protection helped both to (re)establish the protection of valuable knowledge and to shift the focus of protection away from the guild and toward the individual. Although a corporatist governance structure might have encompassed some notion of the social good represented by a public realm of knowledge, with the emergence of the individual as a recognizable social actor, the Venetian city authorities would likely have found themselves attempting to balance their corporatist view of the organization of the city's affairs with demands from individuals to be recognized as worthy of reward in their own right. Thus, this conjuncture of emerging individualism (the sovereign knowledge creator) alongside the relatively rare governance structure of Venice at this time (not based on an individual autocratic ruler) produced a unique opportunity to develop this early notion of intellectual property in the form of public/private bargain over innovation and its dissemination.

The first known attempt to protect craft knowledge in Venice had been a decree issued by the Council of Venice on 21 May 1297 that stated: "If a physician makes a medicine based on his own secret, he too must make it only of the best materials; it all must be kept within the Guild; and all Guild members must swear not to pry into it" (quoted in Bugbee 1967, 20). By issuing a decree to this effect the council gave limitations on the diffusion of knowledge the weight of law rather than merely of guild regulation. Although formally a separate organizational entity, the Senate was able to control the guilds through the choice of magistrates who represented the guild's interests to the government but also played a major role in the guild's governance. Although other officers of the guild were chosen from their own ranks, they were still beholden to the governing magistracy and the regulations it approved. But it is a mistake to see the guilds as merely a method of governmental control of economic life in Venice at this time. The well-established appeal procedures enabled the guildsmen to restrain the practice of guild officers (Mackenney 1987, 21–28). Not least of all owing to the Senate's desire to foster economic well-being, the guildsmen's appeals could lead to shifts in the way they were governed.

There was therefore a well-established link between the guilds and the government of Venice. Through these channels the Senate would have been alerted to the manner in which guilds perceived their knowledge resources, and the guilds would have likely had some impact on how the Senate's members started to think about the value of similar resources for Venice as a whole. Venetian guilds had been responsible for the policing of trade-marks to constrain counterfeiting since the twelfth century, and thus the notion of the importance of a "knowledge" element to commodities was well established in the city (Mackenney 1987, chaps. 1 and 3). Furthermore, for both the Senate and the Council of Ten, which had day-to-day oversight of legislation, responding to pressure from below regarding issues of governance was accepted and quite usual practice (Finlay 1980, 44–59). Thus, the guilds could have made their needs known directly and also through their membership of the General Assembly to which the Senate and council were partly accountable. That the statute of 1474 was the result of pressure from below combined with the city authority's own wishes not only seems likely but would fit with the normal political practices of Venice at this time.

Certain Venetian guilds therefore may have sought to strengthen their control over strategic knowledge by persuading the state to support their efforts in the first instance through customary law, cumulating in the statute of 1474. That said, a number of patents awarded under the statute were granted to non-Venetians, and thus the statute may have actually been more effective at encouraging the importation of techniques and technology. Furthermore, as noted above regarding *privilegi*, new knowledge or innovation was often likely to infringe on guild monopolies, and thus, although innovation within the guild's membership was valued, innovation outside was dangerous and threatening. In any case, as demand rose for cheap consumables (textiles, food), the guilds found themselves increasingly subject to competition from sectors outside their historic cartels (Thrupp 1963, 276). In this sense the guilds' support for patents in Venice may have been a reaction to economic problems of new competition and new technologies. Their leaders, through contacts with the Senate, may have sought laws that would (at least temporarily) guard their knowledge-related advantage. Thus, patents in Venice, even though formally introduced to protect innovation, may have been intended (by the guilds at least) to protect extant knowledge in service of their traditional advantage against non–guild members. The Venetian authorities on the other hand seem to have had more general concerns regarding the economic well-being of the city's economy.

The general economic advantage to Venice was recognized in the preamble to the statute, valuing "devices of great utility and benefit to our commonwealth" (Mandich 1948, 176). Already the strategic argument for economic innovation (which is to say the social value of innovation) is apparent in the minds of the Senate's legislators. Likewise, the issue of *usefulness* is clearly articulated in the statute with the phrase "as soon as [the device] has been perfected, so that it will be possible to use and apply it." The issue of invention (or in contemporary patent terms, *novelty*) within the Venetian territory is also explicitly stated: "any new and ingenious device, not previously made within our jurisdiction" would be subject to the statute. According to Mandich, in this decree "in outline, a requirement of inventive merit seems to emerge, according to which the invention must not be a trifling, all too obvious application of known technology" (Mandich 1948, 177). In the papers regarding Galileo's patent of 1594 for a water pump, it is clear that the Purveyors of the Venetian Commune (directly accountable to the council) had the responsibility for ensuring that potential grants fulfilled these conditions before they were granted (Federico 1926). The distinction between previous monopolies and the reward for invention is made explicit here, as is the formal requirement of a process that begins to approach formalized patent examination.

Those empowered to examine claims for *novelty* and *usefulness* often were unable, however, to completely ascertain a petition's validity, either because in many cases applicants were still in the early stages of developing their particular technological innovation or because previously patents were incompletely recorded. Thus, in a number of cases the patents were awarded, with the provisos "without prejudice to other patents previously granted" or "assuming without deciding that this is a new invention, not heretofore disclosed by others" (Mandich 1948, 187; Prager 1964, 271). If there was a dispute between two applicants, the purveyors (or magistrates) embarked on a fuller investigation. Even then, given the lack of formal criteria for patent submissions and the differing modes of application, the investigating magistrates could never be absolutely sure of their conclusions. The 1474 statute was a blunt and unrefined instrument for the protection of intellectual property. Where there was doubt arising from these inconclusive investigations, it was always resolved in favor of the applicant concerned: the records indicate that between 1474 and 1550 not a single petition for a patent was rejected by the Senate (Mandich 1948, 189). This privileging of the interests of knowledge owners will become familiar as our history progresses.

On the other hand, the Senate was also fully aware of the act's requirement for a device to have been "perfected" in order for protection to be awarded. A considerable number of grants had further tests inserted to ensure that at a later date the shortcomings of the initial investigation into *usefulness* and *novelty* could be made good. In some cases the clause "the patent shall be void, as though it had never been issued" was inserted to cover the instance of an inventor failing the test set at a specified later date. If the device could not be operated, or turned out not to be novel, again the particular patent was canceled. The Senate required the test to show not merely actual use, but successful use vis-à-vis its claimed purpose. Some patents were written to only run from the successful completion of such tests in any case and therefore were only provisional (Mandich 1948, 189). Given Leonardo da Vinci's observation that people with inventions, such as perpetual motion machines, often set out for Venice to seek a patent (Popplow 1998, 109), such tests served a clear purpose of sorting out what was worth awarding a patent to and what was not. Although this system may have encouraged innovation and contributed in some way to Venice's continued prosperity, as time passed other factors started to shift the currents of history away from the lagoon.

While Venice had been a major city economy and a major trade center, it had attracted streams of artisans and entrepreneurs of various sorts. As the city declined in the face of new trade routes and the rise of other European trade centers, the flow of individuals reversed. With the beginnings of decline, artisans left, taking with them their skills, their technologies, and their relatively well-developed understanding of intellectual property that had become relatively commonplace in Venice. As Prager argued, in "most places the patent system was adopted almost exactly as developed in Venice. . . . [A]ll of the basic rules developed in Venice were preserved in the subsequent systems" (Prager 1944, 720). The appeal of the patent system for rulers in whose territories these migrants settled lay in the benefits to the economy overall through the importation of new methods of manufacturing. The competition for these artisans should not be underestimated, and one way of encouraging their immigration was to ensure that their special skills and practices enriched them.

Patents, Printing, and the Venetian Economy

Although it is beyond the scope of this chapter to examine the role of the statute throughout the Venetian economy, it is worth examining one important sector. Printing in Venice exhibits the triangulation we are concerned to reveal especially well: here the links among legislation, technology, and the ideology of ownership can be easily identified. In the late fifteenth century, Venice had become the "capital of printing" after the authorities had struck down de Spira's attempt to set up a monopoly over the industry. Venice had strong commercial links with Germany, and thus when German printers moved to Italy to be nearer their best market, they often chose to set up business in Venice (Gerulaitis 1976, 2).[6] Richard Mackenney suggested that this new trade was the "most significant contribution which Venice made to the civilization of the Renaissance" (Mackenney 1992, 61). There was a well-developed home market, and as Aldus Manutius realized, the concentration of scholars able to translate classical texts into the vernacular for the new popular editions made Venice a magnet for printing activities.

Printing related to intellectual property in three ways during this period. In the first instance, patents were awarded for the actual techniques of printing (most important were innovative typefaces, such as roman and italic). Second, there was also a move toward a system of copyright for the contents of some publications. And third, the increased diffusion of scientific and technical knowledge through the circulation of books in the fifty years after the invention of printing meant that the mere holding of a "secret" process or mechanism was less likely to ensure a monopoly over its use. The printing of books of techniques (often drawn from medieval texts) may have only codified well-known practices, but they often revealed intentionally concealed techniques to a much wider audience (Long 1991, 860n37). Thus, once the limited distribution of information and knowledge had been adversely affected by the explosion in printed materials discussing techniques and "science," the original owners of such knowledge were likely to seek ways of reimposing some form of scarcity to protect their interests.

Therefore, although subject to intellectual property provisions in themselves, the printing trades also had a profound impact on the political economic environment in which intellectual property as a formal institution developed. This burgeoning public domain of information availability contributed to the 1474 statute's very clear stand on novelty. Monopolies would only be awarded henceforth if innovations were new to Venice. The advent of printing prompted knowledge holders to seek protection but also limited that protection to specific sorts of knowledge (the new, the useful). The recognition of what would now be termed *prior art* became much more a case of prior publication of a specific idea or set of supposed innovations.

Alongside the burgeoning institutionalization of intellectual property, the printing trades in Venice flourished. During the two years prior to the statute of 1474, the printing trade had found itself in a crisis of oversupply. The printing of Latin classics far outstripped the demand and left many printers either bankrupt or at the mercy of their creditors. This situation led to some consolidation, with at least one press, that of Vindelinus, passing into the hands of two German entrepreneurs (Gerulaitis 1976, 23; Lowry 1979, 13). The oversupply of (duplicated) texts from different printers could have been avoided through some form of copyright. Given the Venetian authorities' interest in the city's economy, it is possible that this was also a contributory factor in the form of protection laid out in the statute, although there is nothing in its text to directly support such a supposition. Hirsch asserted from his understanding of the Venetian industry, however, that the protection offered printers was not a product of "scruples, nor the attitude of the public [to pirated copies], but [that] economic considerations were responsible for privileges" (Hirsch 1967, 81). Certainly, the industry thrived in Venice at the very same time that intellectual property laws became more formalized.

The Aldine Press, the first "popular" press, printing long runs of around 1,500 per edition, was increasingly active in the twenty years after the passing of the 1474 statute. Linked to a vigorous export trade, for the first time scholars could discover the classics without recourse to the expensive and small editions hitherto produced (Eisenstein 1980, 223). The Venetian printing trade exhibited an innovative and export-oriented character. Publishers and printers were in the market to make a profit, and even in this early period of quasi capitalism the logic of reducing prices (through lowered costs) to expand the market was already affecting the sector as a whole (Gerulaitis 1976, 10–11, 19). But, like content providers today, Aldine and other printers had a problem with counterfeits.

One strategy against imitations was to patent the typeface that was used, and many printers sought this protection. For instance, on 14 November 1502, Aldus was granted a monopoly for all Greek and Latin publications in italic within the Venetian jurisdiction. This grant was the first time a (known) patent was awarded for the use of a typeface, rather than the works printed with it. The grant seems to have caused a major rift between Aldus and the master who had cut the type, who regarded it as his, not Aldus's. Aldus retained the grant, however, and the master, Francesco Griffo (along with others) wasted little time in breaking the monopoly, engendering a controversy over the first use and legitimate ownership of italic that seems not to have been satisfactorily adjudicated by the Venetian authorities of the time (Lowry 1979, 89, 140). The most prestigious printers secured patronage for their expensive editions, which freed them from an overall reliance on profit from their activities. But Aldus Manutius, exhibiting the characteristic modernism of fifteenth-century Venice, took advantage of the economies of scale that could be secured from larger editions, competing with other editions through price and availability. Counterfeit editions remained a major problem, despite the supposed protections (including in Aldus's case not only letters of patent but also a papal bull). Unfortunately, authority over the issue of adjudication did not rest with a single body, and neither was it always easy to ascertain the similarity of the copy, or its date. Although patents, *privilegi,* and other methods were deployed, this was not a complete success.

Aldine used the italics cut in 1501 to support the proliferation of the pocket classics by which the press became known throughout Europe and beyond, becoming perhaps the best known publishing house of the age (Allen 1913, 305). So well known was Aldine that when Erasmus, in 1508, was looking for a publisher who would be able to produce an expanded edition of his *Adages* with some form of protection for Erasmus's "rights" as an author, he directly approached Aldus Manutius. Once agreement had been made to publish, Erasmus moved to Venice for some years to work closely with the publisher. From her close reading of Erasmus's work on the *Adages*, Kathy Eden argued that the author was centrally concerned with his (intellectual property) rights (Eden 2001, 271 passim). It is therefore likely that although the reputation of Aldine for production quality and distribution contributed to Erasmus's choice, his desire to gain some advantage from the Venetian system of protection was also important. It is also likely that Aldus Manutius would have reassured him that the system was quite effective. In the previous year the Aldine Press had successfully prevailed in a legal action over Filippo Giunti, who had counterfeited a number of the publisher's texts (Lowry 1979, 156–158). This action was less successful when it came to the patent for italics, but for Erasmus such actions would have been an attractive bonus to publication with Aldine.

By 1518 problems of counterfeit editions carrying the Aldus mark had become ever more serious, as the preface to that year's edition of *Livy* testifies:

> Lastly, I must draw the attention of the student to the fact that some Florentine printers, seeing that they could not equal our diligence in correcting and printing, have resorted to their usual artifices. To Aldus's Institutiones Gramaticae, printed in their offices, they have affixed our well known sign of the Dolphin wound round the Anchor. But they have so managed that any person who is the least acquainted with the books of

our production, cannot fail to observe that this is an impudent fraud. For the head of the Dolphin is turned to the left, whereas that of ours is well known to be turned to the right. (Quoted in Azmi, Maniatis, and Sodipo 1997, 138)

As would become common, counterfeiting engendered not only a discourse of theft but also a justification of intellectual property based on the just reward for labor; the fraudsters unable to "equal our diligence in correcting and printing, have resorted to their usual artifices": passing off inferior goods under an established mark. The death of Aldus in 1515 coincided with the Venetian authorities' revocation of all previous privileges in an attempt to stamp out the widespread abuse of such monopolies (Prager 1944, 717; Hirsch 1967, 85), however, and therefore in strictly legal terms "pirated" editions from that year and after were taking advantage of the termination of these protections.

Many successful printers deemed protection through grants of *privilegi* over specific texts to be crucial. This reduced competition and established monopolies over their chosen texts. The desire for a form of copyright protection was prompted by some strikingly familiar practices. As Martin Lowry noted, some of the petitions for copyright presented to the Venetian government during the 1490s

conjure up pictures of a sinister underground at work within the industry: its agents sniff out any new and important work, which is in preparation, bribe some disaffected worker, and secure a copy; secret presses mass-produce the stolen text; a cheap version appears on the market before the original, and the poor printer who has invested his money and expertise in the project is left destitute. (Lowry 1979, 14)

Thus, the desire for a legislative settlement regarding the issue of legitimate copyright was hardly a surprise. In addition, almost from the start the Venetian printers were working within a prototypical capitalist structure of production, and within this organizational pattern, secure property rights over the intellectual content of their products were of increasing importance.[7]

In most cases *privilegi*, and after 1474 monopolies (or quasi patents), were granted to the printers, not the authors. Sabellico's *privilegi* of 1486 in regard of his history of Venice, however, allowed him "to choose which printer would publish his book, and any other printer who published it would be fined 500 ducats." This grant was then reinforced by a second *privilegi* three days before official publication, possibly intended to quash rumor and speculation regarding the previous grant's veracity (Chavasse 1986, 26).[8] Other grants included one in 1492 to Petro Francesco da Ravenna for *Foenix*, and showing some inflation in the value put upon putative intellectual property, in 1515 Ariosto's rights to his *Orlando furioso* carried a penalty for piracy of 1,000 ducats (Rose 1993, 10; Eden 2001, 270–271). The key players, however, as would be clear in Britain two hundred years later, were the printers (or publishers) rather than the authors.

Responding to a scramble to secure rights on profitable titles, the earliest formal provision for the protection of copyright (separate from grants of patent for textual content) was formulated by the Council of Ten in Venice, sitting between 1544 and 1545. Their decree "prohibited the printing of any work unless written permission from the author or his immediate heirs had been submitted to the Commissioners of the University of Padua" (David 1993, 52). As with the patent statute, considerable customary practice preceded its formal institutionalization. After 1493, when the Venetian Cabinet set a precedent by giving Daniele Barbaro a ten-year exclusive grant to publish a book by his late brother Ermolao (whose close connections with the Venetian authorities no doubt eased such a grant), and before 1517, any title could be the subject of an award of monopoly. This had led to a rush by printers and publishers to secure profitable titles, either for immediate publication or so the monopolies could be sold on.

In 1517 the Senate restricted *privilegi* henceforth to "new and previously unprinted works" to reduce the number of claims and counterclaims it was required to hear (David 1993, 51). Problems arose again, however. The granting of *privilegi* mushroomed after a lull of a few years, and in 1534 the Senate stipulated that *privilegi* only remained valid if the title was published within a year. This was intended to halt the hoarding of unpublished titles and to stimulate continued expansion of the trade (Gerulaitis 1976, 46). But the problem of counterfeit editions remained.

In 1549 all Venice's printers and booksellers were finally organized into a guild, which allowed a full record of works to be maintained (to police unauthorized reprinting) and also gave the church some assistance in suppressing heretical literature (David 1993, 52). Authors now (as for most of the history of printing) were dependent on the publishers to secure publication of their work through the legal formalization of a protectable (copyrighted) text. Protection relied on the guild's members, and this monopoly fitted well with many European guilds' own perception of their ownership of knowledge.

The formal wording of the law had not made such a turn of events obvious, however. The Council of Ten ordered in the 1544 act that "no printer of this city shall dare to print, or to offer for sale when printed, any works regardless in what language, unless the author thereof, or his immediate heirs, have declared their consent in writing to the Board of Education (*Refomatori*) in the State University of Education" (quoted in Mandich 1948, 204). This phrasing seems to indicate that copyright lay with the author. Indeed, this may be the first time something akin to the author as individual creator was legally codified: certainly the printer and publisher superficially seem to move into secondary positions. The operation of the patent system regarding the practice of printing itself and the prohibition of parallel production of specific texts undermined this position, however. Without rights to the means of reproduction, the Venetian copyright holder was (as is often the case today) at the mercy of a printer or publisher who was (and is) willing to print copies of the copyrighted text.

Nevertheless, Prager argued that "authors went more readily to Venice than to any other city, in their search for publishers. This preference was caused by the copyright tradition at least as much as by the excellence of paper stock and typography" (Prager 1952, 135). And, of course, the excellence in typography was also supported by the Venetian system of intellectual property through patents granted under the statute of 1474. Significantly, as each book carried the printers "device" regarding the grant of patent and the author's formal copyright, so the idea of intellectual property was spread through the export markets dominated by the Venetian presses. Eventually ecclesiastical censorship caused the severe contraction of the book trade in Venice, however. Although the Tridentine Index of 1564 had some adverse effects, it was the Clementine Index of 1596 that caused a general exodus of printers in response to the strict limitation on the types of works that could be legally printed, and within a few months of its publication the number of presses in Venice fell from 125 to forty (Logan 1972, 76). At this point, and linked to the wider issues around the decline of Venice and the rise of its competitors (most significantly, London), the history of patent and copyright moves to Britain.

The Venetian moment produced the skeleton of a system that has been remarkably robust in its central elements. In Venice, the invention of something akin to modern intellectual property was in part a response to a new revolutionary information technology. Printing changed the environment in which knowledge and information could be deployed. It changed the rules of the game for those who sought to profit from their control of ownership of secret processes and techniques, of privileged information, or merely of access to important scholarship. In this period of upheaval in the knowledge environment, practitioners and the political authorities innovated (or elaborated on emerging practices) to produce new forms of property rights. During the fifteenth century the institutionalization of intellectual property not only was directly related to the previous customary practice but remained only one method of providing protection. Depending on the sorts of protection they required, petitioners might seek a patent related to the statute of 1474, or they might petition for *privilegi*, or try to retain knowledge or information through guild secrecy. Protection was supple and related to the needs of the knowledge owner.

Certainly there is a coincidence between Venetian success, its domination of printing (a strategic technology of its time), and the emergence of intellectual property that might imply some causal link. In the conventional justification for patents, this link is axiomatic. Although presented in terms of universal principles, what the Venetian moment reveals, however, is that from its legislative origins, intellectual property was not unduly concerned with the idealized individual and his rights but rather was a city/government-derived strategy for the development of competitive advantage and effective economic organization. Furthermore, the central ideas of intellectual property were developed in the guilds, the private sector, before being adopted by the juridical authorities. The 1474 statute was intended to shore up and improve Venice's position in a number of industrial sectors in response to the problems that were starting to beset their commercial empire at the end of the fifteenth century. But this response was driven by a logic developed not by the legislators but by those who would gain from a formal ownership regime in knowledge. As intellectual property emerged as an institution, whatever subsequent justifications may claim, the rights and interests of the owners of knowledge, not its producers, were regarded as central to legislative innovation.

Elsewhere

Before picking up the history of intellectual property where many accounts start, in the legislative innovations of the British court in the seventeenth and eighteenth centuries, we shall very briefly outline some significant, although broadly independent, developments to one side of our main story. These developments are both interesting and noteworthy for contemplating alternative approaches to the property systems that emerged from the historical trajectory that we examine in detail. More research is needed in this area, and such work would be a helpful contribution toward imagining alternatives to the legal trajectory that we explore here.

The concept of the theft of ideas was also developed in Jewish social practices: reporters of the Hebrew Talmud were required to identify contributors of additions and new principles while making their oral presentation. This requirement finds its roots in Chapter 23 of Jeremiah, which states that "therefore behold saith the Lord. I am against the prophets that *steal my words* everyone from his neighbour" (quoted in Hazan 1970, 24). Victor Hazan suggested that this explains the important principle of Jewish law, dating at least back to 70 A.D., that the reporting of others, words as one's own was unlawful (Hazan 1970, 25). Although the citation of previous contributors is hardly a property right, it does recognize the author as in some manner enjoying ownership of a particular idea, inasmuch as that authorship should be reported to subsequent audiences.

The Chinese also developed many of the technological innovations that prompted thought about property in knowledge in Italy and Europe, without developing the notion of intellectual property themselves. Furthermore, the notion of awarding monopolies sanctioned by the state was also a key part of Chinese imperial economic policy during and after the Han dynasty (Barron 1991, 321). In Europe this laid the grounds for patent statutes, but not in China. Likewise, around 500 years before the invention of movable type in Europe, the innovation that sparked the "Gutenberg revolution" in printing, the Chinese had used this method to reproduce texts (Febvre and Martin 1976, 71–76). This was never fully developed, however, partly because of the large number of characters in written Chinese, but because also to Chinese eyes, movable type worked against the established (and highly valued) traditions of calligraphy (Febvre and Martin 1976, 75). Although individual creativity was valued, the expression was such that a mechanical form of reproduction was not feasible, except through the laborious engraving of plates or blocks (both methods widely used in Chinese printing). And given the low level of literacy, less than 20 percent of the population by the eve of the twentieth century, the (qualified) mass market that printers elsewhere responded to was relatively absent from China for most of the period after the initial technological innovation of printing.

William Alford argued at some length that a form of intellectual property did not emerge, whatever the economic and technological factors, for a specifically political philosophical reason: Confucianism (Alford 1995, 19ff.). The valuing of the past within a complex pattern of social relations led the Chinese to value unencumbered access to the knowledge of the past from whatever source. Although in many ways the Chinese empire might have exhibited some of the elements that could have stimulated the development of property in knowledge, without the requisite political stimulation such developments failed to produce the same results that are evident in Venice and other European cities during the fifteenth century.

In Korea, the court was keen to disseminate knowledge through the printing of books and during the late fourteenth and early fifteenth centuries sponsored in government printing shops the development of new methods of printing to satisfy this policy. The first three sets of movable type were produced in 1403, 1420, and 1434, just preceding Gutenberg's breakthrough, but again there appears to have been no parallel development of the idea of property in knowledge.

Elsewhere, the Balinese did not adopt a principle of intellectual property despite a highly developed practice of artistic expression; they regarded artistic and creative (or innovative) activity as an expression of collective thought. As such there is no intellectual division of labor recognizing a specific class of intellectual producers and thus no need or desire to identify the originators of new expressions or ideas in art or technology. Again, lacking the philosophical structure that stressed the individual as in some way sovereign over his or her own ideas, the notion of intellectual property remained alien (Ploman and Hamilton 1980, 4–5).

These brief examples serve to further emphasize the central argument we are making throughout this book. Intellectual property is the result of developments in *three* specific social areas: the technological, the legal/political, and the philosophical (as regards the conceptualization of the individual knowledge producer). And it is only in the history of modern capitalism, and its expansion through globalization, that the conjunction of all three elements has produced the sort of intellectual property laws that have been consolidated by the Agreement on Trade Related Aspects of Intellectual Property Rights (TRIPs) at the World Trade Organization. In the next chapter we return to this history and examine the more frequently nominated dawn of intellectual property: Britain in the seventeenth and eighteenth centuries.

Notes

1. Charles Carroll has suggested to us in private correspondence that the source for this story is most likely Jeoffrey Keating's *History of Ireland* ([1629] 1854, 2:452).

2. The English industry got off to a much slower start, with publication reliant on patronage and the demand of prominent individuals for much longer than was the case for Venetian printers (see Lathrop 1922).

3. The translation provided in Mandich (1948) is at variance with the text in Phillips (1982), which was adapted from Frumkin's translation (Frumkin 1947) and slightly different from the text provided in Ladas (1975). All four texts, which are reproduced in full in May (2002b), are similar enough, however, to establish the meaning of the act, which is what concerns us here.

4. Harold Wegner reported that Erich Kaufer has argued that the Venetian system was to a large extent a transplant from the Tyrolean region conquered by Venice. As Wegner also noted, however, this argument has received little support from other historians (Wegner 1993, 2–3), and although a certain similarity in practice is noted by Marcus Popplow (1998, 107–108), there remains little evidence of direct influence in this direction.

5. This assessment is not unqualified, however. In a translator's note to Mandich (1948), Prager suggested that "it is not clear whether this proviso in the act means that the inventor shall be the only one to operate the device (a) for the use of the government, or (b) for the use of others. . . . Construction (a) is at least as plausible as (b). It is true that it leads to the question what are the precise incidents of 'operation' (*exercitar*) as distinguished from 'use' (*usar*). The statute is vague in this respect; however, not more so than, for instance, the U.S. act of 1910 as amend-

ed 1918 . . . " (Mandich 1948, 180n37B). It seems that some form of quasi-public interest is implied by this injunction, but this is neither completely clear nor certain, although we draw the reader's attention to the first paragraph of the decree that seems more certainly to imply the social worth and value of innovations being developed in and imported to Venice.

6. This movement to Venice was also part of the dispersion of printers from Mainz (Gutenberg's home town and an early center of printing) caused by Adolph of Nassau's sacking of the city (Thompson [1911] 1968, 8–9).

7. Comprehensive discussions of the Venetian printing sector can be found in Gerulaitis (1976) and Lowry (1979).

8. Ruth Chavasse (1986) discussed the biographical and literary background to Sabellico's publication at some length to support a claim that Sabellico, rather than Erasmus, was the first author to make a living from writing for publication.

4

Commerce vs. Romantic Notions of Authorship and Invention

ALTHOUGH WE have focused on the Venetian moment, other developments in the sixteenth century prefigured the legal innovations in Britain. The influence of the Venetian law was evident on the European continent: forms of patenting were established in Flanders and Antwerp and by the French crown, with grants often awarded to Venetians importing various techniques of manufacture (frequently glassmaking). Such grants were made in the form of personal grants, however; there was no general enabling legislation (Bugbee 1967, 27). It is difficult to be exact about the influence these continental developments had on the making of English law, but it is unlikely that they had *no* influence.

The myth of Venetian political stability and constitutional excellence was well established by the early sixteenth century, although this was partly a product of the city's own propaganda. Freedom from domestic upheavals and political longevity meant that Venetian modes of governance were well respected by the political classes of Italy and across Europe (Finlay 1980, 27–37). In the early seventeenth century, the political classes in Britain often compared Venice to a modern Rome as an exemplar of benign government, and even at the end of the fifteenth century legislators in Britain had already looked favorably on Venetian political practices (Fink 1940). Any legislative innovation characterized as Venetian would have received a sympathetic hearing and was unlikely to be dismissed without careful consideration. Nevertheless, although Venetian arrangements had some influence, when the English government moved to produce a patent law, key elements were uniquely English. Before we examine these British legal innovations, however, we briefly examine developments elsewhere that may have had some additional influence on British patent and copyright law.

75

From Venice to London: Some Continental Developments

By the middle of the sixteenth century, Venetian protection of innovation was becoming known abroad. Venetian glassblowers often introduced rulers to the Venetian model; bringing new methods of manufacturing glass (allowing glass to become a commodity instead of a luxury), and knowing that in Venice such methods could be protected by a patent grant, these emigrants sought monopolies in their adopted countries (Frumkin 1945, 144). A letter of patent from the sovereign allowed them a limited (but sometimes renewable) monopoly for their imported practices, often in exchange for the transfer of technological advances by instructing apprentices. Return to Venice was impossible, as the death penalty awaited glassmakers who breached the Venetian monopoly in manufacturing.

The French crown awarded its first grant in 1551—a ten-year import franchise for Venetian glassmaking techniques to Theseus Mutio, a migrant from Venice (Mandich 1948, 206). Likewise, the government of the Netherlands awarded a number of privileges during the second half of the sixteenth century, again often to Italians. For instance, a group of Venetian glassmakers received grants in 1541 in Antwerp (Frumkin 1947, 52). But grants were not limited to Italians. Abel Foullon, a native of France, was the recipient of what is likely to have been the first French patent for an invention in 1554. His range finder received a ten-year grant not only for selling the invention itself but also possibly a quasi copyright over the instruction manual that accompanied the instrument (Bugbee 1967, 25). Maximilian Frumkin suggested that publication was held back to ensure that others could not pirate the invention despite the crown's required disclosure of the technique (Frumkin 1945, 145). Nevertheless, Foullon received a further patent on a "horseless carriage" four years later (Frumkin 1947, 53), suggesting that relations between the inventor and crown remained friendly whatever his activities regarding the previous grant.

Elsewhere, early patent grants in Germany were often linked to mining, with an early Saxon patent in 1484 awarded to Blasius Dalmaticus for the draining of mines and a grant to the margrave of Brandenburg-Onolzbach in 1535 for an eight-year monopoly for a pump to be used in mines (Frumkin 1947, 53). In 1545 Emperor Charles V granted a twelve-year patent to Hans Hedler for the construction of wind and water mills (Klitzke 1959, 620). Indeed, during the hundred years from 1530 to 1630, various levels of German government (from the imperial to local electors) seemed to have issued around 100 grants of patent. German law at this time was based on a combination of Germanic and Roman customary laws, and like the common law in Anglo-Saxon countries, legal practice was established through court decisions rather than formal legislative development. Thus, by 1600, Hansjoerg Pohlmann has argued, the grant of patent rights had "crystallized into a rule of legally binding custom" (Pohlmann 1961, 123, 125). But even in the 1551 petition for a grant to A. Schultz, for a method of casting, the text clearly states: "under time-honored usage of the Empire the inventors of new things (useful and beneficial to the arts) have always been privileged with grants of rights . . . and have (as is equitable) enjoyed the first fruits of their works" (quoted in Pohlmann 1961, 126). Innovation was to be recognized and rewarded, and this was regarded as a timeless principle, not a new legal practice.

During the sixteenth and seventeenth centuries, in the German states, patents often were denied on factual grounds, including rudimentary tests of novelty and utility, rather than on the grace (or otherwise) of the court. This practice indicates some form of patent examination (which included the use of external experts to assess the applications) (Pohlmann 1961, 126–129). Some of these applications also seem to refer to the public bene- fit of the grant. One application Pohlmann referred to invokes the appli- cants' desire "that their newly invented device be published in the common interest and particularly for the benefit of the mining art" (quoted in Pohlmann 1961, 130). Thus, a public-regarding aspect to the grant was also starting to be deployed. In an interesting parallel to German policy, during the seventeenth century the Pascal family (father and son) struggled to develop a form of patent examination in France. Although separate from the court's actual granting of patents to individuals, Frank Prager suggested that their work on how patent specifications were to be written and how innovation was codified in such grants had a significant long-term impact (Prager 1964). Applications had sometimes included a discourse on the invention or practice, as a way of substantiating the veracity of the claim, but the Pascals tried to set some standards for the form and content of these statements in support of grants.

During the mid-sixteenth century, a number of Italians had settled in Antwerp (then part of the Netherlands) and established new industries. Of the twenty-three patents issued in the Netherlands between 1560 and 1580, five were to Italians (Walterscheid 1994a, 714n68). In the United Provinces, applicants were required to clearly set out the matter to be cov- ered by the grant of patent, with many of these specifications examined by a committee set up for the purpose. As in other countries, novelty remained geographically specific, with first importation of a technique or innovation sufficient to gain a patent (Walterscheid 1994a, 714–715). As in Venice, printing was an important industrial sector, where patent grants were used to establish profitable opportunities for entrepreneurs. By the seventeenth century, as part of the licensing of the printing trade in the Netherlands, exclusive licenses to print specific titles were required in certain subject areas (most important were theological and devotional literature), whereas more popular works could be printed under a general license. As Paul

Arblaster pointed out, however, "printers were free to apply for such a legally enforceable monopoly on works for which it was not in fact required, in order to enjoy the benefits of exclusivity" (Arblaster 2001, 182). These exclusive licenses, voluntarily applied for, indicate an interest in solutions to competition.

In the early sixteenth century, authors such as Erasmus were starting to garner a reputation sufficiently distinct from their printers to cause some problems in the industry. Certainly, despite the innovations in quasi or prototypical copyright protections in Venice, much of the print trade in Europe merely reprinted "unauthorized" volumes originally printed by others. Erasmus may have stumbled onto one strategy for dealing with such copies. In a letter from 1516, Erasmus's Parisian publisher Badius observed: 'Your fame is now so great that when a new edition of any of your works comes out, with indication of revision, although there may be nothing new added, people do not touch the earlier issues" (quoted in Allen 1913, 320). Of course, equally, publishers reprinting unauthorized editions might also utilize the claim of revision or "new edition." Nevertheless, what is clear is that the author's repute (and the desire to gain an author's most recent work) played a role in the industry, which hints at a more individualized notion of authorship already emerging, as well as the value placed on "newness."

In the seventeenth century, the Frankfurt Book Fair was an established and crucial part of the (international) industry, and the Frankfurt Town Council was at the forefront of attempts to find ways to limit the unauthorized copying of books. At the end of each fair, printers were required to present to the bürgermeister a list of those books they would publish before the next year's fair. Thus when specific books appeared on more than one list, there was time to resolve the issue of who owned the *privilege* to print the title. As no publisher could bring books to the fair without the consent of the council, this procedure limited duplicate editions (Thompson [1911] 1968, 83–85, 99–108). The fair's size, the international character of the sellers, and the volume of books sold mean that it is not clear, however, how effective such measures were. As these lists were also used for censorious purposes, not merely the protection of the "rights" of publishers, they may not have been complete in any case.

These important practical, customary, and legal developments were to a large extent lost to the wider historical development of European intellectual property law, however, by the upheavals of the Thirty Years War (1618–1648) (Pohlmann 1961, 122).[1] The conflict effectively dismantled the centralized imperial legal structure, and many legal innovations were lost. Subsequent legal institutions of intellectual property in Germany trace their roots little farther back than the nineteenth century. Although the Netherlands benefited from the Thirty Years War, inasmuch as it removed a major competitor for their printing sector, this did not lead to any particular innovation in prototypical copyright protection. If anything, as far as authors' rights were concerned during this period, the Netherlands developed a considerable reputation for the "piracy" of books from elsewhere in Europe (Bugbee 1967, 49), as there were no laws proscribing such methods.[2]

Finally, before moving on to a discussion of the British innovations in patent and copyright, it is as well to briefly mention the development of trademarks up to this point. By the fifteenth century, in many cities merchants' guilds maintained registries of trademarks (*handelsbuecher* or *Livres de Commerce*) where both local and foreign (trade)marks were recorded. Gerald Ruston reported books from Danzig (dated 1420) that listed marks for traders from the city and from England, Amsterdam, and Genoa; another from Antwerp (dated 1556) gave marks from Venice and Genoa (Ruston 1955, 139). Furthermore, city authorities often punished infringements of these marks. The elector of Palatine had an innkeeper publicly hanged who was using the *Rudesheimer* mark on bottles of inferior wine, in violation of a statute recently passed to halt this practice. Across the continent the use of a false mark on cloth of gold or silver was treated as "coining" (counterfeiting currency) and was accordingly also routinely punished by death (Ruston 1955, 141). The medieval guild system had already prompted widespread laws for the punishment of unauthorized usage of (trade)marks, and their vigorous defense continued into this period.

In the sixteenth century, the requirement to mark for guild information purposes was widened to include some notion or property-like transferability. For instance, in the Guild Statute of Lübeck of 1547, the baker's mark was attached not to the individual but to the business, allowing it to be transferred as part of the assets when the business was sold (Paster 1969, 560). The Privy Council in Britain and various other authorities on the continent used marks to control and shape economic development within their jurisdictions. The mark itself was still established by use, *not* by a grant or award, however, even though it was moving toward its more modern role as a business asset.

Having established that the innovations regarding intellectual property in the seventeenth century (for patents) and eighteenth century (for copyrights) were hardly unprecedented, we now move to examine the widely recognized legal innovations of the 1624 Statute of Monopolies and the 1709 Act of Anne. Given the weight accorded to these moments in most accounts of the emergence of intellectual property, we examine the context of these pieces of English legislation at some length. This serves two purposes: first, they were important and innovative legislative settlements, although perhaps not unprecedented; second, owing to their general identification as the birth of *modern* intellectual property, they have considerable contemporary influence on debates around intellectual property.

British Innovations in Patents

Up until the early seventeenth century, in many European countries grants of patent were subject to the vagaries of political power and personal relationships. Although there had been moves toward a more formalized system of granting patents across Europe, Britain was the first state to establish relatively modern legislation to govern intellectual property, utilizing a systematic method of granting patents and later copyrights. One possible reason that the next stage of legal innovation was in English law may be that, given the political structure of France, Italy, and Germany, Britain was the only country in which social, political, *and* economic conditions existed for the development of a more robust law for the granting of something approaching modern patent monopolies (Federico 1929, 295). The legislation also reflected the practice and policy of the court during the previous hundred years, during which the importation of technologies and the notion of mercantilism had been central elements of Crown policy.

Jeremy Phillips made a strong case for one route by which knowledge of Venetian and continental practices was brought to the attention of the Elizabethan court. In 1559, Jacobus Acontius seems likely to have received the first patent issued in Britain explicitly for innovation. While living in Venice he had registered a patent there, and when he emigrated, Acontius took with him the notion that the innovator should receive certain benefits and rights relative to his invention (Phillips 1982; see also Klitzke 1959, 634). As there were also many domestic reasons for adopting the practice of patenting innovations, this direct link should not be overemphasized, although neither is it insignificant.

It is worth noting the argument that Jacobus Acontius made when he petitioned Elizabeth for his patent:

> Nothing is more honest than that those who by searching have found out things useful to the public should have some fruit of their rights and labors, as meanwhile they abandon all other modes of gain, are at much expense in experiments, and often sustain much loss, as has happened to me. I have discovered most useful things, new kinds of wheel machines, and of furnaces for dyers and brewers, which when known will be used without my consent, except there be a penalty, and I, poor with expenses and labor, shall have no returns. Therefore I beg a prohibition against using any wheel machines, either for grinding or bruising or any furnaces like mine, without my consent. (Quoted in Phillips 1982, 71; Klitzke 1959, 633)

Here we can see the notion of the inventor as a legitimate recipient of reward, underlined by the comment added to the grant itself: "At his suit: it is right that inventors should be rewarded and protected against others making profit out of their discoveries" (quoted in Phillips 1982, 71). This seems to be the first recorded philosophical combination invoking both natural rights *and* labor (or effort) to justify the award of a patent (Mossoff 2001, 1274). In addition to the mercantilist support for granting patents for strategic reasons, at least one inventor already saw the advantages for his own welfare and may have conceived of any linked rewards in terms of *rights* rather than prizes or bounty.

Elizabeth I's chief minister, William Cecil (later Lord Burghley), saw patent grants primarily as a device to attract foreign technologies. The Tudors had both encouraged national industry and supported national security through awards to German armorers, Italian shipwrights, and glassmakers of monopolies on their various trades and techniques (Federico 1929, 294). Where some sort of importation of technique or innovation was concerned, as Christine MacLeod suggested, patentees "were required to implement their 'invention' without delay and ensure its continuance by communicating the necessary skills to native workmen [and the] grant was revocable if these conditions were not met" (MacLeod 1988, 11). But the revelation of secret or new processes was less important than it would become as legislation matured. Rather, Cecil was more interested (utilizing the mercantilist logic of the time) in expanding trade, both by the reduction of imports through domestic production and the export of the goods that any particular patent recognized. If a grant might harm those already active in a specific trade, patents were seldom granted; if they were, they attracted considerable infringement, requiring courts to deal with arguments regarding their legality.

Before Elizabeth gained the throne, there was a reasonably settled process of awarding grants, and the Elizabethan court's practice was not necessarily innovative. Her court often issued patents to either support courtiers in financial difficulty by enabling them to profit from monopolies or to reward favorites (in lieu of any other reward for duties undertaken on her behalf). Furthermore, these grants delegated powers to the patentee, which gave commoners the same rights as the Crown (in the area of the grant, at least) to supervise, search, and seize the goods of infringers as well as the ability to levy fines and penalties for infringement (Walterscheid 1994b, 864). This practice led to a large number of disputed or objectionable grants, made to individuals who were not the inventors, nor even specialists, in the particular fields of endeavor. Some were awarded when the processes (or derivations) were already well known. Starch, salt, paper, saltpeter, and glass all came under the control of the queen's favorites (or debtors), causing enormous price rises (which is one reason for the price issue being part of the 1624 statute).

After Parliament's attempt in 1601 to pass a bill reforming the Crown's granting of letters of patent and considerable public disquiet, the queen herself undertook to reform the practice. Her ministers would not have been able to halt legislation in Parliament, and thus, to retain some authority, she canceled the worst of the monopolies and allowed the remaining grants to be examined by the courts without her restraint. Thus, while she retained the ability to issue grants, these became subject to judicial review and challenge by those aggrieved, or their representatives. These reforms did not last, and similar problems reemerged under James I.

In 1610, James classified the types of patent he would grant in a declaration that became known as the *Book of Bounty*. Patents were to be granted for "projects of new invention so they be not contrary to Law nor mischievous to the state by raising prices of commodities at home, or hurt trade, or otherwise inconvenient" (quoted in Hill 1924, 408). These sentiments became part of the 1624 statute. But before the statute was enacted, in 1621 the new Parliament investigated abuses under various patents, canceling many and requiring others to be tested in court (Federico 1929, 302). Although the Crown (most especially Charles I) continued to abuse the system to some extent, the statute of 1624 codified into law for the first time those legitimate practices in regard to patents that made up common law.

The British patent for invention, provided for in the Statute of Monopolies of 1624, was, as William Cornish argued, "plainly devised as an exception, for good economic reason, to the general campaign against royal monopolies . . . those who brought technical ideas into the Kingdom, even if they were not their ideas, were 'inventors'"(Cornish, 1993, 50n10). Furthermore, Paul David argued that the fourteen-years duration of early English patents, with the possibility of seven-year extensions, "was not fixed arbitrarily: seven years was the term of service of an apprentice, and so the protection afforded was to last for at least two generations of trainees" (David 1994, 134). The focus on the instruction of apprentices reduced any need to have patents carefully specified, as training in the practical use of a technique provided the dissemination required. Certainly under Elizabeth, the instruction of "native apprentices" was a key undertaking required from most (if not all) patentees (Klitzke 1959, 639). Prior to the statute, grants had been of ten or twenty years and only sometimes of multiples of seven.[3]

Patents (in the modern sense) were allowed by virtue of section 6 of the 1624 Statute of Monopolies, which excepted them from its proscriptions:

> Provided also and be it declared and enacted that any declaration before mentioned shall not extend to any letters patent and grants of privilege for the term of fourteen years or under, hereafter to be made, of the sole working or making of any manner of new manufactures within this realm, to the true and first inventor and inventors of such manufactures, which others at the time of making such letters patent and grants shall not use, so as also they be not contrary to law, nor mischievous to the State, by raising prices of commodities at home, or hurt trade, or generally inconvenient; the said fourteen years to be accounted from the date of the first letters patents, or grants of such privilege hereafter to be made, but that the same shall be of such force as they should be if this Act had never been made, and of none other. (Quoted in Federico 1929, 303)

Although this merely codified preceding practice, the statute at last provided a clear benchmark against which applications could be assessed. It also provided for the first time a fixed (and clear) term for the grant of patents and shifted the legal apparatus of patents from the court to the judiciary. In the main the exception seems meant to act in the way that Cecil's policy had in the previous century—to support and encourage the development or importation of innovations that benefited English trade.

In his commentary on the statute, published five years later, Sir Edward Coke stated that for a patent of invention to be valid under the exemption established by section 6 it must have seven properties:

1. the term of patent must not exceed fourteen years;
2. the patent "must be granted to the first and true inventor";
3. "it must be of such manufactures, which any other at the making of such Letters Patents did not use";
4. it "must not be contrary to law";
5. it must not be "mischievous to the State by raising of prices of commodities at home";
6. it must not "hurt trade"; and
7. it must not be "generally inconvenient" (Walterscheid 1994b, 876).

Although many terms may indicate a significant continuity with modern law, we should be careful to recognize the divergence of meaning over time.[4] Thus, the second criteria actually includes first importation into Britain, and the third, which might seem to be similar to the modern notion of "novelty, is here more concerned with use (or "working") rather than actual novelty itself. This was interpreted at the time, however, as meaning that a patent could not be issued if the knowledge of the invention had become known and been used (by fair means or foul). This may explain why specification was not mandatory, as revelation before the sealing of the patent would undermine the application itself if such a description got into the wrong hands.

It is interesting to note that the use of the words "shall not use" in the statute was replaced by "did not use" in Coke's commentary. The latter would indicate some concern as regards the limitation of patents to activities not currently being carried out (which is a reflection of the previous use of grants for common industries but also indicates a focus on *innovation*). The former is more like a modern limitation on future activities of non-patentees (which may reflect a desire to allow patents to continue to cover extant industries, a practice Coke wanted to resist). Coke's invocation of "not contrary to law" prohibits the patenting of mere improvements; legal patents must be innovations of some sort. The last two points reflect the continuing importance of mercantilism for the British state.

As MacLeod suggested, although intended to "proscribe the Crown's abuse of its dispensing powers, the Statute's role as the legal basis for the patent system was a curious side-effect, a quirk of history" (MacLeod 1988, 15). It was patents' exceptional character as regards the statute that allowed their continuance, rather than the prohibition that befell other monopolies. When the monopoly rights grounded in the recognition of property in intellectual "objects" were first recognized, therefore, their potential scope was regarded as a problem rather than a just reward. Their recognition was an exceptional compromise, not a general allowance of monopolies. And indeed Coke's commentaries attempted to limit grants to innovative practices.

Nevertheless even this exception was not without its critics at the time, with both Francis Bacon and Samuel Hartlib arguing that the protection offered inventors did not go far enough. When philosophers and commentators thought about how innovation itself should be promoted, direct grants and state support were often the preferred option. This led William Petty to argue in 1648 for a state-sponsored research institute that would allow the frequent and speedy development of useful innovations and technologies. To some extent, the Royal Society took up this role itself during the eighteenth century.

During the interregnum, in any case, very few patents were upheld, and the abuse of monopolies came in the popular imagination to be one of the chief causes of the English Civil War (MacLeod 1988, 16). Therefore, it is perhaps unsurprising that the later Stuart monarchs amended their behavior. Although monopolies including grants of patent were still issued to courtiers and their clients, the practice of issuing grants that covered a whole industry's operations, with the exception of glassmaking, were no longer used. And even the Duke of Buckingham's post-interregnum monopoly on glass (the quality of whose products increasingly worried the Venetians, whose own industrial secrets were increasingly violated by emigrants) was only for certain procedures, allowing another patent to be issued during its term for a different process. Indeed, this monopoly seems to have had a beneficial effect on glassmaking in England, leading to lower prices and an improvement in quality (MacLeod 1988, 26). This change reflected the wording of patents that after the Restoration included the invocation that the "sole use and benefit" of an invention was not intended to forbid the use of other methods for producing the same or similar articles.

Although in the last quarter of the seventeenth century the government engaged in straightforward mercantilist practices of supporting domestic industry and import substitution, this did not amount to a fully developed industrial policy of patent provision. Patent grants were for the Crown to conduct what business or commerce it so desired, especially when such activities might potentially contravene the areas of activity of specific guilds. The Crown's interests lay mainly in the areas of currency and military supplies, however, and therefore, although other inventions were often not protected by patents, anything that involved the conduct of warfare (especially on the high seas) was readily granted protection by the Crown to enhance the country's security and power projection capabilities. Patent grants also always allowed the Crown and military authorities to conduct security-related affairs without respect for any rights thereby awarded. This compromise remained a problem for patentees for much of the next two centuries but was hardly novel; the Venetian statute had ensured that where the governing authorities' interests were concerned, patents were no guarantee of protection.

The 1624 statute included no element of public specification. Some applications, such as Robert Crumpe's often-noted patent of 1618, included quite detailed discussion of what would now be termed "prior art," but these were the exception and not the general practice (Walterscheid 1995a, 783–785). Although specification emerged more fully in the early eighteenth century, examination, rather than mere registration, only became mandatory in the 1883 Patents Act, despite the rudimentary practices that had been established in Venice and Germany.[5] Unlike the Netherlands or France, grants were issued without substantive investigation of their claims. It was left to the courts to arbitrate disputed grants.

Patents started to be used as claims both to originality and to authenticity of a specific product, a role that guilds had for long held to be their own. As MacLeod put it, the "publicity value of these patents was not lost on established city tradesmen, who, as the cloak of guild protection grew threadbare, were increasingly feeling the chill winds of competition" (MacLeod 1988, 87, 188). This is not to say that the guilds put up no resistance. Between 1688 and 1718, the Guild of Clockmakers spent over £500 to defeat three patents and two acts that threatened their collective livelihood. Other guilds attempted to dispute grants but were not always successful, and some took to harassing the applicants to try to forestall the process. Whether or not guilds were an obstruction to innovation, their role as conveyers and protectors of specialized knowledge was dealt a severe blow by the expansion in use of patents that sidelined (or sometimes directly contravened) their efforts on behalf of their members.

It would be a mistake to assume that a fully fledged modern patent system emerged with the Statute of Monopolies. As would become apparent over the following 200 years, this "essentially negative" piece of legislation had not established a mechanism suited to inventors' needs in the Industrial Revolution (MacLeod 1988, 1). The Privy Council refused to concede jurisdiction to the courts, leaving patents in a strange no-man's-land, based on both royal prerogatives and the statutory instrument. The lack of a settled patent law led to confusion but also to lively debates about how such rights, as might be obtained through the avenues available, might be justified and be legitimized (Mossoff 2001, 1277). Thus, in a patent monopoly case in which the East India Company was the defendant, Hugo Grotius is cited in support of the grant. Adam Mossoff suggested that this is "momentous in the development of patents," as it established that courts would accept natural rights philosophers as reputable authorities on the problem of patents. In this case Grotius's conception of a property right (requiring *use* and *occupation*) was limited to preexisting tangible goods, however, and did not serve the patentee well (Mossoff 2001, 1281–1282). Despite these doubts and confusions, patents slowly became an accepted part of industrial practice.

As increasing numbers of innovations and industrial processes were protected by patents, it became increasingly imperative for new innovations to seek such protection before an "impostor" received a grant. If protection was available, then inventors and entrepreneurs wanted such protection for themselves to fend off competition. It remained a complex and expensive process, however, that was relatively underused (Federico 1929, 305). The grant of patent rights did, however, start to transform innovation into alienable property that could be bought and sold, transferred, and (to some extent) subdivided to raise money. In this sense the attraction of applying for a grant became a part of the increasingly market orientation of a nascent capitalist society.

Rather than being the result of some new period of inventing and innovation, recourse to patents had profoundly social roots. MacLeod concluded that if patents "can be taken as a gauge of anything, then it is primarily of the increasing awareness of the patent system's existence and a defensive—or opportunist—reaction to it. This was itself symptomatic of improved communications, particularly between London and the provinces, and the consolidation of a national market" (MacLeod 1988, 157). The rise and expansion of the patent system therefore had little do with inventiveness and much more to do with the rise, expansion, and growing institutionalization of the capitalist mode of market organization. The philosophical recognition of man's inventive nature certainly played a part in the justification of these new "rights," but this must be located within the wider political economic shifts of the time.

Whatever the intent of the statute, and even though it certainly laid the foundation for later patenting practice, for the next century the councilor courts continued to adjudicate in much the same way they had before passage of the act (Walterscheid 1995a, 773). This may have been partly because few wished to exploit their apparent new right to test royal grants in the common law courts and partly because the Privy Council retained significant powers over the validity of patents, ensuring that little common law activity could easily take place. Only when the Privy Council divested itself of this role in 1752 did rulings over patents finally arrive in the common law courts (Walterscheid 1995a, 775). In this sense, although patenting and the legal foundations for modern intellectual property were advanced by the Statute of Monopolies, the modern system remained to be established. The next major development in the genesis of intellectual property would come nearly a century later and revolve around the idea of artistic creation, authorship, and the "invention" of copyright.

British Innovations in Copyrights

Although the English innovation in patents was part of a historical process of legislative development stretching across Europe, in copyright legal innovation was more localized. British printers had been attending the Frankfurt Book Fair since the fifteenth century and thus, for the more internationally minded stationers, Venetian and continental ideas about protecting stationers' "right" over publications would have been known, if not necessarily adopted. The Frankfurt Book Fair was also a place where scholars and writers could meet to exchange ideas, make contacts, and arrange for the foreign publications of their works (Thompson [1911] 1968, 57–59). Certainly, we can presume that conversation would have turned to the possibilities of authorial remuneration, and hence the Venetian system would hardly have been unknown to writers of other nationalities.

Nevertheless, the new copyright legislation that was developed at the beginning of the eighteenth century emerged much more directly from British domestic political demands and was nearer its modern successors than the patent legislation of eighty years before. Venetian books had been widely exported throughout Europe in the seventeenth century, and the notion of privileges to protect books from unauthorized copying had been disseminated via this route. Likely influenced by Venetian practices, in 1501 Conrad Celtes was awarded a privilege for his edition of the works of

Hroswitha of Gandersheim, for the German-speaking areas of the continent, and the first French privilege related to book publishing was granted six years later (Hirsch 1967, 85). The guild monopoly model of publishing, which had flourished in fourteenth- and fifteenth-century Venice, was an important exemplar for managing the torrent of printed works produced in this period.

In Britain, the court organized this new industry, like others before it, into a guild-monopoly by the grant of a monopoly in 1557 to the English Stationers' Company. To allow Mary Tudor's court to suppress publication of seditious material, the company was given the power to search any printers' or booksellers' premises for unauthorized works. As David pointed out, "whether censorship was obnoxious or desirable in their opinion, they had a strong economic motive to enforce their monopoly by suppressing publications not licensed by the Crown" (David 1993, 53). The immediate roots of British copyright lie in this industrial/sectoral regulation linked to the Crown's interest in censorship. Although the Crown supported the introduction of printing into Britain in the late fifteenth century for mercantilist reasons (printing was already proving to be a strategic technology), its expansion as a commercial sector worried successive monarchs. An industry that sought potentially high selling content was seldom afraid of printing works that dissented from the rule of the Crown. Thus, industrial control always needed to balance issues of economic development with the censorship requirements of particular rulers, and in the Statute of Monopolies, James I explicitly exempted printing (alongside innovation) from the overall ban on monopolies, to allow such control to continue.

Prototypical copyright at this early stage was seldom the protection of a particular text, but rather of the guild members' right to publish free from the competition of other printers. Indeed, in 1533 Henry VIII had ensured that English booksellers would not suffer competition from abroad by forbidding (on pain of confiscation) the importation of books bound abroad. The booksellers themselves might import sheets, but profits were secured by imposing a monopoly on finished volumes. This might well have been intended to help the new industry, but it also meant that the flow of foreign texts (that after Henry's break from Rome might be uncomfortable politically) would be controlled (Bugbee 1967, 50). The printing industry eventually supplanted scribal publication, but during the seventeenth century the (relatively) large-scale scribal copying of manuscripts remained another way for authors to "publish" their work.

Given the censorship role of the Stationer's Company, scribal publication flourished on the margins because for many dissenters it was the only way of securing wider circulation of their views (Love 1993, 189). Even for less contentious authors, given the guild monopoly on printing, in many cases scribal publication offered a more profitable avenue for the reproduction of their works (until demand reached the level at which copying became unfeasible, given the emerging economies of scale for print) (Love 1993, 59). Although space precludes an extended discussion of the realm of scribal publication in the century prior to the Act of Anne,[6] the copying of texts by hand represented a significant (if small-scale) alternative to the monopoly of the stationers. Although we can only speculate, it certainly seems possible that as authors frequently used both scribal and print publication, they attempted to assert similar levels of control that they had over scribal copies in the print realm.

Despite the claims for the St. Columbia dispute mentioned in Chapter 3, a more likely candidate for the first "copyright" dispute may be the "piracy" of a book written by Wynkyn de Worde and published in 1523. Like many later disputes, the argument concerned a cheap reprint of the original edition. The second "authorized" edition (published ten years later under a royal privilege) contained an explicit attack on the printer of the cheap edition for pirating an author's work. This case is not well documented, however,[7] leaving the first *privilege* or patent awarded to an author rather than a bookseller or printer being that granted to John Palsgrave in 1530 for a French language textbook. Palsgrave was the royal chaplain, however, which may have accorded him special treatment, and the grant itself was only for seven years (the standard, apprenticeship-related length of grant). More usually at this time monopolies were organized on the basis of content and the control of the publisher, although in some cases this *was* linked to the actual author.

The Elizabethan court's widespread issuing of restrictive monopolies, not over particular titles but over entire classes of books (such as law books), undermined the guild's ability to control the trade in the interests of *all* its members. Frequently, the demand for books could not be met by the privilege holders, and this then spurred the "illicit" supply of books not licensed by the guild. These other printers attempted to cover their tracks by copying not only the text and lay-out of texts when a monopoly was held but also the name and details of the patentee on the title page. To themselves (and, it should be added, in their defense in court) they argued that they were driven by the exorbitant prices and poor quality of the products of the guild monopolists. Such arguments did little to convince the court of the value of a free-for-all, and in 1559 Elizabeth issued an injunction complaining of the "publication of unlawful and infamous books and papers" (quoted in Bugbee 1967, 51), requiring that all publications be licensed, a form of control that would be utilized and refined considerably over the next century (both by monarchs and by Parliament during the interregnum).

Following a decree in the Star Chamber in 1586 that made it clear that privileges could be passed on from father to son, it became apparent to the poorer elements of the book trade that profitable books might never return to the trade as possible titles for publication. Therefore they felt little compunction in seeking their livelihood from counterfeiting these titles. These printers were well organized, and despite continued pressure to suppress their activities, they seem to have managed to continue to disrupt the guild's activities throughout the sixteenth century.[8] In essence the guild was attempting to monopolize the new printing trade on behalf of its members, but there were insufficient opportunities for all journeymen and apprentices to profitably practice their art without infringing the wide licenses granted to guild members. The interests of the authors were hardly considered; any nascent notion of copyright was almost entirely concerned with the livelihood of the printers and stationers.

In the late sixteenth century, the printers who had originally dominated the Stationers' Company through their monopolization of technology (both as regards skill and control of the actual physical machinery) started to lose influence to copy-holding booksellers (Feather 1994a, 199). More printers emerged from the ranks of apprentices as the printing industry expanded. The technology itself became easier to acquire as it became better known, leading to the dilution of the monopoly over the production function even within the Stationers' Company (and outside). The copy-holding booksellers, however, managed to maintain their title- (and genre-) based monopolies on new and existing books. By the end of the century, power in the guild had shifted to the booksellers, although their control of the guild was no more helpful to individual authors than had been the rule of the printers.

For much of the seventeenth century, the Stationers' Company continued to exercise some control over the nascent system of copyrights through the registration system for its members. During the interregnum their monopoly was abolished, however, not from any hatred of copyrights but rather as a reflection of the new rulers' mistrust of censorship as well as of the monopolies so assiduously exploited by the Stuarts. Following the demise of the Star Chamber (which had ended the Stationers' monopoly), the new Parliament forbid the members of the guild to "print or reprint anything without the Name or Consent of the Author" (quoted in Rose 1993, 22). Rather than any particular recognition of authorial rights, this ban was primarily meant to ensure that libelous or blasphemous literature could be traced, with anonymous works the responsibility of the printer.

This stance on the part of Parliament established a link between authorial permission and reproduction that would become increasingly central to copyright's development with the Act of Anne some decades later. Indeed, the role of the author as producer of texts would be emphasized in the Act of Anne, not on the basis of authorial rights but rather primarily as a rhetorical device to attack the previous monopoly of the stationers (Patterson

1968, 147). Not all authors saw the parliamentary acts as necessarily in their interest. In *Areopagitica* (1644), John Milton very pointedly complained about the operation of these new laws, but on the other hand, explicitly exempted from this criticism of the ordinance "that part which preserves justly evry mans Copy to himselfe" (quoted in Bugbee 1967, 52) suggesting that although possibly merely rhetorical, the appeal to an author's right had some other currency.

Although reinstated in 1660, the decline of prior censorship in the late seventeenth century led to the lapse of the Licensing Act (which had supported the stationers' monopoly) in 1694. Combined with the increase in the number of presses, the next fifteen years exposed the stationers to unrestrained competition. Their complaints and petitions finally enabled them to gain some renewed protection in the Act of Anne in 1709[9] (more correctly, A Bill for the Encouragement of Learning by Vesting the Copies of Printed Books in the Authors, or Purchasers, of such Copies, during the Times therein Mentioned). This act, the first formalized copyright statute, had two central concerns: to encourage the writing of books that would be useful to society and (more important for the printers) to prevent widespread counterfeiting. Authors, or those to whom they assigned their rights, retained an exclusive right for a limited period to print such works: twenty-one years for existing titles; fourteen years for new books, with an additional fourteen-year right of renewal. The Stationers' Company was required to register all works and to indicate whose work was assigned to whom and who held the right to print the work (with the list open to all, not merely members of the guild). The act also established the system of "copyright deposit," with all publishers being required to lodge copies of their books or other publications with the nine "deposit" libraries (including the royal library and the universities of Oxford and Cambridge), that continues to this day.

To a large extent the act recognized the role of the company under existing common law (and like the Statute of Monopolies, in many ways codified existing practice). Conversely, the use of the royal prerogative and the licensing acts in the latter part of the previous century had diluted the efficacy of the stationers' registration system (Walterscheid 1996: 97), and thus the Act of Anne went some way toward clarifying the award of literary property by mandating a single system. The act responded to the demands for statutory protection from the stationers, but through time limits and opening registration beyond the guild, limited and constrained the power of those who had petitioned for it in the first place (Patterson 1968, 13). As enacted, the 1709 statute provided for two forms of copyright: the statutory copyright for new books; a continuation of the stationers' copyright for already published works (but extended to twenty-one years from the date of the act); and the printing patent (which covered entire classes of works—

almanacs and law books being the most prominent monopolies) by omitting any limitations on such grants (Patterson 1968, 143, 148–149). Thus, rather than a fully developed unitary copyright system, the Act of Anne retained some of the prior legal complexity in this area while moving elements of protection toward the modern model.

The licensing acts (from 1662 to the last, which expired in 1679) had effectively allowed stationers to claim a perpetual copyright. These acts had also prohibited the printing (or importing) of any book without the consent of the copyright owner, with a fine divided between owner and the Crown (Davies 2002, 11). This second element was a crucial aspect of the Act of Anne, which sought to recognize and institute the rights of authors to control their works. Additionally the act recognized the public interest in expanding the supply of cheap books by instigating a price appeal system. All this is encapsulated in the first few sentences of the act, which set out its overall purpose:

> Whereas Printers, Booksellers and other Persons have of late frequently taken the Liberty of printing, reprinting and publishing, or causing to be printed, reprinted and published, Books and other Writings, without the Consent of the Authors or Proprietors of such Books and Writings, to their very great Detriment, and too often to the Ruin of them and their families: For preventing therefore such Practices for the future, and for the Encouragement of learned Men to compose and write useful books. . . . (Davies 2002, app. 1, ¶ 371)

The stationers may have taken tactical advantage of the emerging notion that authors had rights over their work to push for this legislation (Abrams 1983, 1142), but the recognition of authorship is also placed at the center of the act's *own* justification for legislation.

In the pamphleteering prior to the act, it is worth noting that Daniel Defoe (author of what is often identified as the first English novel, *Robinson Crusoe*) argued that legislation was needed to "put a Stop to a certain sort of Thieving which is now in full practice in *England*, and which no law extends to punish, viz. some Printers and Booksellers printing copies none of their own" (quoted in Feather 1980, 29). Defoe argued that this not only robbed authors of their just rewards but also allowed poor reprints and abridgements to appear under the author's name without his authorization; a direct defense of authors' rights partly reflected in the Act of Anne. Thus, the first copyright act represents the summation of pressure brought to bear on the Houses of Parliament by the book trade and authors themselves and followed the failure of a number of proposed acts on the book trade to successfully navigate the legislative process.[10] Indeed, as John Feather noted, the stationers "saw the Bill as being for their protection, not for the protection of authors and certainly not to encourage authors to enjoy the profits of their work after publication" (Feather 1980, 36). The guild's representatives managed to amend the draft bill to move it more toward this notion of protection and to keep the legal recognition of authors' rights in check.

The Act of Anne reflects the four central tenets of modern copyright law: the recognition of "natural rights," a "just reward" for authorial labor, the stimulation of creativity, and some clear social requirements (Davies 2002, 13–17). The first two reflect the more general influence of John Locke and the new politics of individualized property rights emerging at this time, whereas the third and fourth represent a more public-regarding view of the role of copyright; the stimulation of activity, as well as a public interest in the establishment of a mandated public realm of "free" texts.

Although largely recognizing and instituting extant guild practices, it is important to note that the act included a recognition of the possibility of authors themselves owning copyrights. Whereas previously only the printer could have enjoyed copyright, now authors/proprietors (which is to say non–guild members) could also seek protection. To prevent the monopoly over copyrights from being reintroduced, the act made provision for an alternative (nonguild) register of copyrights that would undermine any attempt by the guild to deny an author copyright by refusing to register a particular text. Lyman Patterson argued that the rights of the author in the act should not be overstated, however: "The steps an author took to obtain a copyright for his own work were no different from those required for any-one else" (Patterson 1968, 13). Authors' rights were not elevated *above* those of printers, rather they were made equal: the "only difference between an author's securing a copyright and another's securing a copy-right was that the author did not have to purchase the right" (Patterson 1968, 146). Although Patterson accords little weight to this difference, to us it seems fundamental; from whom else could a copyright be purchased in the *first* instance but an author (at least for new works)? This is a signifi-cant move into the realm of property in the production of authorial outputs, the clear commodification of literary property.

Like the Statute of Monopolies that had instigated patent as a by-prod-uct, the Act of Anne was primarily concerned with regulating the printing trade and only as a secondary concern established a *potentially* common law copyright for authors. It is most significant that the statute separated the question of literary property from censorship and introduced a new struggle over the meaning of authors' property rights. The act clearly distin-guished between the rights to the authorial work and the means of its repro-duction (the book itself), and the phrase "books and other writings" hinted that copyright might be extended to other forms (Stewart 1977, 85). The subsequent history of copyright is partly the story of this potential to expand its scope.

Despite the Act of Anne, the issues of ownership at the heart of copyright were not fully tested in a common law court until the famous cases of *Millar v. Taylor* in 1769 and *Donaldson v. Beckett* in 1774, cases that have a totemic importance in all histories of copyright. These cases followed a series of unsuccessful attempts by the stationers to effect the continuation of their monopoly rights through further legislation amending the Act of Anne.[11] Although the precedent established by *Millar v. Taylor* was subsequently struck down, the case finally set out the clear link between authorial function and copyright. The interest of the case lies in the judicial opinions as regards the character of copyright, and it is these (rather than the decision itself) that have become so important in the historical narrative of copyright.

In supporting a common law copyright (instead of merely the statutory one), Mr. Justice Aston concluded that "a man may have property in his body, life, fame, labors and the like; in short in anything that can be called his . . . [and] I do not know, nor can I comprehend any property more emphatically a man's own, nay, more incapable of being mistaken, than his literary works" (quoted in Patterson 1968, 170). Furthermore, in agreeing with this position, Lord Mansfield argued that the rights of the author should be upheld

> because it is just, that an author should reap the pecuniary profits of his own ingenuity and labor. It is just, that another should not use his name, without his consent. It is fit that he should judge when to publish, or whether he ever will publish. . . . It is fit, he should choose to whose care he will trust the accuracy and correctness of the impression; in whose honesty he will confide, not to foist in additions. (Quoted in Davies 2002, 30; Abrams 1983, 1153; Patterson 1968, 170–171)

And Mansfield went on to argue that without this control the author was unable to exercise rightful discretion over the published work.

Patterson concluded that the "two opinions of Mr. Justice Aston and Lord Mansfield say, in effect, that copyright contains two basic rights of the author, a right to the rewards of his labor, and a right to protect his fame" (Patterson 1968, 171). It is well known that Justice Yates, dissenting from the majority view upholding the plaintiff's rights to publication, examined not the basis on which the right could be established but rather its social effects. Focusing on the limitations on diffusion that an effectively perpetual copyright would establish, Yates argued that copyright should be limited to the statutory right established in the Act of Anne; that, in effect, the protection should be limited for reason of the public good (Abrams 1983, 1155). He stressed that "the inconvenient consequences the public might feel [if perpetual copyright were enacted] . . . [i]nstead of tending to the advancement and the propagation of literature . . . it would stop it; or at least might be attended with great disadvantages to it" (quoted in Davies 2002, 30). Yates's concerns were more widely held than his minority view in this case might have indicated, and the precedent of *Millar v. Taylor* lasted only five years, even though the case itself was not appealed.

A second, linked, case, *Donaldson v. Beckett*, finally settled the issues that had destabilized copyright in Britain in the eighteenth century. The justices struck down the notion of a common law copyright vested in authors, or for that matter their assignees (the stationers), and replaced it with the limited protection that had been envisaged by the Act of Anne. Prior to *Millar v. Taylor* there had been some confusion and some variance in practice, which was brought to an end by the assertion of perpetuity in copyright secured by the stationers in that decision. Reflecting the suspicion of monopolies, as well as a public-regarding interest in the flow of printed works (as set out by Yates in his dissent), however, *Donaldson v. Beckett* clarified the position in favor of a limited copyright.

The outcome ended the notion that the copyright was a publishers' right and firmly placed the justification for copyright as a right of authors (Patterson 1968, 172–179). Many commentators at the time noted that although stationers had claimed to be purchasing a perpetual monopoly over a title, the price offered seldom reflected the expected income from more than a couple of years' sale. Indeed, as A. S. Collins noted: "If booksellers had being paying for perpetuity before 1774, prices for copyright must have fallen seriously after the adverse decision. That they did not fall, but even maintained the steady rise of recent years, is conclusive proof that perpetuity had been no concern" (Collins 1926, 80). Thus, *Donaldson v. Beckett* established time-limited copyright and rejected the *direct* comparison between literary property and real estate (although the metaphorical link between real estate and *intellectual property* was far more resilient).

Musical composers did not fare as well as literary authors during the eighteenth century. Music was not covered by even the rather chaotic and uncertain system that was available to authors. Composers could try to obtain patents or privileges for specific works, and in the sixty years after 1709 about sixteen such grants were made. Given the explosion of printed music in that century, however, most composers were at the mercy of what rewards they could gain from an industry that thrived on the unauthorized reproduction and distribution of increasingly well known standard musical works (Hunter 1986, 277 passim). As Peter Tschmuck suggested, however, there is little conclusive evidence that this was a major problem for composers at this time. Vienna in the late eighteenth century enjoyed one of the most productive periods for music composition (in what we now term "classical" music). With an almost complete absence of copyright protection for composed works, however, composers often sold specific compositions to more than one publisher, receiving no protection from unauthorized editions. Certainly there were major conflicts between composers and publishers, but creativity can hardly be said to have been stifled (Tschmuck 2002). Viennese musicians and composers mostly earned a good living from performance, and composition was primarily seen in performance terms, not as a product for reproduction and sale.

In Britain (where performance was considerably less profitable), two prominent composers (C. F. Abel and J. C. Bach) petitioned the lord chancellor in 1774 over an unauthorized edition of one of Bach's works printed by Longman and Lukey. When the case was finally heard in 1777, Lord Mansfield concluded that music was covered by the Act of Anne, as it explicitly encompassed "books and *other* writings," and that therefore music would be considered as included within copyright legislation (as then recently formalized in *Donaldson v. Beckett*) (Hunter 1986: 279, emphasis added). Alongside the extension of copyright to artist-engravers, this expansion set the tone for the continued widening of the activities that might be commodified through copyright, and in the nineteenth century protection was accorded to sculpture (1814), dramatic works (1833), and fine arts (1862). As the years wore on, more and more creators came to enjoy rights similar to those of writers.

Once the twenty-eight-year limit that the 1709 Act had legislated was finally applied in practice, the profitable trade in annual reprints of popular titles could not support copy-holding publishers forever. To find new books to publish where a monopoly could be maintained for the mandated period of twenty-one years, the stationers needed to deal with authors. This may have encouraged them to act more generously than in the past, and by putting authors in a stronger position vis-à-vis the trade, authors' rights became more effective (Feather 1987, 25). This period also saw the move from intensive reading (focusing on a few books that would be read and reread) to extensive reading (the serial reading of books *once*), which along with expanding literacy vastly expanded the market for *new* titles. This demand, the expanded possibility of asserting authorial rights, and the emergence of the author as a respectable member of society meant that authors such as Defoe, or Diderot in France, who were able to live by their work, were important examples for aspiring writers (Hesse 2002, 32). Increasingly, individual creators started to move to center stage in the law of intellectual property.

Now that both copyrights and patents were limited in time and scope, the emergence of a more generalized conception of *intellectual property* (*rights*) was possible. Early patents reflected the desire of rulers to capture new technologies for their national economies, but copyrights arose more as the result of pressures brought by the industry that copyrights were to govern. As the printing industry matured and technological changes reduced the costs of publication, the regulation of competition became more pressing, but the importance of the creating individual was still given little weight. Patents could be granted to whoever brought the idea to the attention of the court, and copyrights were the result of attempts by the printers and stationers to secure their rights to publish free from the competition of others. Early copyright in England was a statutory, not a natural, right; it regulated the production of copies of literary works and was not designed to confer property rights on an author.

Technological and economic shifts prompted the development of a legal institution related to specific views of the sort of ownership of knowledge that might be legitimate or "efficient." The need to capture new technologies for national economic development, alongside the expansion of the market for books brought about by printing, were important elements in political pressure to establish early intellectual property rights. These important changes also led to political pressures to attempt to have the products of other creative processes covered by copyright laws (including printed textile patterns and other works of artistic craftsmanship) in various sectors of the developing capitalist economy. But national differences remained crucially important.

The Early Modern Period of Intellectual Property

In Britain and then, in response, across Europe (and finally in the United States at the end of the eighteenth century), notions of copyright and patent started to enter the generally accepted universe of social facts. The idea that individuals in some way "produced" knowledge became increasingly prevalent and supported the development of intellectual property across the European continent. This is not to say that these ideas where received without criticism or debate or that all forms of modern intellectual property were equally embraced at this time. Rather, legislation followed specific national paths and was dependent on the sociolegal culture of particular national jurisdictions as well as the shape and trajectory of economic development.

Prior to the rise in advertising across the capitalist world, for instance, trademarks had little real economic significance, although during the nineteenth century their perceived asset value started to be more widely recognized. But even in the eighteenth century the awards of damages for mark infringement in civil cases, outside of those areas where the Crown might require capital punishment, started to rise. For instance, in 1777 in the case *Carbrier v. Anderson*, the court awarded damages of £100 to the plaintiff for the use by the defendant of Carbrier's name on five watches that he had made (Paster 1969, 565). But this was more the exception than the rule. Indeed, as Edward Walterscheid noted, although intellectual property was certainly emerging in Britain during this period, and if sometimes patent monopolies had a rightslike character, "nowhere prior to the French law of 1791 was there any legal *guarantee* of a property right or patent privilege" (Walterscheid 1994b, 715; emphasis added). Thus, until the late eighteenth century, no formal intellectual property *rights* can be said to have been enacted; intellectual property remained more a privilege than a right for the first 150 years of its formal history.

Debates about the transformation (in Britain and elsewhere) from feudal social relations to the nascent capitalistic model have been subject to extensive analysis and debate. Here we focus only on the issues that are directly relevant to the history of intellectual property, however, while recognizing that this narrow focus may frustrate those who wish to make a more general argument about the political economy of the "great transformation." Given the central role of technological innovation in any account of the arrival of modern capitalism, the argument that patents helped encourage further innovation was common.

Adam Smith in his *Lectures on Jurisprudence* (published in 1766) saw patents as a "rare example of a harmless exclusive privilege" that had clear benefits as regards the support of invention (MacLeod 1988, 197). And in his famous *Inquiry into the Nature and Causes of the Wealth of Nations* (first published in 1776), Smith justified patents and copyrights as monopolies on the grounds that they were "the easiest and most natural way in which the state can recompense [companies] for hazarding a dangerous and expensive experiment, of which the publick is afterwards to reap the benefit" (Smith [1776] 1993, 418). In the most famous award of a patent monopoly of the period, however, the arguments about public good were a little more difficult to sustain.

The disputes that were prompted by James Watt's patents raised important issues regarding intellectual property, and because steam power was common to a number of industries, these disputes had a wide impact on technological advance as well as the legal realm. For those seeking parallels with more recent history, it is crucial to note that Watt did not want a patent on a specific steam engine but rather sought to patent the "method of diminishing the consumption of fuel" in steam engines. He already understood that to patent a specific engine would lead his competitors to specify some small changes and claim their steam engine was a new invention (Robinson 1972, 120). Thus, to constrict the possibility of "inventing around" his patent, he sought a wider-ranging patent to cover the technological method, and once granted it is perhaps unsurprising that it was challenged on the basis of its specification.

In the key case, which Watt won (*Boulton and Watt v. Bull*), judgment hinged on whether the patent grant had been for the principle of the expansive force of steam or a practical method for harnessing such force

(Robinson 1972, 122). Watt avoided the claim for the principle of steam power but retained a wide enough scope to ensure most engines infringed his patent. His company also relied on trade secrets when certain aspects of its work were too important to risk specifying in a patent. Thus, the steam indicator, which they used to improve the performance of individual engines, was never patented but was used secretly at the works to enhance performance of their engines, an innovation that gave them a clear competitive edge (Frost 1991, 147). This indicates a clear appreciation of the public-regarding aspect of a patent application; information so protected entered the public realm. Where use would reveal the method, patents were useful; where the method could remain hidden, trade secrecy was better.

Watt's successful protection of his invention was not so much by virtue of the patent system but by his idiosyncratic manner of handling his patents and by the courts' latitude toward his actions; both of these factors stemmed from his fame rather than his innovation. Not only did Watt actually manage to evade the requirement to fully disclose his invention but also—in the words of John Farey, giving evidence to a select committee on patents some years later—"engineers who wanted to make steam engines, had to go and steal knowledge of his invention from his factory, or from examining engines made by him, with as much difficulty as if he had never had a patent" (quoted in Robinson 1972, 138). In other words, Watt sought the private right of protection for his invention while avoiding the public-regarding aspect of full disclosure through specification. This may have been partly because patents themselves were not fully understood by the judiciary and partly because through their social contacts and their wealth, Matthew Boulton and Watt were able to influence the courts decisively in Watt's favor (Robinson 1972, 138–139). This advantage was unavailable to most other patentees.

Watt and his business partners believed that the term of the central steam patent was not long enough to recoup their investment, not least of all as after the grant Watt had not immediately been able to manufacture a steam engine that worked. To this end, in 1775—six years into the term of the patent—Watt sought an extension from Parliament (Frost 1991). The extended period that was secured from Parliament after their examination of the facts allowed Watt to enjoy a thirty-one-year patent on his invention. This caused two problems in the supply of steam technology. First, unless prospective users were prepared to wait, and could afford the license fees, they had to settle for inferior engines or build illegal machines. Second, to some extent the Watt patent also stifled and constrained further innovations of this important technology for at least two decades. These two factors had the striking effect of halting the development of steam-driven rotary movement for some years, until Watt's business partners could convince him of its utility.

Likewise, high pressure steam had to await the end of the patent to be developed into a usable improvement (Frost 1991, 145–146). Indeed, the patent so alienated the Cornish mining industry that at the beginning of the nineteenth century various mine owners and others instigated a more collective approach to innovation, publishing improvements to their steam engines in *Lean's Engine Reporter*. Joel Lean, a well-known Cornish "mine captain," toured the county and published each month a report of improvements made and incremental inventions made. Alessandro Nuvolari argued that this spurred increased innovation and technical improvement and led to Richard Trevithick's forgoing any patent claim for his work on high pressure steam (Nuvolari 2001). Here, the full exploitation of a patent grant (by Watt) instilled a reaction by innovators that did not regard patenting as the best way to spur inventive activity, looking to a more collective innovation model instead. To some extent the relatively small community of Cornish mine owners enhanced the possibility of developing technologies outside the patent system, but even so this suggests that patents did not fully support all modes of commercial activity. Thus, the notion that patents helped the diffusion of innovation is hardly a straightforward depiction of the system's effects at this time.

Nevertheless, the widely held perception that Watt was an industrial genius—an individual at the height of his mental power—aided his attempts to control the industrial fruits of this genius. Here, the influence of Newtonian mechanics on the recognition of individual genius should not be underestimated. Where there was once predestination and fate, now God had been reduced to the maker of the universe (the initial "winding of the clock" as it were). Humans stepped to the center stage as the agents of invention. Providence and discovery were replaced by invention. As ideas about natural rights started to become more well known and influential on British society, so the assertion of rights over innovations became linked with the innovating mind, the creative genius.

Invention was linked with effort; Bernard Mandeville stressed in the *Fable of the Bees,* for instance, that skill and industry were the source of all improvements (MacLeod 1988, 209). The ingenuity of artisans, improving through use, remained the dominant concept of industrial and process improvement into the eighteenth century. But as the century progressed, so too the notion of a property right in invention and innovation (industrial and artistic) gained ground. The discourse of property rights became more explicit in patent applications (not least of all Watt's), and the notion that there might be some property-related value in ideas or knowledge became more widespread (MacLeod 1988, 198; Walterscheid 1996, 100). In the last decade of the century, the French Revolution gave the notion of a property right in knowledge a further and major boost.

In both France and in the American colonies, the common law traditions of British patent protection were rejected and rights-based legal struc-tures instituted, based on Thomas Paine's notion of the "rights of man." In 1790, the French National Assembly declared that "it would be a violation of the Rights of Man . . . not to regard an industrial discovery as property of its author" (quoted in MacLeod 1988, 199). Similarly, as we discuss later, the protection of intellectual property in the nascent United States of America was based directly on a notion of individual rights, although even in US law there is a considerable continuance as regards the public-regard-ing elements of patent and copyright law. The notion of property in knowl-edge entered the mainstream of political economic relations during this period.

The growing value of patent grants during the eighteenth century led to an increase both in the interest in securing grants of patent and also in the challenges that might be mounted by those whose interests were compro-mised. As large-scale manufacturing was developed, the ability to secure initial protection for the investment needed became increasingly attractive. Patents were a way of capturing the funds that were flowing to London without the inventions actually ever reaching production (MacLeod 1986). In the wake of a number of "stock-jobbing" scandals and then the South Sea Bubble, the government began to distrust joint-stock enterprises and worry about rampant stock market speculation. Therefore, between 1720 and 1832 the government regularly inserted a clause into patent grants ren-dering them invalid if more than five people received the benefit of the grant (although this rose to twelve for the twenty years after 1832) (MacLeod 1988, 55). It is possible, although of course difficult to prove, that this discouraged certain enterprises from taking out patents on certain inventions and innovations. Certainly, into the nineteenth century this reduced the utility of patents to an emerging group of large corporations, which would come to dominate the realm of intellectual property in the twentieth century.

Walterscheid argued that the eighteenth century saw an expansion of discussion about the justification of the protection of patents and copyrights because there was a perception that the court system in Britain was hostile to the protection of the nascent intellectual property rights (Walterscheid 1996, 102–103). The Lockean model of property ownership was a political rhetorical device of some currency, and after 1750 Locke's ideas were often referred to in disputes regarding the protection of patents and copyrights (Mossoff 2001, 1297–1302). Thus, it is perhaps no surprise that the emer-gence of a political philosophy of an individualized form of personality, alongside its aesthetic portrayal, fed into the legal form of commodification that copyrights and patents expressed. As Peter Jaszi put it, the notion of "authorship" that was established in the Act of Anne, although not yet fully developed, "was a charged receptacle, prepared to collect content over the next century" (Jaszi 1991, 471). Having been deployed by the booksellers and stationers as a rhetorical weapon to secure their property, the notion of authorship was (re)captured by authors to serve their (different) interests. As part of this shift, Jaszi also noted the rise of the term *work* (or *works*) for the output of the author (Jaszi 1991, 472–475), a change that firmly inserts the notion of authorial function into a discourse of commodity and nascent capitalist social relations (leading to a position that *work* should be rewarded, with property, following Locke).

By the end of the eighteenth century, invention was regarded as a matter of synthesis rather than analysis. Rather than merely being an extension of what had gone before, invention became potentially infinite, and the notion of continuous innovation emerged around this time. Christine MacLeod suggested that this increasing emphasis on

> the efforts and "genius" of the individual fostered an "heroic" explanation of invention, which was to come to fruition in the nineteenth century when inventors and engineers were indeed lauded as national heroes. For the present, invention was still a largely anonymous achievement. . . . Yet invention was now recognised as the achievement of individuals; they were more than the agents of Providence, and without their efforts there was no God-given guarantee that an invention would be made by someone else. (MacLeod 1988, 220–221)

The encouragement of the individual in his role as genius, as hero, justified the temporary suspension of the free market to allow the owner of an idea to profit from that which he had invented. The Statute of Monopolies exception regarding patents therefore seemed like an excellent device for rewarding innovation. Although the American and French revolutions produced genuine new laws for the protection of innovation, the English continued with a strange hybrid, an exception rather than a positive law. Eventually in the mid-nineteenth century, reform would become unavoidable, but for perhaps much longer than might have been warranted the English law carried on adapting and hedging an old law to do new things, in a parallel to the craft model of adaptation rather than synthetic innovation.

By the time the intellectual property laws were renewed in the nineteenth century, developments in Europe, again, had begun to have an influence on British legislation. In France the idea of a right approximating to copyright had originally emerged with the granting of *privilèges en librairie* to both authors and publishers in the early sixteenth century. Usually limited to ten-years' monopoly, these grants were intended to allow an investor to recover his original outlay, with the book passing into the realm of the "free copy" once the grant's term had expired. Despite being granted to authors *or* printers/publishers, generally the cost of printing and distribution encouraged authors to transfer those grants they did gain to printers for a fixed sum (Birn 1971, 136–137). These grants were controversial, however, and many printers outside Paris refused to recognize the limitations they imposed. For most of the century the *privilèges en librairie* was subject to challenge and amendment[12] while moving ever closer to a system that started to recognize the rights of authors as flowing from some conception of natural law. In this sense, the developments in France were part of the wider move to the conception of the author as a creative *individual* who enjoyed certain rights over his efforts. Despite being formulated (in outline, at least) by the ancien régime, the revolutionaries felt it necessary to enact a new law of copyright that accepted this view of the author.

Unlike the underpinnings of the Act of Anne on the other side of the channel, in postrevolutionary France copyright was conceived of as *le droit d'auteur* that, rather than a positive legal right created by a legal instrument, was a natural right established through an act of creation and then merely recognized or—more precisely—formalized through legislation (Burkitt 2001, 159). Here the notion of a natural right of authors, a right accruing to genius, finds its origins as a justification for the awarding of property rights. This individualization of the "author" was tempered by the recognition of the author as servant of a public domain, however. Hence, although according these rights to authors for their lifetime, public enlightenment was to be encouraged by a revocation of these rights on death (Hesse 1990). The revolutionary law, although according new (moral) rights to authors, also was the first to explicitly recognize the existence of the public domain. Certainly such a domain was clearly implied in the earlier British law, but in the French law of 19 July 1793, the public realm (and its benefits) became an explicitly recognized legal entity.[13]

In the realm of the protection of property in inventions, French legislators seemed to have taken more explicit notice of how the British dealt with such issues. The ancien régime had operated a system of *privileges* for the establishment of monopolies in invention. During the eighteenth century, the French system centered on a public examination of patent applications, which served to ensure that inventions entered the public domain, not least of all by keeping a public repository of all machines that were granted *privileges* (Hilaire-Pérez 1991, 919). Alongside the *privilege* system, a system of financial reward was also run by the Bureau of Commerce to directly reward inventors (funded from an import levy on goods from the French West Indies). In some cases this allowed the state to intervene when inventors claimed they were not receiving sufficient reward and hence tried to limit the diffusion of their techniques and innovations.[14] These arrangements in the second half of the century started to be criticized, however, by those who drew a link between the liberal policies of the British government and the accelerating economic development on that side of the channel.

Despite early hostility to patents in the Revolution, by 1791 a group of dissatisfied inventors petitioned the National Assembly for the provision of a patent law and cited the British system. The French patent law was enacted in the same year (Frumkin 1947, 55–56). This law was preceded by a series of acts that had culminated in the act of 1787, which accorded designs clear property status. These acts, following the first in 1711, were intended to help support the French textile industry and had originated with the silk manufacturing guild, not the various governments under which they had been passed (Prager 1944, 730). Indeed, it is far from clear that the pre-Revolution court had any desire to recognize industrial (or intellectual) property outside the realm of textiles.

Only with the 1791 act was intellectual property finally recognized more widely in France, although the revolutionaries backed away from this stance a mere four years later. Having reintroduced a notion of recompense (that is, a return to the notion of the privilege, from which previous patent law largely stemmed) in 1795, subsequent legal commentary in France started to identify a tension between the necessarily limited grants of rights under intellectual property law and the overall theory of property. Hence, the 1844 patent law avoided all reference to intellectual *property,* and the French High Court declared in 1887 that there was no such thing as intellectual property at all (Prager 1944, 735). On the other hand, the notion that national control of inventions was important continued throughout this period, with patents being rendered void in France if an inventor attempted to secure a patent for his invention in another national jurisdiction (Khan 2002, 16). This attempt to limit the international diffusion of French innovations suggests that the importance of ownership of such innovations continued to influence national policy, whatever the discussions regarding the appropriate use of the notion of property rights in information and knowledge.

Although the French and British might well have wished to limit the diffusion of new technologies (especially in the textile industries), elsewhere the utilization of *privileges* and other forms of quasi patents continued to be developed for clearly mercantilist reasons. For instance, in Victor Amadeus's attempt to secure complete independence for Piedmont from the domination of France, artisans such as Francesco Suarz—who could bring with them important techniques (in this case the dyeing of cloth)—were awarded monopolies over specific technologies. These grants allowed the artisan to benefit from the exploitation of the technology but also required the education of locals in the imported techniques (Dolza and Hilaire-Pérez 2002, 27–28). Even these awards were not necessarily well received by others, however, and political remonstrations led, one year before Victor Amadeus's abdication, to the setting up of the Royal Council of Commerce, among whose duties was the oversight and issuance of future privileges.

The council continued to work on balancing the needs of society (for training and new technologies) with the desire of owners to profit from their (often imported) innovations well into the second half of the century, until emerging arguments about free trade started to undermine some of the mercantilist claims for regulations on which it was based. What is clear here, however, is that the idea of regulating through grants of patentlike monopolies over technology had considerable political resonance across the continent as individual rulers discovered the importance of economic development in the emerging international economy.

The modern period of our history of intellectual property sees ideas about owning knowledge and information, which had been developing for many centuries, galvanized and transformed by the new industrial society (most obviously in Britain and France, the most economically developed countries of the time), where property was more than mere possession but rather the basis upon which to build economic relations. The idea of intellectual property spread outward from Britain, linked with the emerging capitalist institutional practices being developed as feudalism was transformed. On the continent in the early nineteenth century, the expansion of Napoleonic France led countries such as Spain to adopt patent legislation based on the French model. Recognizing the individualism at the center of US intellectual history, the US Constitution—unlike European grants that generally accorded patent privilege to those who were first to file (whether they were the inventors or not)—recognized the moment of innovation as establishing rights against other applicants. In the hands of the drafters of the US Constitution, the rights that should be accorded an innovating individual start to emerge as a key justification for awarding property in knowledge and information (reflecting the French revolutionary patent law of 1791 that had established that the inventor had a natural property right in his invention). Prior to this, some of the North American colonies had already started to legislate some sort of patent grant, not as a sovereign grant but as a fulfillment of the (natural) rights of the inventor; of these, South Carolina in 1691 may have been the first. In the next chapter, we move to the consolidation of the shift from grant to *right* and to the interaction of the accelerating Industrial Revolution and the burgeoning modern capitalist system.

Notes

1. Space precludes a detailed history of the German book trade; a good account can be found, however, in Thompson ([1911] 1968, chaps. 1 and 3).

2. Ironically, one of the main "pirates" was the Elzevir family of Leyden and Amsterdam (Bugbee 1967, 49), whose company (now called Elsevier) went on to become one of the major publishers of science periodicals and are often currently

attacked for using the copyright system as a major element in their high subscription price business model.

3. See the early grants of patent listed in Hulme (1896, 145–150) from 1561 onward.

4. This and the following paragraph summarize points made by Walterscheid (1994b, 876–879; 1995a).

5. D. Seaborne Davies explored early English patent specifications at some length but concluded that the precursors to patent specification he identified "were seeds that fell on rocky ground" (Davies 1934, 272).

6. Harold Love (1993) surveyed this phenomena in great detail, and the treatment here can only hint at the breadth of his scholarship in this area.

7. This case is briefly reported by W. F. Wyndham Brown (1908, 56) but appears in no other accounts available to us.

8. A detailed and fascinating account of these activities can be found in Judge ([1934] 1968), on which these remarks are based.

9. As Edward Walterscheid (1996, 96n101) noted, there has been some confusion about the date of the act: "It was enacted in the calendar year 1709 and became effective in April 1710. But at this time the beginning of the year in England was March 25." Only the Calendar Act of 1750 would institute the modern year, hence there is some confusion about whether the Act of Anne should be dated 1709 or 1710.

10. The history of the attempts to get an act passed is detailed in Feather (1980).

11. See Patterson (1968, 154–158) for the series of failed attempts in Parliament.

12. These events were recounted in some detail in Birn (1971) and Hesse (1990).

13. Carla Hesse (1990) discussed at length the debates in France and the series of legislative changes that produced this shift toward an explicit public domain.

14. Luisa Dolza and Lilianne Hilaire-Pérez (2002) discussed the case of John Kay (who introduced the flying shuttle and carding to the French textile industry from England) as a specific example of how the French authorities might aid grant holders.

5 ———

The Nineteenth Century: Technological Development and International Law

AS OUR ACCOUNT of the history of the development of intellectual property recognition and protection has already demonstrated, this process involves a complex yet identifiable relationship among three major factors. First, it reveals shifting ideas or conceptions of ownership, authorship, and invention. These ideas denote what counts as property and who shall lay claim to it. Second, this history reflects changes in the organization of innovation and the production and distribution of technology. Third, institutional change is intimately connected to these shifting ideational and material forces. Institutionalization of these changes in law alters power relationships and inevitably privileges some at the expense of others but is also affected by specific actors furthering *their* interests. Up until this point, we have described the faltering development of both general ideas about and particular manifestations of intellectual property that led to the development of a recognizably early-modern system of rights. These (intellectual) property rights were situated within broader historical structures of an emergent global capitalism and served to either reproduce or transform these structures. Depending on the world in which one lived, the counterfeiting of intellectual properties may have been construed as theft *or* as an important tool of social policy for the public interest. Definitions of what constituted property depend upon time, place, the constellation of interests and degree of competition present, stage of economic development, and political economic power. Insofar as intellectual property was, and is, an instrument of public policy, all of these factors are relevant.

As we have established, historical change is hardly linear. The history of intellectual property rights (IPRs) is a history of contestation. The inherent tensions in the idea of intellectual property recurrently resurface under philosophical, technological, or institutional pressure. Questions and problems that arose in the two millennia before the Venetian moment continue to reverberate through the subsequent and increasingly international history of intellectual property. Therefore, this chapter highlights some key moments in nineteenth- and early-twentieth-century law, when again particular ideas and economic circumstances converged to privilege particular agents and alter the institutions of intellectual property.

We begin by discussing the idea of intellectual property as public policy and go on to describe the diversity of law in the nineteenth century, demonstrating the variety of ways in which different countries used intellectual property policies to encourage economic development. This diversity underscores a range of possible approaches to intellectual property protection, exemplified by the "patent controversy" between 1850 and 1875. This controversy was resolved in favor of intellectual property rights and marks a key settlement in the history of intellectual property law and its relationship to international trade. The next section discusses the multilateral institutionalization of this resolution in the Paris and Bern conventions. We then move to examine the role of Thomas Edison and his use of patents as a business strategy and the emergence of the works-for-hire doctrine in US copyright law; we conclude with a discussion of the German chemical industry's new business model and the rise of patent cartels.

Intellectual Property as Public Policy

Romantic notions of inspired and creative genius offered a powerful image of the status of intellectual property. Indeed, advocates for rights in such property often evoked these romantic notions to justify natural rights in an individual's creations. But as we have seen, it is not the only way to think about such rights. During the latter part of the eighteenth century and the early decades of the nineteenth century, social utilitarianism challenged these subjectivist notions of universal natural rights in one's intellectual creations (Fisk 2003, 9–10; Woodmansee and Jaszi 2004, 2–3). Utilitarian conceptions emphasized the social or collective process of invention and authorship. These competing doctrines embody the continuing tensions inherent in intellectual property rights between individualized and collective models of creativity and invention. As a matter of public policy, utilitarian notions are designed to reward creation and diffusion, whereas natural rights or romantic notions privilege the goal of stewardship or the right to "manage" one's property after it is created.

Mark Lemley usefully contrasted these conceptions as "ex ante," in the case of the utilitarian/public goods justification, and "ex post," in the romantic/private reward justification (Lemley 2004, 129). As William Fisher pointed out, under the incentive/public goods justification, "like other 'monopolies,' patents and copyrights were dangerous devices that should be deployed only when absolutely necessary to advance some clear public interest" (Fisher 1999, 11). Conversely, advocates of the romantic/private reward justification argued that the extension of intellectual property rights was necessary to give existing copyright owners incentives to preserve any work they had already created. Thus, according to Lemley, under this view "the optimal right would appear to be perpetual: if only ownership gives efficient incentives to use, the right of stewardship . . . should never end" (Lemley 2004, 135). These apparently philosophical differences have had obvious and sharp policy ramifications throughout our history, and Lemley identified ex post justifications as profoundly antimarket (Lemley 2004, 148–149). Thus, even as the development of modern capitalism started to accelerate and expand, its logic of marketization and commodification severely divided political opinion.

Throughout its history, intellectual property protection, intentionally or not, has always been a form of public policy. Intellectual property rights can serve particular developmental goals or can thwart them. We have already noted that during the fourteenth century patents were grants of privilege awarded to those who brought new techniques into a sovereign's territory. Rulers sought to attract and retain talented artisans in their territory, inspired by the mercantilist goals of limiting imports and promoting exports. Furthermore, the diversity of intellectual property policies between countries was, and remains, in part a function of their different stages of development. A technological leader generally will prefer strong protection of its innovations, whereas a follower will favor access over protection. Here, the case of Richard Arkwright, a friend of James Watt, is instructive: Arkwright's patent disputes demonstrate the public policy aspects of intellectual property policy and were concluded quite differently from Watt's own cases. Unlike Watt's experience, in Arkwright's cases the social good of promoting access to and use of his inventions was favored over his individual rights to control the use of his creations. The decisions in his cases animated a countermovement to shift the balance in favor of the private rewards of property, to (re)establish the level of protection that Watt had secured.

In 1781 Arkwright pursued his first infringement case, relating to a patent he held for methods of spinning cotton, but the court ruled that his patent was invalid because rather than disclosing his invention, he "did all he could to hide and secret it" (quoted in Moore 1998, 20). He then sued a neighbor, Peter Nightingale, four years later over an alleged patent infringement. Nightingale's defense again focused on the patent specification, specifically whether a competent person could build the machine based upon it, but this time the court ruled in Arkwright's favor. Barrington Moore argued that this victory actually made Arkwright's situation worse, because the Lancashire spinners now feared the prospect of being forced to pay Arkwright license fees to use his equipment. The spinners sought to get the verdict annulled that same year and ultimately prevailed, with Arkwright losing his patent owing to its ambiguous specification. According to Moore:

> The legal representative of the Lancashire spinners took the high moral ground of public and national interest. Arkwright's patent represented a monopoly. Legal recognition of the patent would enable Arkwright, already a rich man, to choke off the livelihood of thousands of hard-working people. Moreover, it would in time destroy the flourishing British textile industry in which England already led the world. (Moore 1998, 21)

Arkwright lost both of his patents, and his two trials cost him £1,911 (Jeremy 2004, 6). This case demonstrates that property holders did not automatically win and that courts tried to balance diverse public goals.

This judgment reflected the continuing assumption by the courts that intellectual property rights should be considered grants of privilege that were explicitly recognized as *exceptions* to the rules against monopolies. Considering patents to be privileges underscored their temporary and unstable nature and specifically highlighted the fact that what may be granted may be taken away when such grants conflict with other important social goals. The case of the Lancashire spinners pitted the right to labor, and continued British economic hegemony, against the right to monopoly. The outcome of the case also set into motion another political dynamic that energized patentees' activities, however. It is significant that Arkwright's losses in court mobilized a broad quest for stronger patent rights.

In 1785, after the court canceled his second patent, a number of patentees and a "putative Patentee's Association" met and resolved to "unite in defense of their respective rights and to agree upon a mode of application to Parliament for the better security of their inventions" (quoted in MacLeod 2004, 14). Manufacturers were above all concerned with protecting their escalating investments in factory production. Christine MacLeod maintained that the manufacturing interests played a major role in shaping the patent system during the nineteenth century. The manufacturers were most concerned with "the security of their intellectual property and the development of institutions that would decrease the risk and uncertainty of managing it—primarily a cheap and fast way to settle disputes over the ownership and infringement of patents" (MacLeod 2004, 14). Again, as this emphasizes, the development of intellectual property legislation often has been subject to the mobilization of interest to establish and reinforce positions of advantage, especially when such advantage has been threatened by a public-regarding intent articulated by courts or through legislation. The historical picture reveals a recurrent tension that has not always been resolved in favor of property holders. For every Watt there was likely to be an Arkwright: the balance between private rights and public-regarding social benefits remained part of a national, and highly conflictual, set of deliberative processes in the courts.

The International Diversity of Law

The intellectual property landscape of the nineteenth century was a patchwork of diverse national laws and approaches to intellectual property regulation. As a matter of public policy, most states by now had adopted intellectual property policies to encourage the migration of useful inventions to their territory and to facilitate the access of the reading public to an extensive range of published materials. These policies included introductory patents, compulsory licensing, "working" requirements, differential treatment for citizens versus foreigners, and (by contemporary standards) weak or lax intellectual property protection. For instance, the early British patent system was designed to introduce foreign technologies to the kingdom and granted monopoly privileges not to inventors but rather to those who brought the invention to the knowledge of the public. By contrast, the early US patent system was established to provide incentives for domestic innovation while denying protection for foreign technology. US copyright policy also was designed to promote learning, public access, and protection of the public domain (Patterson and Joyce 2003). In general, innovators tended to seek higher levels of intellectual property protection. Imitators and technological "latecomers" sought maximum access to intellectual property at minimal or no cost.[1]

The British dominated the first Industrial Revolution (roughly the 1780s to the 1840s) with their mining and steam engine technology and the mechanization of the textile industry. Patents did not play a major role in the emergence of the cotton industry, however, in part owing to the way that the sector was initially organized.[2] As MacLeod pointed out: "The diffusion of a manufacture over a wide area, often in remote cottages, made enforcement very difficult. . . . [After 1770] the removal of cotton and worsted spinning into the factories prompted an upsurge in patents in those sectors. Not only was a patent easier to police in a factory-based industry, but it was also potentially more valuable as these industries grew exponentially" (MacLeod 2004, 10). Also from a potential patentee's point of view, the British administration of patent law up until 1852 left much to be desired. Patentees faced a cumbersome bureaucratic maze, high costs of securing and defending patents, and deep uncertainty that deterred many efforts to prosecute possible infringement (MacLeod 2004, 6). Therefore, as was the case with Watt and his steam indicator, often innovators relied on secrecy or restrictive covenants to control their new technological innovations.

On the European continent, France had a well-developed patent system. The French had established their system in 1791 with patents of introduction, patent rights restricted to France (French patentees could not patent abroad), and a working requirement in which all patents had to be worked in France within two years of the grant (Beatty 2002, 127). Spain's first official patent law was imposed by the French in 1811 after the Napoleonic invasion; it is not surprising that it resembled French law. Spanish rulers modified it slightly in 1820 and 1826, but the basic contours remained the same. J. Patricio Saiz Gonzalez characterized Spain's system as based first on French law and then more generally on an emerging body of practice by "follower and latecomer countries whose governments attempted to develop processes of innovation, modernization and economic growth over and above intellectual property rights" (Gonzalez 2002, 51). In the mid-1830s, and between 1849 and 1878, the Spanish government actively blocked numerous invention and introduction patents that were not worked within the specified time frame (Gonzalez 2002, 67). Indeed, between 1826 and 1907, 75 percent of registered inventions lost their monopoly rights within three years, transferring that technical information into the public domain. Therefore, for most of the century Spain balanced intellectual property protection with an express, and often enacted, commitment to public access.

In the Netherlands, between 1860 and 1865 the lion's share of patents granted each year also covered inventions made abroad (at least 124 out of 140). It seems that many citizens did not see granting such rights to foreigners as being beneficial, however. A Dutch pressure group representing small and medium-sized enterprises successfully lobbied for the abolition of the Patent Act as an "obstacle to the growth of industry and prejudicial to the national prosperity" (quoted in Cullis 2004, 39). This political pressure led the Dutch to abolish their patent system altogether in 1869. As the Dutch were "followers" in economic and technical fields, Roger Cullis argued that this "gave small companies, and those that were just starting up, protection from the disruption and expense of litigation and thus improved their chances of survival" (Cullis 2004, 40). Without having to pay royalties, the Dutch could produce goods equal in quality to foreign goods for much reduced costs. Despite remaining outside the international system of protection, however, arguments continued to rage in Dutch politics about the morality of the national position. Finally, the objections of their trade partners and the Dutch government's own embarrassment over its isolationist position led the Netherlands to reinstate a patent law in 1912 (Schiff 1971, 77–81). For many Dutch business groups, their traditionally outward (trading) orientation had eventually led them to accept that nonnationals should have the same rights they accorded themselves.

The Swiss also had no comprehensive patent law between 1850 and

1907, and therefore during this time many Swiss companies were free to imitate or modify others' inventions. Indeed, although there had been a spasmodic enactment of privileges and some early forms of patents across a number of the cantons, there was little political interest in the protection of intellectual property at the federal level until late in the nineteenth century (Ritter 2004, 470–473). By the 1880s the political and business elites of Switzerland engaged in a heated political argument over patenting, however. Quite apart from the morality of their position (and here, like the Dutch, many found themselves in an awkward position relative to their trading partners abroad), many Swiss policymakers were concerned that their lack of patent legislation opened them up to international retaliation in other economic and/or policy areas (Schiff 1971, 89). Although these and other domestic pressures led to the enactment of patent legislation in 1888, as Eric Schiff pointed out, this was "probably the most incomplete and selective patent law ever enacted in modern times" (Schiff 1971, 93). The most important omission was patents for chemical compounds, but under continued pressure from both the German and US governments (at the behest of their chemical sectors), the Swiss revised their law in 1907. The revision extended coverage to chemical processes, although *substances* remained unpatentable in Switzerland for another half century.

Across the Atlantic, the US patent laws of 1790 and 1793 had offered strong rights to citizen inventors. Only inventors, not "introducers," could patent, and using the system was inexpensive in order to encourage broad domestic participation, with fees at around a twentieth of those charged in Britain. US law also included working requirements up until 1908 (Merges 2000, 2221). Not only were foreigners and foreign inventions ineligible for US patents before 1836, but when nondomestic applications were allowed, they were subject to higher fees (Beatty 2002, 126–127). On the other hand, noting the debates regarding the danger of monopolies that had underpinned patent legislation in Britain, the framers of the US Constitution also clearly limited the extent of the rights conferred to ensure that both copyrights and patents should be strictly limited in duration to serve the public interest (Ochoa and Rose 2002). Thus, the US system was designed, for clearly political reasons, to discriminate in favor of US inventors. Discrimination against foreigners served the public interest and was a common policy to encourage technology transfer. As David Jeremy noted: "[I]f both citizens and aliens were denied the possibility of a patent for introducing a foreign invention, foreign inventions could be introduced to America without the additional cost of the inventor's monopoly rights. The USA had access to the world's technology at a lower cost than other nations" (Jeremy 2004, 3). This asymmetry between British and US patent laws favored "inventors in the developing, follower, economy of the USA, rather than the more industrialized, leading, economy, Britain" (Jeremy

2004, 4). During the nineteenth century the notion of national treatment, which would become so central to US policy in this area at the end of the next century, was completely absent.

It is hardly surprising that Britain and the United States experienced considerable friction over copyright policy as well. British authors and publishers complained of widespread piracy of British books abroad. Here the United States was hardly alone: reprinting foreign books was perfectly legal in many other countries. Nevertheless, reprinting texts by popular British authors such as Charles Dickens was a thriving industry in the United States and represented a major lost market for British rights holders. For example, in 1843 a US copy of Dickens' *A Christmas Carol* cost six cents, whereas a British edition cost the equivalent of $2.50 (Hesse 2002, 41). The British book trade recognized that this was reducing potential profits and eliminating major export markets for legitimate British editions (Feather 1994b, 154). Both British *and* US authors unsuccessfully lobbied the US government to establish US recognition of foreign copyright claims. US authors were interested in such recognition because of US publishers' predilection to publish British works, which were not copyright protected, instead of US ones, which were (Nachbar 2002, 45). As Carla Hesse noted, this led US authors to appeal to Congress "to encourage American letters by preventing cheap reprints of unauthorized British texts" (Hesse 2002, 41). The US publishers prevailed, however, employing the discourse of public interest in defense of their position. A prominent Philadelphia publishing house, Sherman and Johnson, sent the following appeal to Congress in 1842: "All the riches of English literature are ours. English authorship comes to us free as the vital air, untaxed, unhindered, even by the necessity of translation, into the country; and the question is, shall we tax it, and thus impose a barrier to the circulation of intellectual and moral light? Shall we build a dam to obstruct the flow of the rivers of knowledge?"[3] When the interests of authors and publishers were different, it was the publishers' commercial interest that triumphed.

At this time, then, it is fair to say that US policy reflected the utilitarian justification of the public interest (Perelman 2002, 16; Vaidhyanathan 2001, 8). As a developing country and an importer of "literary and scientific creations," the United States sought to retain the right to appropriate the ideas, scientific inventions, and literary creations of the leading countries (Hesse 2002, 40; see also Goldstein 1994, 182–183; and Clark 1960, 26–29). By contrast, net exporters such as France, England, and Germany invoked what Hesse has characterized as a "natural rights doctrine" that stressed a "universal moral and economic right enabling authors to exercise control over their creations and inventions and to receive remuneration" (Hesse 2002, 40). By the middle of the century, Europeans had negotiated an extensive network of bilateral copyright agreements, prompting a growing demand for their codification into an international treaty reflecting this claim of natural rights. Americans were reluctant to participate in such an undertaking, however, not least of all as US policymakers did not begin to share this European perspective on copyright until the late 1880s.

From the Patent Controversy to Paris and Bern

Between 1850 and 1875, a controversy raged between those seeking to defend the protection of innovation and invention through the patent system and those contrasting this protection with the needs and demands of an international system of free trade. The controversy highlighted the tension between free trade and intellectual property but also reflected the inherent tension in intellectual property rights on which we have focused.[4] Free trade liberals criticized the monopoly aspect of intellectual property and tried to undermine the patent system by arguing that invention was social, objective, and a product of technological change, rather than the result of individual genius (Fisk 2003, 9). Using numerous examples of simultaneous invention to buttress their case, they suggested that it was far from clear that anyone really needed the incentive of a patent to invent (MacLeod 2004, 5). Opposing groups and committees were formed to protect the rights of inventors; patent lawyers, engineers, and large companies, who stood to gain from continued patent legislation, mobilized their political forces to support patent rights. Not all inventors or commercial interests supported patents, however; those who had fallen foul of their enforcement in the past had few illusions about the beneficiaries of the system.

The abolitionists focused on three main (still familiar) arguments. They argued that claims that there was a "natural" right to own intellectual property obscured the very necessary legal *construction* of IPRs, which—unlike material (rival) property—are not characteristically scarce. Second, although they accepted that arguments about just rewards had some weight, the abolitionists noted that seldom were the rewards distributed fairly and seldom did the actual innovators garner these rewards. Third, despite the claimed "incentive to invent," patents were actually a disincentive to rival inventors once first inventions were patented. Furthermore, mankind had seemingly been quite innovative throughout history without recourse to intellectual property (Machlup and Penrose 1950). To convince business interests of the case for abolition and to offer an alternative to mere reform, however, initially those against the patent system suggested a system of direct grants and government support for inventive activity (Batzel 1980, 192). These ideas failed to convince industrialists, who were often suspicious of this sort of state involvement. Although the abolitionists certainly stimulated a forthright debate, their dependence on largely pragmatic arguments opened the way for reform rather than the elimination of patents (Batzel 1980, 199). In the end, supporters mobilizing narratives of justification similar to those relied on today won. As Mark Janis noted, although the critics retreated, patents' supporters shared "many of the concerns promulgated by the patent abolitionists" (Janis 2002, 947), even if they reversed the argument.

The abolitionists had seen the nonavailability of patents in some jurisdictions as giving those countries an unfair advantage and therefore suggested that patents should be abolished to reestablish free trade. Conversely, the internationalist position sought to widen the scope in order to halt, in the words of John Stuart Mill, "attempts which, if practically successful, would enthrone free stealing under the prostituted name of free trade" (Mill 1871, 2:552). Hence a central element of the move to internationalize IPRs was a direct reaction to a forthright debate regarding patents' shortcomings and, significantly, "theft" by foreigners. But in marked contrast to contemporary arguments, free trade advocates regarded intellectual property rights as a privilege that could *not* be supported between jurisdictions, as it constrained the free trade in goods that included claims of intellectual property. This political dispute was perhaps the last time that free traders would undertake a concerted effort to suggest that intellectual property rights were illegitimate and fundamentally inconsistent with free trade.[5]

Therefore, through extensive propaganda supporting the rights of the patent holder versus the infringer and, perhaps more important, because of the decline of support for free trade itself, the champions of patent protection eventually won (Machlup and Penrose 1950, 4–6). A further spur to a patent-favoring settlement came when in Britain the domestic patent controversy was resolved in 1883 with reforms that increased access to the patent system (MacLeod 2004, 5). A more open system, alongside a political shift that began to see free trade as less of an overall benefit, caused opposition to the constriction of free trade by patents to lose its momentum. The abolitionists also supported an international agreement because, as Moureen Coulter pointed out, "the idea of an international agreement was the only thing that made continued domestic protection tolerable" (Coulter 1991, 176). Intellectual property was still regarded as a restriction of trade, but such restrictions, as long as they served the national interest (and were applicable to all), were no longer regarded as problematic. In the coming century, this frank recognition of potential conflicts between international trade and intellectual property would disappear from mainstream discourse. On the other hand, it is important to note that this period marked the full development of the discourse justifying intellectual property rights as an acceptable and legitimate form of monopoly; a discourse that would now start to drop the pejorative term *monopoly* from most discussion.

Henceforth, intellectual property usually would be regarded as a direct reward for intellectual labor (Locke's labor desert), as part of the inalienable right of individuals to be associated with their innovations (the Hegelian narrative), or perhaps most clearly for reasons of economic "necessity," to ensure the efficient use of resources. The idea of property in knowledge was accepted among the governments, policymakers, and commercial interests of the increasingly developed industrialized countries, partly for pragmatic reasons and partly owing to the intense lobbying of the 1860s and 1870s. This paved the way for the international market in products that stemmed from the manipulation and control of knowledge to become formally organized on the basis of multilateral legal structures.

This establishment of the justification for patents is another important moment of settlement. The fact that by the end of the nineteenth century the rights of owners to own intellectual property, through the analogy to material property, were rendered unproblematic represents a key moment in the development of the global intellectual property rights structure. Although technologies were only just emerging that would transform the use of knowledge in economic organization and production, and although institutional development remained spasmodic, the increasing political solidification of ideas of intellectual property based on the rights of owners was crucial for the next stage of the international development of intellectual property rights in legislation. The decline of objections to the restriction of completely free trade cleared the way for a greater coordination of cross-border recognition of patent protection to replace the essentially territorially delimited provision then current. The complex of bilateral treaties was replaced by an emergent multilateralism of intellectual property conventions with cross-border reach.

This important shift in ideas about intellectual property was accompanied by economic and technological changes that together drove the establishment of multilateral institutions governing intellectual property. Intellectual property, both patents and copyright, became the basis for a new business model for investment and production. The period from about 1870 into the early 1900s was marked by shifting conceptions of ownership; at the same time, economic and technological leadership shifted from Britain to the United States and Germany. The first Industrial Revolution had been driven by the invention of the steam engine, the spinning jenny, machine tools, and the development of the textile, iron, and shipbuilding industries. The second, roughly from 1870 to 1914, was driven by chemicals, steel, oil, and electricity.

The four decades before the outbreak of the Great War (World War I) witnessed the swift expansion of world commerce facilitated by significant improvements in transportation and the commercial development of telegraphy. In the United States, the development of railways created a huge domestic market and facilitated mass production that fueled US economic growth. Furthermore, the expansion of the economies of scale (due in part to the expanding US domestic market) that could be captured by larger corporations in this growing market allowed significant gains for workers and other non–capital owning groups/classes (Resnick and Wolff 2003). Thus, the nascent US corporate capitalism, by expanding productivity through technology and organization but at the same time producing a significant rise in the standard of living of its workforce (however precarious such advances might be for individuals), laid the foundations for a new period of modern capitalism. Large corporations were now able to dominate market sectors (nationally and increasingly globally) on the basis of technological and organizational advantage. New industries (and leading sectors) allowed the United States to capitalize on its abundant raw materials and Germany to profit from its well-organized scientific education.

In many cases, "myth-making" inventors, such as Thomas Edison and Werner Siemens, were at the helm of these changes. Significantly, these business leaders pressed for higher standards of patent protection and also sought protection for the results of corporate research and development. An 1871 US Supreme Court decision (*United States v. Burns*) amended the 1791 Patent Act to permit employment contracts to include a clause requiring employees to assign patents or other invention rights to the employer.[6] Indeed, as William Kingston contended, without this change in the law "the R&D of in-house research laboratories and workshops, such as Edison's at Menlo Park, would have been impossible to finance" (Kingston 2004, 4). In Germany, Werner Siemens became a member of the German parliament in order to get the 1877 German Patent Act passed. As the Siemens Corporation needed large numbers of employed inventors in its research labs, Siemens wanted to ensure that its patents would belong to the firm and not to the individual inventors that the company employed. As in the United States, the 1877 German law created this option, a major legal development to which we return below.

In 1873 the Austro-Hungarian Empire hosted a World Exposition in Vienna. US inventors refused to take part out of concern that their inventions would not adequately be protected, and German inventors shared this reluctance. This led the empire to adopt a temporary law providing for protection for foreigners in order to encourage foreign inventors' participation; the protection would last for the duration of the exposition. Following this compromise and as a result of German and Austrian patent attorneys' and engineers' intense lobbying efforts, the government held the 1873 Vienna Congress to address inventors' concerns (Dutfield 2003, 55). William Siemens, brother of Werner Siemens and founder of the Siemens Corporation, chaired the congress, where German participants predominated, and only 13 of the 158 participants represented other countries' governments (Porter 1999, 265). The Vienna Congress endorsed international patent protection but retained support for compulsory licensing as an instrument of public policy. The overriding objective was to establish a system in which states would recognize and protect the rights of foreign inventors and artists within states' own jurisdictions (Okediji 1995, 137). Conferences in Paris (1878 and 1880) developed the idea further, and a final conference in 1883 approved and signed the Paris convention, which was completed by an Interpretative Protocol in Madrid in 1891. The 1883 Paris Convention for the Protection of Industrial Property covered patents, trademarks, and industrial designs (World Intellectual Property Organisation 1988, 49–50). Member countries also constituted an International Union for the Protection of Industrial Property. The patent controversy was therefore ultimately laid to rest, and the victors' perspective became enshrined in this new multilateral treaty.

Private sector actors (including forty-eight Chambers of Commerce) had played a prominent role at the 1878 Paris conference. Tony Porter suggested that these private sector actors were, in effect, asking states "to provide a regime within which a new level of negotiated private arrangements could be brought about" (Porter 1999, 266). In addition, the role of US and German interests in these deliberations marked a radical change in intellectual property preferences from those of followers to those of leaders seeking enhanced protection.[7] The antipatent mood of Europe vanished as the continent's governments retreated from free trade, and powerful industrial sectors sought protection for their products. The Netherlands had abolished its patent system in 1869 but reinstated it in 1910. In 1887 Switzerland finally enacted its first (modern) patent law, under German pressure; as noted above, however, the coverage attained was far from comprehensive.[8] It would be a mistake to assume that international pressure was entirely predicated on the morality of each country's position (although this did carry some weight). Especially in the Swiss case, the interests of the German chemical sector and their desire to halt the theft of their innovations by the growing Swiss sector prompted their demands for legislative changes. As before and after, commercial interests were important in prompting political pressure for change, even if this interest was (and is) often masked by moral arguments.

In copyright, fierce competition among French, Belgian, and Swiss publishers and a dense network of bilateral treaties throughout Europe inspired a quest for a broader multilateral agreement that would incorporate the doctrine of national treatment. Governments quickly became disenchanted with reciprocal treaties, however, because their effects were never equal (Goldstein 1994, 181). A number of countries had refused to make such deals with France in the first half of the nineteenth century, believing that France would get the better end of any bargain, but in 1852 Napoleon

III promulgated a decree that made the counterfeiting of foreign works in France a crime punishable by law (Clark 1960, 134). In effect, this meant that France would extend copyright protection to works from foreign countries whether those countries' legislation protected French works *or not* (Goldstein 1994, 181–182). Within ten years of this French initiative, twenty-three additional countries signed copyright treaties with France, demonstrating a general intention to establish the international governance of copyright provided that the benefits were shared relatively equitably.

In 1858 the French author Victor Hugo convened a Congress of Authors and Artists in Brussels that affirmed the principle of national treatment for creative artists and authors. At a subsequent conference in Paris, that accompanied the Paris Universal Exhibition of 1878, Hugo launched the International Literary Association (later the International Literary and Artistic Association) under his founding presidency, which held a number of meetings (London 1879, Lisbon 1880, Vienna 1881, Rome 1882), culminating in the 1883 congress in Bern. Chaired by Numa Droz, this and subsequent conventions explicitly set out to follow the example of the Paris Convention for the Protection of Industrial Property and to produce a multilateral copyright agreement (Ricketson 1987, 49ff.). This process finally produced the Bern Convention for the Protection of Literary and Artistic Works (1886). The United States was excluded from Bern, however, because it retained a provision in its copyright laws requiring authors to register their work in Washington, D.C., and send a copy to the Library of Congress. These terms were inconsistent with the Bern convention that made the acquisition of copyright automatic upon authorized publication in any member state. Bern signatories could not require registration as a precondition for granting copyright.

The underlying principles of both of these initial multilateral intellectual property agreements were nondiscrimination, national treatment, and the right of priority (protection to the first to invent or create, rather than the first to file or reproduce). Under this system, states were free to pass legislation of their own design but were obligated to extend their legislative protection to foreigners of member states. These conventions neither created new substantive law nor imposed new laws on member states; rather, they reflected a consensus among member states that was legitimated by domestic laws already in place (Okediji 1995, 137). This consensus was slower to form on the other side of the Atlantic, however.

The copyright battles of the nineteenth century between the British and the Americans had increasingly pitted two US factions against each other, requiring some compromise between competition and security. According to Hesse, "trade protectionists, printers' unions and publishing houses, whose fortunes were rooted in pirating British literature argued against any international agreement. On the other side, advocates of indigenous authors allied themselves with partisans of free trade and international copyright, claiming universal rights of authorship" (Hesse 2002, 41). It was not until the 1880s, in the face of ruinous competition from new "penny press" publishing houses in the Midwest, that the older East Coast publishing interests changed their tune. Elite publishing houses converted to the cause of international copyright based on a shift in their perceptions of self-interest, leading the move to international copyright to look increasingly like a source of economic salvation rather than ruin (Woodmansee and Jaszi 2004, 11). Hesse suggested that these publishers altered their business strategies and their arguments about intellectual property because

> [t]hey realized that they would be better positioned than the new generation of publishers to sign exclusive copyright agreements with foreign authors that would be enforceable in the United States. . . . American theologians, including the Reverend Isaac Funk, now denounced the "national sin of literary piracy" (which had allowed him to make his fortune on his pirated *Life of Jesus*) as a violation of the seventh commandment. (Hesse 2002, 42)

Thus, the combination of a changing domestic market and the shifts in the international sphere encouraged some (although by no means all) US publishers to modify their position on copyright.

As in many cases in the past, the battle lines were drawn between competition and control. The American Copyright League was formed in 1884 to represent the elite US publishing houses such as Putnam, Houghton, Scribner, and Harper. These publishers lobbied hard for copyright reform. Even though prominent US authors such as Harriet Beecher Stowe and Mark Twain had already argued for the United States to offer copyright protection for foreign works, it was only the additional pressure that the publishers brought to bear that resulted in policy change. Moral arguments notwithstanding, they (not their penny press competitors) could afford to pay for licenses to reproduce foreign works. The exclusion of the United States from Bern prompted the league to push for changes in US law to conform to the Bern convention, although southern Democrats bitterly opposed any effort to open US markets to foreign competition. To appease the printing workers' unions, the final compromise of 1891, codified in the Chace Act, provided that foreign authors could obtain copyright protection only if their work was published in the United States not later than it was published in its country of origin, and foreigners' works had to be printed in the United States or printed from type set in the United States (Feather 1994b, 168). This so-called manufacturing clause went directly against the Bern convention, and therefore the United States remained outside the agreement until 1986, when the clause was allowed to expire. In 1891, Congress signed an international agreement with England, however, for reciprocal copyright protection (Hesse 2002, 42). The use of such bilateral agreements that the Paris and Bern conventions had sought to end continued by virtue of US domestic policy.

Thomas Edison: Patents as a Business Strategy

Just as ruinous competition in the late 1880s had prompted a redefinition of the established US publishers' interests in intellectual property protection, a similar dynamic animated a major shift toward stronger patent protection. In the new business model developed during the second Industrial Revolution, patents played a major role; for example, in the United States alone, between 1840 and 1910 the annual number of patents increased more than fiftyfold (Jenkins 2004, 1). The rise of large managerial firms in the chemical and electrical industries, such as Siemens in Germany and Edison in the United States, introduced a new way of organizing innovation and attracting finance capital. Then, as now, new firms (or established companies starting new ventures) needed to raise capital, and patents became increasingly integral to this process.

The story of Thomas Edison's transformation from "Yankee genius" to predatory businessman illustrates this larger trend. Edison became famous for his inventions in telegraphy; popular mythology notwithstanding, Edison was a latecomer to electric lighting. Well known in the telegraph industry, Edison approached successful telegraph entrepreneurs to help him to establish the Edison Electric Light Company. The general counsel of Western Union, Grosvenor P. Lowrey, advised Edison to set up a corporation to finance research and to take out patents (Cullis 2004, 15). Western Union itself had already pioneered a strategy of patenting and cross-licensing inventions with competitors in order to secure market shares (Jenkins 2004, 12–14). The president of Western Union, a major stockholder in the Gold and Stock Telegraph Company and a partner in J. P. Morgan, backed Edison, and a company was set up to own and/or license all of Edison's electrical inventions except those concerned with telegraphy (Cullis 2004, 15). Edison's mentors at Western Union, William Orton and Marshall Lefferts, promoted a business strategy of market dominance by controlling the fruits of innovation through control of existing patents and of future patented inventions. The idea was to maintain control over innovation, manage patents so as to create barriers to entry, and prepare patent applications with broad claims (Jenkins 2004, 32). Reese Jenkins has argued at some length that "Lefferts taught Edison the business importance of patents and of 'covering the field' with patents and with broad claims within patents" (Jenkins 2004, 14). Lefferts introduced Edison to a patent attorney,

Lemuel Serrell, who taught Edison to keep scrupulous records for the Patent Office and for litigation.

The establishment of corporate research laboratories, such as Edison's in Menlo Park, New Jersey, and the adoption of patent amendments in US law in 1871 to allow employers to require employees to sign over any patent rights in their work-related innovations spurred the development of a new way to organize research and development. Patent attorneys played a key role as agents of the industrial research system and as campaigners for heightened patent protection (Drahos and Braithwaite 2002, 43–48). Litigation was a sport for the rich and as Cullis pointed out, during the last quarter of the nineteenth century, successful lawyers were some of the most highly paid professionals in the country (Cullis 2004, 2). Nevertheless, Edison was extremely litigious and used predatory patenting strategies to good effect. For example, even though the British inventor James Swan invented and exhibited the incandescent filament lamp before Edison, Edison preempted any patent application by Swan by filing a British patent with extremely broad claims. When Swan established a company in Britain to manufacture his lamps, Edison immediately filed an injunction to stop Swan from infringing his patents. Ultimately Edison was able to wield his patent-based power to get Swan to agree to amalgamate the two companies as the Edison and Swan United Electric Light Company Ltd. (Cullis 2004, 30). Even though Swan had contributed most to the actual invention, Edison's patent enabled him to maintain a monopoly position.[9]

Responding to growing competition in the sector, between 1885 and 1901 Edison initiated over 200 infringement lawsuits, spending about two million dollars on litigation (Cullis 2004, 36). Even when Edison technically lost, the costs of litigation ran many small competitors out of business, and after this spate of aggressive lawsuits, competition virtually disappeared. By 1893, Great Britain had only seven producers in the lamp business, not all of which actually produced lamps (Cullis 2004, 34). The 1888 ruling in *Edison and Swan Electric Light Company v. Holland* strengthened Edison's monopoly position by accepting quite dubious claims regarding the veracity of the patent's specification.[10] Edison was accused of "unfair exploitation of the rules of legal etiquette and avaricious patent claims" to "gain ascendancy over competitors" (quoted in Cullis 2004, 33). Although the court was hardly friendly to Edison (whose conduct had attracted unfavorable comments from the bench during the case), the patent was upheld, revealing to competitors that Edison's position was essentially unassailable.

In 1886, at the height of a high-profile Edison case, one outraged commentator, James Swinburne, decried Edison's tactics and highlighted the unfortunate consequences of Edison's monopoly:

> The first effect of a lamp monopoly will be that prices of lamps will remain high or go higher, and will be no stimulus to improvement in their quality because there will be no competition. People often grumble at the price of lamps. Prices have to be high because it takes a long time to get a factory into working order, as the making of lamps is new to all the hands, an enormous amount of experimenting, and that on a commercial scale, is needed before lamps can be made cheap and well. A factory takes about two years to get into swing, but after that lamps can be made very cheaply. The actual labor and material in practice comes to about fivepence halfpenny per lamp sent out when made on a small scale. These are the actual figures. On the scale of manufacture of a large company the lamps should be sold at a shilling or eighteen pence. (Swinburne 1886, 132)

Today, advocates of access to generic medicines to address the human immunodeficiency virus/acquired immunodeficiency syndrome (HIV/AIDS) pandemic are making the very same arguments.[11]

Copyright and Works for Hire

Edison's use of patents as a business strategy accompanied the rise of the multinational corporation organized to conduct industrial research. Legislative changes permitting employers to claim ownership in the innovations of employees supported the further development of this type of firm, but corporate ownership was not limited to patents. Changes in legal doctrine and challenges in the courts in the 1860s introduced the notion of "works for hire" in copyright. The development of this works-for-hire doctrine is noteworthy because it not only was highly contested but also presented a peculiar melding of Romantic conceptions of authorship with overtly utilitarian purposes that reflected changes in business organization. Once again this shift was informed by political contestation, changes in the realm of ideas, and responses to technological change.

In contrast to narratives emphasizing the relentless expansion of copyright over time (Litman 2001; Vaidhyanathan 2001), Catherine Fisk highlighted the ambiguity and the uncertainty accompanying this ultimate shift from individual to corporate authorship (Fisk 2003). In the United States before 1860, the rule was relatively straightforward, and those who were hired to create works retained ownership of the copyright. After 1860 courts began to recognize employers' rights in copyrighted works of their employees, however. Initially, the court recognized employers' rights only in the case of an express contract in which the employee signed over his or her rights. This view gradually changed to recognition of employers' rights as an *implied* contract. Finally, Fisk argued, with the rise of the modern corporation "courts came to understand that a corporation—the quintessential 'corporate' (as in collective) author—should own the rights to the work created by all of the persons who worked for the corporation" (Fisk 2003, 32). Building on the already established recognition of a singular corporate personality in law, it was clear that any intellectual property rights that were to be recognized should to be accorded to the company rather than to any of its constituent employees.

Between 1860 and the early 1900s the legal status of copyright in employees' works was ambiguous at best. Sometimes the courts invoked Locke's theory of labor desert to justify employee ownership, whereas in other cases DeFoe's "brat of the brain" paternity metaphor was invoked to uphold employees' rights (Fisk 2003, 36). An 1861 court case, *Keene v. Wheatley,* produced the first published opinion that articulated a "default rule of employer ownership" (Fisk 2003, 40; emphasis added), but it was not until the adoption of the 1909 copyright law that this was codified in legislation. From 1861 to 1909, court decisions were not consistent, and Fisk argued that "the law of employee copyrights was highly uncertain and the results of cases were quite unpredictable" (Fisk 2003, 47). The unsettled nature of the law led many employers to provide express contracts to secure more reliable ownership of their employees' work, rather than risk litigation over increasingly valuable commodities.

The idea of corporate authorship in works for hire is a peculiar amalgam of Romantic notions of authorship and social utilitarianism. Fisk referred to the notion of corporate authorship as "the ultimate legal fiction underlying modern copyright law" (Fisk 2003, 55). Martha Woodmansee and Peter Jaszi argued that this conception reflects

> a simple working out of the basic premises of the Romantic conception of authorship: inasmuch as an employer holds contractual power to assign tasks, it constitutes "effective cause" of its employees' creative labor, and the product thereof constitutes work "made for hire." In this way— through a spelling out of the implications of Romantic ideology—corporate legal authority over the work of individual creators was secured. (2004, 7)

Thus, copyrights were awarded to the initiating action of the employer, whatever subsequent creative input was contributed by the employee.

At this time courts were also increasingly struggling with the introduction of new media, such as advertising and motion pictures, trying to establish how such media did or did not fit under copyright. The utilitarian impulse is evident in Justice Oliver Wendell Holmes's 1903 opinion in *Bleistein v. Donaldson Lithograph Co.* The case involved two printers, one of whom accused the other of infringing his copyright by reproducing circus advertising posters that he had prepared. Both the trial and appeals courts had upheld the defendant's right to reproduce the posters on the grounds that advertisements were not eligible for copyright. Holmes stated, however:

> Certainly works are not the less connected with the fine arts because their
> pictorial quality attracts the crowd and therefore gives them a real use—if
> use means to increase trade and to help make money. A picture is none the
> less a picture and none the less a subject of copyright that it is used for an
> advertisement. And if pictures may be used to advertise soap, or the the-
> atre, or monthly magazines, as they are, they may be used to advertise a
> circus. (Quoted in Goldstein 1994, 61)

This ruling broadly expanded copyright protection, reversing years of
precedent in one decision. It was a short step from circus posters to motion
pictures, and the *Bleistein* ruling opened the door to expanding copyright
for new media.

In 1909 Congress finally passed revisions to US copyright law that
explicitly introduced the notion of corporate copyright and works made for
hire (Vaidhyanathan 2001, 101). Just as in the case of patents, the rise of
the modern corporation facilitated this change. As Fisk pointed out, "the
kinds of materials that were subject to copyright had expanded to include
more materials prepared in a collaborative way in a corporate setting. It
became apparent that employee ownership of copyrights thwarted publication of encyclopedias by making it difficult to obtain renewals" (Fisk 2003,
67–68). Since only copyright holders could obtain renewals, without corporate authorship a publisher would have to track down each and every contributor in order to obtain a renewal on an encyclopedia copyright. Items
like encyclopedias and maps were so clearly the product of collective creation, in a way that plays and paintings are not, that a works-for-hire doctrine seemed preferable to the French notion of moral rights that implied a
continued stewardship of one's creation. In the deliberations over the 1909
law, however, some participants expressed the concern, related to "moral
rights," that the firm might degrade the employee's creation and sully the
employee's reputation. Nevertheless, as Fisk again suggested, "the kind of
works subject to copyright had begun to include things less intellectual, and
as the replacement of small partnerships by large corporate enterprises was
well underway, the moral claim of the firm seemed stronger (and the notion
of corporate authorship less fictional) just as the moral claim of the
employee waned" (Fisk 2003, 69–70). If the corporation could have a single (collective) personality in law, then there seemed to be little reason to
deny that it could also enjoy those rights accorded creators, when its activities facilitated and organized such creation.

The Ascendance of the German Chemical Industry:
A New Business Model

The development of the German dyestuff industry in the 1860s introduced a
new business model, eclipsing the inventor-entrepreneur with professional

research and development departments (Dutfield 2003, 75). German industrial policy supported the development of industry by protecting German companies from foreign competition and permitting cooperative interfirm alliances to fix prices and rationalize their sales networks. Beginning in the mid-1860s, German interest groups representing the chemical industry lobbied hard for national patent laws.[12] Although eager for domestic patent protection, Werner Siemens worried that British and US firms would take out patents and then fail to work them in Germany. Therefore the German Patent Law of 1877 that he worked on included a working requirement whereby if a patent was not worked in Germany within three years, the government could withdraw the patent. The chemical industry was divided over whether patents should cover processes or products or both, and the final bill covered processes, not products, in line with the wishes of the Chemical Association.

To enable firms to claim patent rights in employees' innovations, German patent law excluded the term *inventor* in favor of *applicant*. German law also reflected the chemical industry's commitment to a research strategy of process innovation and a marketing strategy of product diversity, allowing German firms' process patents (related to extensive industry tacit knowledge) to strengthen their position in the industry. As in the case of the Edison companies, strong patent positions (that is, massive holdings of patents) could help block research by rivals and facilitate market domination. Despite having no provisions for patenting chemical substances (as opposed to processes), German companies took advantage of such provisions in other countries, the most important of which were the United States and Britain; the German companies followed this practice especially where foreign laws did not include working requirements, such as in the United States (after 1908). In 1912, 98 percent of chemical patent applications in the United States were assigned to German firms and were never worked in the United States (Dutfield 2003, 82). Americans, outraged by this asymmetry, proposed the abolition of product protection but were outflanked by leading industrialists, such as Edison; their bankers, such as J. P. Morgan; and their patent attorneys.

The Germans came to dominate the pharmaceutical industry before World War I. The dyestuff producers Bayer and Hoechst moved into pharmaceutical production and invested their huge dyestuff profits into further research and development. The German corporate model, organized to conduct industrial research, spread rapidly in the first ten years of the twentieth century. In the United States, General Electric, Westinghouse, AT&T, International Harvester, Parke Davis, and E. R. Squibb, just to name a few, set up research labs (Braithwaite and Drahos 2002, 454). Eastman Kodak set up its industrial research lab in 1912 (Jenkins 2004, 42). US companies also began to establish patent departments that became central players in their corporate strategies. These companies came to regard patents as strategic business assets that could be used not just to protect inventions but also to raise capital and to force cross-licensing with rival firms (Merges 2000, 2220). Corporate patent departments policed patenting activity, and DuPont especially earned a reputation for being particularly tough by preventing its employees from publishing scientific papers (Braithwaite and Drahos 2002). Alfred Chandler has suggested that these US management "techniques and procedures perfected in the first years of the [twentieth] century . . . have remained the foundation of business administration" (Chandler 1977, 289). Certainly US corporations developed the manner in which production (or services) were to be organized in modern capitalism (building on the example of the German pharmaceutical sector), and alongside the application of "scientific" management, utilized patents to build competitive advantage.

Between 1870 and 1911, the number of US patent grants shot up from 120,573 to more than one million (Braithwaite and Drahos 2002, 460). Although in the early days most patents were granted to individuals, by the beginning of the twentieth century most patents were being issued to corporations. In follower states, such as Spain, between 1878 and 1907 the bulk of patents granted went to foreign, nonresident companies (Gonzales 2002, 73). As Edward Beatty pointed out, the dramatic expansion of trade and foreign investment in the last quarter of the nineteenth century, coupled with the 1883 Paris convention, sparked "patent law reforms [that] yielded an increasingly homogenous landscape in a process that was not complete until the eve of World War I" (Beatty 2002, 143). This also meant that countries that "found themselves increasingly part of the globalizing economy of the late nineteenth century could not avoid international pressures to offer patent protection to foreign inventors. Moreover, domestic elites around the world . . . had also largely adopted the liberal arguments that linked property rights with incentives to invest" (Beatty 2002, 132). It seemed that the discourse eliminating the tension between free trade and intellectual property rights had triumphed, and the patent controversy had been left behind (although recent political commentary suggests it has *not* been forgotten).

Early in the twentieth century patent-based cartels emerged. Just as Edison had bought up, absorbed, or merged with rivals under predatory patent litigation, numerous companies consolidated and set up cross-licensing, price-fixing, and market-dividing arrangements. For instance, in the electrical industry, in 1897 General Electric formed a cartel, the Incandescent Lamp Manufacturers Association, to control prices and market shares (Cullis 2004, 37–38). Very few firms remained outside of this group, which made a price-fixing agreement with Westinghouse underpinning price rises of about 30 percent for electric lamps (Jenkins 2004, 26). The US bank panic and depression of 1893 left General Electric surrounded by weakened competitors that it proceeded to acquire under the rubric of the National Electric Lamp Company—a stratagem designed to create the appearance of independence (Jenkins 2004, 26–27). General Electric used its patent licensing power to acquire further relevant patents, charge higher royalty rates, prohibit others from exporting without General Electric's permission, and lead European cartels. As Jenkins pointed out, "the company's strong patent position gave an initial near monopoly position from which it then exercised its financial and market power to maintain a dominant American and world position until after World War II, decades after its key patents had expired" (Jenkins 2004, 28). These strategies were hardly unique, and increasingly patents were used to organize cartels to dominate particular industrial sectors and constrain competition.

In Britain, British Thomson–Houston, Siemens, and the General Electric Company pooled their patents and collectively controlled the industry (Cullis 2004, 40). In 1912 they formed the Tungsten Lamp Association (TLA), which included almost all of the significant producers in England. In 1915, Robin Electric, excluded from the association, mounted a public interest challenge to the TLA's price fixing. The judge ruled in favor of the TLA, however, stating that "although poor families could not afford electric lighting, there was no evidence that the price was so high as to be a serious burden to the consumers" (quoted in Cullis 2004, 42). Faced with potentially ruinous competition and dumping just after World War I, the leading European and British electric lamp producers negotiated an international agreement to rationalize competition in 1925. The Phoebus agreement, a private multilateral agreement administered in Geneva, was designed to divide markets and to exchange technical information and patents. Patent ownership was used to induce independent companies to enter into contracts with quota restrictions and agree to observe set prices (Cullis 2004, 43). This agreement remained in force up until the outbreak of World War II.

Similar arrangements flourished across sectors in the interwar period, and the patent system became a central mechanism facilitating cartel solidarity. This was not limited to industrial sectors but also included minerals and agriculture (American Cotton Oil, Corn Products, and National Lead also had research labs that facilitated strategic patenting activities) (Braithwaite and Drahos 2002). In 1939, the proportion of goods sold under cartel control in the United States was roughly 87 percent for mineral products, 60 percent for agricultural products, and 42 percent for manufactured products (Porter 1999, 266). In sector after sector, risk was subordinated to security and control.

The development of intellectual property policies in the nineteenth century reflected the conflicting imperatives of risk versus control, or competition versus security, with the balance shifting over time. Patents and intellectual property protection were not crucial to the emergence of the cotton industry in Britain, and James Swan did not deem them to be particularly important until Edison unleashed his litigious strategy. In general, follower states were wary of too much protection, and new economic sectors often flourished without it. The end of the patent controversy and the multilateral agreements of Paris and Bern ushered in an international era of intellectual property protection, displacing the prior national patchwork that had kept transaction costs of international commerce high. As the United States and Germany began to emerge as industrial powerhouses, their interest in intellectual property protection grew. Often in response to competition, ruinous or otherwise, industrialists and publishers lobbied for stronger intellectual property protection.

Notably, the situation at the end of the nineteenth century seems to have been quite similar to the situation at the end of the twentieth and beginning of the twenty-first. States, responding to pressures of economic globalization, are increasingly adopting intellectual property policies that mirror those of the technological leaders in the hopes of securing increased investment and technology transfer. Lest one believe in the inexorable march of expanded property rights through time, it is important to remember that although the United States changed from being a technological follower to a leader over the course of the nineteenth century, its intellectual property policies did not always reflect the preferences one would expect. Even though in copyright US law demonstrated relatively steady expansion, the story in the patent area was quite different. This continuing US ambivalence about strong protection in the twentieth century is the subject of the next chapter.

Notes

1. This was not the case in every instance. As MacLeod wrote: "In the wake of bitter resentment against Watt's patent for the separate condenser, Cornish engineers turned their backs on the patent system. Cornwall's share of patents for steam-related inventions fell to under one percent of the national total in the period 1813–1852. The start of this period saw Richard Trevithick and Arthur Woolf erecting (unpatented) high-pressure steam engines in Cornish tin and copper mines, where high coal prices made thermodynamic efficiency of particular concern" (MacLeod 2004, 12). And also see our discussion of Cornish practices in Chapter 4.

2. This situation is not unlike the contemporary case of software in which production was decentralized and widely dispersed. This sector prospered prior to its integration into the patent system. Industry worked around the absence of patent protection. See Merges (2000, 2229–2230).

3. US Congress, *Public Documents Printed by Order of the Senate*, 27th Cong., 2nd. sess., vol. 4, no. 323.

4. A comprehensive discussion of the debates in Britain can be found in Coulter (1991).

5. For a contemporary statement of this position, see Jagdish Bhagwati, who likens international protection of intellectual property to a Mafia racket (quoted in Nisse 2003; see also Bhagwati 1998).

6. *United States v. Burns,* 79 U.S. (12 Wall.) 246 (1871).

7. For a fascinating discussion of the evolution of the German position, see Kronstein and Till (1947).

8. As Kingston pointed out: "The German chemical industry financed three referenda in Switzerland until it got the patent legislation it wanted there to prevent free-riding on its inventions by local firms" (2004, 5). Also see Ritter (2004) for a discussion of the role German pressure played in the Swiss political deliberations of the time.

9. Edison was not always so successful, however. His attempts to lever his patents into control of the market for new technologies to produce sound failed, and his company withdrew from the music (record) industry well before it started its meteoric expansion in the twentieth century. See Barfe (2004, chap. 1).

10. *Edison and Swan Electric Light Company v. Holland,* RPC 459 (1888).

11. See, for example, remarks of James Love in Warner (2002).

12. This paragraph and the next are based on remarks in Dutfield (2003, 76–79).

6

The Twentieth Century: Intellectual Property Rights Consolidated

ACROSS THE world in the twentieth century, there was an expansion of intellectual property laws, but most of this new national legislation broadly reflected the earlier developments that we have discussed in previous chapters. This continuity was the result partly of the adoption and adaptation of existing laws from other countries ("legal imports") and partly of the continuing imposition of legal instruments by colonial occupiers (at least in the first half of the century). In this chapter we focus on the way in which intellectual property was expanded, but also contested, in the United States, as it seems to us that these developments are crucial for understanding the contemporary *global* politics of intellectual property. Therefore, this chapter presents the evolution of the US position from skepticism about intellectual property protection and monopoly power to a vigorous advocacy for dramatically expanded global (intellectual) property rights. Building on the issues raised at the end of Chapter 5, we discuss the trust-busting movement of the late nineteenth century and the rise of patent-based cartels. We then situate the skepticism about intellectual property rights (IPRs) after World War II as part of a broader ideological current. In the next two sections we examine the resurgence of property rights, with a particular focus on patents, and then discuss trends in twentieth-century copyright. Finally, we outline the political economic background to the recent multilateral intellectual property settlement in the World Trade Organization (WTO), before offering some conclusions from the twentieth-century trajectory presented here.

Trust-busting and Cartels

The first big wave of corporate mergers began in the late nineteenth century, proceeding from tactics such as those that Edison had pursued. In the wake of the US bank panic and depression of 1893, US public opinion initially was not so critical of this quest for market control. In 1901 the *New York Daily Tribune* reflected the optimism behind corporate consolidations: "[A] new era has come, the era of 'community of interest,' whereby it is hoped to avoid ruinous price cutting and to avert the destruction which has in the past, when business depression occurred, overtaken so many of the competing concerns in every branch of industry" (quoted in Perelman 2002, 171). The trust-busting movement in the late-nineteenth-century United States had done little to undermine these industrial cartels.

Farmers had lobbied strongly for controls over private monopolies, but these were aimed more at consumer goods industries such as fuel oil, sugar, matches, linseed oil, and whiskey (Cullis 2004, 48) rather than the whole industries organized under some of the cartels. Congress responded with the passage of the Interstate Commerce Act of 1887 and the 1890 Sherman Antitrust Act. The acts were not much utilized until Franklin Roosevelt's administration in the late 1930s and early 1940s, when the first funds were allocated to the Justice Department for enforcement measures. Early government cases focused on sugar and whiskey, and the government lost the first six out of seven cases it brought to the courts (Cullis 2004, 49). In 1911 the US Justice Department filed an antitrust suit against General Electric (GE) for its "shell game" of disguising acquired companies as independent entities, which enabled it to obscure its price-fixing activities. The consent decree obligated GE "to cease all the alleged practices *except* 'the use of patents for market control'" (Jenkins 2004, 27; emphasis added). Consequently, General Electric retained its patent monopoly, and thus the 1911 case did little to change GE's market dominance in the US lamp industry (Cullis 2004, 50). As the optimism of the turn of the century regarding consolidation faded, so public opinion turned against the huge corporations that were exploiting market control to transfer vast wealth "from the public to themselves"; Congress responded by passing the Clayton Antitrust Act of 1914 (Perelman 2002, 171). The US entry into the Great War slowed the trust-busting momentum.

Not all industries supported cartels. For example, the US pharmaceutical industry objected to the German chemical cartels, arguing that US firms were victims of unfair German competition. They complained that overly strong intellectual property protection harmed the development of the US pharmaceutical industry; German companies were insufficiently disclosing information in their patent applications, and they were abusing trademark protection to prolong their control over their chemicals (Dutfield 2003, 114). In 1919 the American Pharmaceutical Association lobbied for chemical product protection to be rescinded (or if retained, made subject to compulsory licensing) and for patents to be allowed only on chemical processes. They also argued that trademarks should expire at the same time as the patent expired. The association's utilitarian argument was noteworthy:

> It should be understood that the patent and trademark laws, like all other laws, are primarily designed to benefit the public at large and only secondarily to benefit the individual. . . . There are some who assume that the object of the Patent Law is to protect inventors in their so-called natural right to the exclusive manufacture and sale of their inventions and the object of the Trademark Law is to protect and foster monopolies. Nothing is further from the truth. The objects of the Patent and Trademark Laws are altruistic not egoistic. (Quoted in Dutfield 2003, 114)[1]

As the mightiest industries in the United States, such as the electrical industry, in fact were flourishing under strong intellectual property protection, however, the government did not accede to the pharmaceutical lobby's desire to weaken protection.

The entry of the United States into World War I gave the government an incentive to promote self-sufficiency in drug production. Overreliance on enemy supplies was dangerous, and in any case, the cessation of German imports spurred the development of a domestic drug industry. Under the Trading with the Enemy Act of 1917, the US government seized 4,500 German-owned US patents (Drahos and Braithwaite 2002, 56). These patents did not disclose sufficient information to be particularly helpful to US industry, but the seizure was noteworthy because it reflected the government's willingness to use industrial policy to promote a domestic drug industry. Furthermore, German firms such as Merck lost their US branches (Dutfield 2003, 101). Domestic chemical producers formed a Chemical Foundation in Delaware in 1919 and purchased German patents from the Alien Property Custodian at bargain basement prices (about fifty dollars per patent) (Drahos and Braithwaite 2002, 56). The US industry was able to break away from the previously dominant German corporations but also discovered the value of patents as a means for controlling pharmaceutical markets.

Cartels dominated the interwar period. This era epitomized the resurgence of economic nationalism and spelled an end to the late-nineteenth-century international liberal economic order. Indeed, many US, German, and British industrialists viewed cartels in a positive light during the interwar period. Although the 1890 Sherman Antitrust Act had prohibited horizontal mergers, the leading US firms still were able to use intellectual property policy strategically to control competition and promote corporate growth. General Electric and DuPont both used patent licensing to participate in interwar cartels in chemicals and electrical equipment while formally complying with antitrust law. As David Mowrey and Nathan Rosenberg

suggested, "U.S. participants in these international market-sharing arrangements took pains to arrange their international agreements as patent licensing schemes, arguing that exclusive license arrangements and restrictions
on the commercial exploitation of patents would not run afoul of U.S.
antitrust laws" (Mowrey and Rosenberg 1998, 19). Patent attorneys such as
Edwin J. Prindle, in the late nineteenth and early twentieth centuries, promoted patents as an indispensable business tool. Rather than highlighting
their widely touted and purported role in encouraging innovation, Prindle
argued that "patents are the best and most effective means of controlling
competition. They occasionally give absolute command of the market,
enabling the owner to name the price without regard to cost of production"
(quoted in Braithwaite and Drahos 2002, 457). Patents were now to be used
to control markets for purely commercial reasons, rather than as any
response to the public good of supporting innovation.

Research-based industrial corporations sought to obtain as many
patents as possible, so that they could cross-license them with competitors
and thereby obtain all the necessary components for manufacturing their
products. Managements wanted to bargain from a position of strength, and
a strong patent portfolio provided such strength. Following the lead of the
German chemical industry, corporate patent departments created patent
thickets around particular technologies to keep competitors out of product
lines. When DuPont established such a position in cellophane, it warned
Union Carbide that any company trying to manufacture cellophane would
come up against "many patents in view of the long time we have been
working on cellophane and the amount of work which has been done not
only to strengthen the position but to build up a defensive patent situation
as well" (quoted in Braithwaite and Drahos 2002, 459). Dividing markets,
limiting production, and fixing prices were all possible through patent
licensing; in addition, despite remaining a national monopoly, patents could
also be used as a basis for founding international cartels (Braithwaite and
Drahos 2002, 461). Noting the example of DuPont and others, Robert
Brady, in his extended critique of the political influence of business, suggested that patents were a "springboard for enhancing market, price, production, capacity and numerous other controls which greatly transcend the
normal limits" of corporate power (Brady 1943, 230).

It is not surprising that patent laws came under critical scrutiny, and
trustbusters in all branches of government called for a rolling back of the
patent system. Congressional hearings between 1938 and 1941, for
instance, sharply criticized patent-based cartels in glass container manufacture (Perelman 2002, 23–24). The US Justice Department's Antitrust
Division was given more resources and, under the vigorous leadership of
Thurman Arnold, initiated about 180 antitrust actions between 1938 and

1942 (Drahos and Braithwaite 2002). Earlier the US Supreme Court, in its ruling against Standard Oil in 1931,[2] had stated:

> If combining patent owners effectively dominate an industry, the power to fix and maintain royalties is tantamount to the power to fix prices. Where domination exists, a pooling of competing process patents, or an exchange of licenses for the purpose of curtailing the manufacture and supply of an unpatented product, is beyond the privileges conferred by the patents and constitutes a violation of the Sherman Act. (Quoted in Perelman 2002, 24)

Just as *The Economist*, a prominent supporter of free trade, had called for the abolition of patents during the patent controversy of the nineteenth century, in 1942 the business magazine *Fortune* decried cartels and recommended the introduction of compulsory licensing, so by "abolishing the protection which the patent system gives to monopolistic practices" (quoted in Porter 1999, 270). Entry into World War II dampened the anticartel mood insofar as some US cartels were key suppliers of essential technologies, but the US government still seized penicillin process patents under compulsory license to ensure adequate supply.

The pharmaceutical industry in the United States really came into its own during World War II. In the 1920s, Pfizer chemists had developed a fermentation process to obtain citric acid in large quantities. This production method became the basis for the mass production of penicillin during the war. As Braithwaite and Drahos pointed out, Pfizer grew into the single biggest supplier of penicillin to the Allies, even though the company had been subject to a compulsory license requiring it "to share its penicillin production techniques with other U.S. manufacturers in order to meet the demand of the Allies" (Braithwaite and Drahos 2002, 465). The wartime demand for antibiotics spurred intense competition and improvements in production methods. As had happened in the electric lamp industry during the late nineteenth century, "ruinous competition" in the pharmaceutical sector inspired a concerted patent-based strategy reminiscent of Edison's. Companies discovered and marketed increasing numbers of effective but essentially quite similar antibiotics. After the war, as competition increased and production methods improved, antibiotic production became wildly competitive: between 1946 and 1950 the price of streptomycin dropped seventyfold; per dose prices for penicillin dropped from twenty dollars during the war, when the government was the sole buyer, to one dollar in 1946 and to ten cents in 1949 (Dutfield 2003, 118). The pharmaceutical corporations needed to rein in this excessively competitive market.

Like Edison before them, and particularly like the German dyestuff producers that the US pharmaceutical industry had complained about in 1919, US drug firms adopted strategic intellectual property policies. As

Michael Perelman suggested, "rather than symbolizing the pinnacle of market success, intellectual property rights are an expression of the failure of the market. Patents and other intellectual property rights come to the fore when markets threaten to self-destruct" (Perelman 2002, 15–16). Indeed, the avoidance of self-destruction during the war, through the use of intellectual property rights, meant that the sector emerged into the postwar world in a strong position to take advantage of the partial destruction of the German industry. Combining trademark and patent-based protection strategies, the drug companies increasingly and aggressively asserted their rights in the courts, keeping competitors at bay and maintaining price levels for the full life of the patent grant. The companies utilized three strategies: (1) they restricted patent licensing to a small number of companies, (2) they incorporated restrictive provisions into patent-licensing agreements (such as prohibiting foreign sales, requiring purchases of intermediate compounds from licensors, or requiring licensees to sign over rights in any follow-on innovations), and (3) they cooperated with competitors by sharing patents and fixing prices (Dutfield 2003, 118–119). Sometimes they used all three strategies simultaneously.

One of the more glaring instances of this approach was the antibiotics cartel that Pfizer, Cyanamid, Bristol, Upjohn, and Squibb organized. This cartel lasted from 1951 to 1961. They all had developed a form of tetracycline, but only Pfizer and Bristol were awarded patents, and the other companies' patent applications were rejected. Knowing that the patents would be attractive targets for litigation, the five companies agreed to recognize Pfizer's patent and to limit competition (Dutfield 2003, 119). As John Braithwaite has argued, the patent, in effect, provided "a cover for conspiratorial behavior to partition a market which in the absence of the patent would have been clearly illegal" (Braithwaite 1984, 184). These companies kept the price of tetracycline constant and were able to organize a cartel-like structure, with the price for tetracycline the same across thirteen countries (for which price data were available) (Braithwaite and Drahos 2002, 464). Although levels and scope of patent-based control varied, the arrangements depicted here were far from unusual.

Skepticism About Intellectual Property Rights After 1945

After World War II, the victors retrospectively associated economic nationalism with militarism, identifying Germany and Japan as the key examples. The United States, as the strongest victorious power, took the lead in discrediting economic nationalism and promoting a new postwar economic order based on multilateralism and, in response to the Great Depression, a welfare-state version of economic liberalism (Ruggie 1998, 62–84). This perspective was institutionalized in the Bretton Woods organizations (the International Monetary Fund, the World Bank), the United Nations, the General Agreement on Tariffs and Trade (GATT), Marshall Plan aid, and the European Economic Community. This perspective was further reinforced through US military occupation of both Japan and Germany, during which time the United States worked to reshape Japanese and German corporate governance regimes (Porter 1999, 269). The United States succeeded in delegitimizing cartels (associated with Japanese and German militarism) and promoted its own form of corporate governance—highly centralized oligopolistic, nonfinancial corporations epitomized by the automobile industry—as consistent with freedom, democracy, and competition (Porter 1999, 270). US policy specifically targeted the horizontal interfirm cooperation that was prevalent in Germany and Japan. As in the case of the rise of the British cotton industry, the patent system had played a minor role in the emergence of the US automobile industry, and thus the explicit use of this organizational model by the occupiers downplayed patenting as a commercial strategy.

This marginalization of patenting also reverberated in US law. Between the 1940s and 1970s, aggressive antitrust enforcement and judicial attacks on patents constituted what David Silverstein has referred to as patents' "Dark Ages" (Silverstein 1991, 304). For instance, the US Supreme Court struck down tying arrangements (requiring a purchaser of a patented item to buy an unpatented item with it) as being inconsistent with the overriding public policy of promoting free competition.[3] Patent rights increasingly were (again) construed as monopolies, market power was the presumed motive for applications, and IPRs were subordinated to the dominant antitrust policy. The concept of patent misuse reached its zenith in a series of cases in the 1940s, including the *Mercoid* cases[4] and *Morton Salt Co. v. G. S. Suppinger Co.*[5] As James Kobak suggested, these decisions alarmed patent attorneys because "misuse became a *per se* defense that an infringer could successfully use to escape all liability. In this respect it proved to be a real windfall for patent infringers" (Kobak 1998, par. 7). Referring to the doctrine of patent misuse at this time, William Nicoson complained that "in this welter of opportunity for judicial absolution, it must be a dull rascal indeed who cannot make piracy pay" (Nicoson 1962, 76n21).

Reflecting this political context, the previously mentioned antibiotics cartel was sharply scrutinized by a US Senate Subcommittee on Antitrust and Monopoly, led by Senator Estes Kefauver (Braithwaite and Drahos 2002, 464). The investigation not only exposed the companies' shadowy practices but also led to numerous civil and criminal lawsuits. The companies involved ended up paying hundreds of millions of dollars to settle these various lawsuits, and the committee itself criticized the pharmaceutical industry for raising prices and making excessive profits. It assailed the firms for using patents for the purpose of profiteering and made it clear that the public was not well served by the companies' actions. The government ultimately failed to prove its case that the pharmaceutical companies had either violated antitrust law or defrauded the Patent Office and was unable to introduce legislation that would have drastically weakened patent rights (Dutfield 2003, 119–120). Only the rise of generic competition finally helped to bring the prices down.

This antipatent environment, characterized by vigorous antitrust enforcement and judicial attacks on the scope and validity of patents, led many US businesses to question the economic value of patent protection. More often than not, the courts presumed patents to be invalid, and patent-ees were criticized for setting monopoly prices for inventions that were already in the public domain (Dreyfuss 1989, 6). Would-be domestic competitors had little to fear from infringing behavior. For example, in 1976 when Eastman Kodak sought to develop an instant camera to compete with Polaroid, its development committee issued an internal directive that stated: "Development should not be constrained by what an individual feels is potential patent infringement" (quoted in Silverstein 1991, 307). The patenting practices that had helped underpin corporate power earlier in the century were constrained through a lack of governmental support. The dependence of intellectual property on legal (policy-related) action was its fatal weakness as a strategy for controlling markets, when such support was withdrawn.

Therefore, since patents were frequently held to be invalid and infringers faced low penalties that usually amounted to payment of a royalty, US businesses sought other means of protection from competition, such as trade secret protection, government subsidies combined with high secrecy levels (in the defense industries), and "voluntary" export quotas (for the automobile industry) (Silverstein 1991, 291). Not all sectors could take advantage of these alternative forms of protection, however; the effective neutering of the US patent system between the 1940s and the early 1980s seems to have had a particularly deleterious effect on US consumer electronics companies. In this environment, Silverstein claimed that "few American businesses were willing to undertake the financial risks of commercializing new technologies" (Silverstein 1991, 305). Therefore, although US firms pioneered technologies such as the transistor, the video cassette recorder, and the integrated circuit, other countries, most notably Japan, successfully commercialized these US inventions. By the late 1960s Japan had begun to dominate the consumer electronics market with a series of technologies, many of which had been originally developed in the United States.

Property Rights Resurgent

Congress first began to address this lax patent environment by passing the 1952 Patent Act. This act reflected the wishes of corporations that had amassed huge patent portfolios for greater protection and clarified the notion of patent power as the power to withhold. Specifically, the act ratified the acceptance of the so-called blocking patent, which was tantamount to a negative right: a right to exclude others from using an invention. This clarification supported the corporate practice of developing blocking positions to counter rivals' strength in new technologies, and as Robert Merges pointed out, "overwrote some critical anti-patent decisions of the Supreme Court from its most virulent anti-patent era (roughly 1930–1948)" (Merges 2000, 2222–2223). Despite a continuing distrust of the power awarded patent holders in some sections of government, this legislative move (re)established the withholding power of patents.

It was another twenty years, however, until a number of US industries really started to lobby hard for stronger intellectual property laws. Producers of brand-name luxury goods sought stronger trademark protection, and research-intensive sectors such as agricultural chemicals and pharmaceuticals sought higher levels of patent protection. By the early 1980s, these companies were joined by copyright interests (especially in film, music, and software) and became a potent political force for change in US intellectual property law and policy. Quite swiftly they were able to force intellectual property protection to the top of the domestic political agenda, but perhaps more startling is how quickly the United States and its corporations succeeded in institutionalizing this new approach globally.

Supreme Court rulings, from 1980 onward, began to signal a new attitude toward patents. In its ruling in *Dawson Chem. Co. v. Rohm & Haas Co.*,[6] the Court stated that "the policy of free competition runs deep in our law . . . but the policy of stimulating invention that underlies the entire patent system runs no less deep" (quoted in Kastriner 1991, 20). For the first time since the *A. B. Dick* case in 1912,[7] the Supreme Court placed the public policy of supporting patent rights on an *equal footing* with the public policy of supporting free competition, and for Lawrence Kastriner this "effectively ended the era of anti-trust dominance over patent law in the eyes of the judiciary" (Kastriner 1991, 20). This "equal footing" was short lived, however: the rights of owners of intellectual property soon became *more* important as these owners were increasingly likely to deliver economic and competitiveness objectives valued by the US government. This led the US government to establish the Court of Appeals for the Federal Circuit (CAFC) in 1982 that institutionalized a more pro-patent approach. The creation of the court was explicitly animated by pedestrian concerns, such as docket management for a grossly overburdened Supreme Court, but as Merges argued, "just under the surface . . . the creation of the Federal Circuit had a clear substantive agenda: to strengthen patents" (Merges 2000, 2224). The era of weak patent rights was indeed drawing to a close.

The debates over the creation of the CAFC are instructive insofar as they provide insight into the diagnosis of the patent problem and anticipate the proposed benefits of such a court.[8] The central problem that CAFC advocates identified was uneven application of patent law in the various circuit courts. Some circuits favored infringers, whereas others favored patentees. For example, between 1945 and 1957, a patent was nearly four times as likely to be enforced in the Seventh Circuit as in the Second Circuit (Dreyfuss 1989, 7). Infringers scrambled to have their cases heard in the lenient circuit courts, whereas patentees fought to have their cases heard in the stricter Fifth, Sixth, and Seventh Circuits. Forum shopping and requests to have patent infringement appeals transferred to different circuits injected considerable uncertainty into patent litigation. When the Industrial Research Institute surveyed 250 companies engaged in industrial research on the question of a single patent court, the vast majority of respondents indicated that the uncertainty, complexity, and inconsistencies in patent enforceability eroded the full economic value of the patent (Lever 1982, 198n61). In this convoluted legal environment, patents were not considered to be sufficient incentives to invest in research and development (Dreyfuss 1989, 7). Furthermore, forum shopping increased the length and cost of litigation and made it difficult for patent attorneys to provide advice to clients.

The stakes had risen sharply after the 1972 Supreme Court decision in *Blonder-Tongue Laboratories, Inc. v. University of Illinois Foundation,* which barred a patent owner from relitigating patent validity against a new defendant. Thus, owners had only a single chance to defend their patent, and if the case were tried in an antipatent forum, the patent holder would not merely be losing the case but would forgo the patent completely (Silverstein 1991, 309). In this high-stakes, and inherently unpredictable, environment, proponents of a CAFC argued that a single court would eliminate forum shopping and inconsistent court rulings, provide more uniformity in patent law, and thereby facilitate innovation by reducing doubt as to what protection was available for inventions (Lever 1982, 198–199). These arguments for predictability, and a reduction in diversity, also would be successfully deployed in the negotiations that two decades later led to the establishment of the Agreement on Trade Related Aspects of Intellectual Property Rights (TRIPs).

Opponents of the CAFC questioned the extent to which forum shopping was a problem. They also raised concerns that a patent court, like any specialized court, might be prone to isolation and susceptibility to special interest groups. If the court were to become either pro-patent or antipatent, the dangers of concentrated judicial decisionmaking power could have a negative impact on the law (Lever 1982, 202-4). In the end, supporters of the CAFC addressed most of the objections raised by opponents and were able to establish a forum that was to have significant future influence over the development of the global governance of intellectual property rights.

The activation of the CAFC in 1982 ushered in a more vigorous approach to the enforcement of patent-holders' rights in the United States. The CAFC's decisions have reflected a more pro-patent approach and have supported higher awards of damages than the decisions of the previous Courts of Appeal. The CAFC has invigorated the presumption of validity of patent rights, making challenges harder to sustain (Dreyfuss 1989, 26). Unsurprisingly, under the CAFC, references to patents as "monopolies" have all but disappeared (Kastriner 1991, 9). Indeed, two decisions in 1983 and 1986 respectively emphasized that courts could issue permanent injunctions once a patent had been held valid and infringed. This signaled a further shift in public policy in favor of patent holders insofar as the court ruled that "public policy favors 'protection of rights secured by valid patents,' adding that 'public policy favors the innovator, not the copier'" (Kastriner 1991, 13–14).[9] This is clearly a far cry from the earlier judicial suspicion of the monopoly aspects of patent rights. The 1986 CAFC decision in *Polaroid Corp. v. Eastman Kodak* ruled against Kodak for infringing on Polaroid patents, issued an injunction, and assessed staggering damages; as Silverstein noted, "the outcome effectively restored to Polaroid a virtual monopoly over the United States market in instant photography" (Silverstein 1991, 307). The Kodak-Polaroid case was widely regarded as the most striking instance of an increasingly pro-patent sentiment in US courts. In Kastriner's judgment, this case demonstrated that "a successful patent infringement case can eliminate a competitor from a business, as well as costing the infringer over a billion dollars in damages and related costs" and signaled to businesspersons that infringement was "no longer an economically feasible option" (Kastriner 1991, 15).

The 1980s therefore ushered in a rededication to a conception of intellectual property protection as a system to protect and exclude, rather than one based on competition and diffusion.[10] Changes in the domestic environment for intellectual property protection were embedded in a broader set of concerns raised by the shifting structures of global capitalism. Competitiveness concerns, especially as regards the increasingly important high-technology sector, animated a number of significant changes in US policymaking and its institutions. In the realm of policy, the relaxation of formerly stringent antitrust policies facilitated an environment more favorable to US intellectual property owners, whereas institutional developments, such as the creation of the CAFC, paved the way for intellectual property owners to promote their private interest. This fortified the perceived connection between intellectual property rights and competitiveness. In this sense, the *Kodak* case brought US jurisprudence back full circle, back to the *A. B. Dick* philosophy championing protection, exclusion, and opportunities for extracting monopoly rents. It symbolized the emergence of US patent law out of an era of judicial skepticism that had characterized much of the twentieth century. The signals were unmistakable, and the trends captured by the case alerted US business that patents would be upheld and could be counted on as valuable economic resources.

Combined with the US relaxation of antitrust enforcement, this facilitated increasing economic concentration within many prominent sectors and is particularly apparent in the life sciences industries. In a familiar pattern, the life sciences sector consolidated into larger corporations that adopted a new business model in response to declining revenues. As Graham Dutfield summarized:

> During the 1970s, US chemical giants like Dow, American Cyanamid, DuPont and Monsanto encountered decreased profits [and] higher costs. . . . They responded by moving into or increasing their involvement in fine chemicals sectors like agrochemicals and pharmaceuticals. These offered much higher profit margins, especially with the availability of effective monopoly protection through the patent system. (Dutfield 2003, 148)

He further pointed out that in the agro-biotechnology field, "six companies are responsible for three-quarters of all US patents granted to the top 30 patent-holding firms. These are Monsanto, DuPont, Syngenta, Dow, Aventis and Grupo Pulsar" (Dutfield 2003, 154). Drahos and Braithwaite have referred to these life sciences corporations as "biogopolies" and liken them to the chemical cartels that persisted through the interwar period (Drahos and Braithwaite 2002, 150–168). In what Merges has referred to as "pigging out at the IP trough," recent trends threaten to choke off innovation (Merges 2000, 2233). Technological advances and shifts to increase the protection of patent rights have been instrumental in the consolidation of the commercial control of the sector, leaving any public-regarding, pro-competitive aspects of patent rights in bioresources as merely the residual after all other private (commercial) rights have been exercised.

The economic concentration in this sector is not just a function of expanded property rights, relaxed antitrust scrutiny, and the development of powerful new biotechnologies. An increasingly expansive definition of patentable subject matter has also contributed to this trend. Beginning in the early twentieth century, the patent profession broke through a huge conceptual barrier by arguing that substances that occurred in nature, but had been isolated and purified, were actually patentable (Braithwaite and Drahos 2002, 463). This version of the labor-desert theory opened the door to a series of further expansions as regards what constitutes patentable subject matter in the life sciences. Most important was the (in)famous 1980 Supreme Court decision in *Diamond v. Chakrabaty*, which held that a new manmade oil-eating bacterium could be patented; this decision led to expanded rights of ownership in living things. In 1987 Harvard researchers Phillip Leder and Timothy Stewart won a patent on a transgenic mouse, having developed a strain of mice for cancer research by inserting a cancer gene into mouse egg cells (Sell 2003, 111n15). It is perhaps more worrisome that James Boyle has documented a case in which doctors in California were awarded patent rights for their patient's cells, after the patient had unsuccessfully sued the doctors for rights in his own spleen (Boyle 1992). As new technologies opened up new substances and processes to commodification, the rights of commercial actors (partly legitimated through narratives of effort and reward) were deemed to outweigh any natural rights we might have presumed that a patient would have in tissue from his or her *own* body.

Twentieth-Century Copyright

Copyright in the United States has expanded in a manner similar to that of patents as a result of intensive private sector lobbying and government acquiescence to, and support for, its demands.[11] In Jessica Litman's masterful survey of US copyright law (Litman 1989), she revealed a pattern of incremental change in which private sector stakeholders drafted narrow legislation that favored their interests. The context-specific nature of the legislation renders it inflexible and unable to adapt to technological change. Therefore, each time a new technology appears, whether player pianos or computer software, the process repeats itself to the detriment of the public weal. Narrowly tailored, industry-specific provisions are added to the legislative array, and copyright owners receive broader and more expansive rights. Litman documented the process of negotiated bargains among industry representatives that has resulted in a striking expansion of copyrightable subject matter. As she pointed out: "The dynamics of inter-industry negotiations tend to encourage fact-specific solutions to inter-industry disputes. The participants' frustration with the rapid aging of narrowly defined rights has inspired them to collaborate in drafting rights more broadly. No comparable tendency has emerged to inject breadth or flexibility into the provisions *limiting* those rights" (Litman 1989, 333; emphasis added). The legislative process has tended to exclude the public and thereby has privileged the private interests of authors and owners at the expense of the public interest in the use and reuse of copyrighted information (Aoki 1996, 1310). The interests of those present at the negotiating table are accommodated; the interests of those who are either absent or uninvited are not.

The example of the music industry at the start of the twentieth century exemplifies this trend. As new technologies of music reproduction were developed and taken up by the music-listening public, the interests of copyright holders shifted and changed as regards their rights to reproduction. Although the 1909 Copyright Act stipulated that an infringing performance act would have to be both public and for profit, the status of background music in clubs and restaurants and unlicensed dance hall performances was unclear. In 1913 a group of writers and publishers formed the American Society of Composers, Authors, and Publishers (ASCAP) to issue performance licenses to cafés and bars. Its initial efforts to entice bar and restaurant owners to buy licenses for the rights to play compositions by ASCAP members went nowhere, but in 1914 ASCAP sued a restaurant for performing an ASCAP show without a license. In 1917, Justice Oliver Wendell Holmes delivered his opinion in the case and supported a broad reading of the Copyright Act. He stated that "if the rights under the copyright are infringed only when by a performance where money is taken at the door they are very imperfectly protected" (quoted in Goldstein 1994, 70). Armed with this new rendering of commercial performances as being "for profit," ASCAP pursued its licensing plans and proceeded to collect as many copyrighted compositions into its repertoire as it could.

Noting that ASCAP operated as a monopoly, Litman suggested that it seems "theatre and [radio] station owners gave copyright infringement little thought until ASCAP showed up on their doorsteps demanding royalties. When ASCAP went to court and got injunctions, radio stations and motion picture owners went to Congress to seek ASCAP's abolition" (Litman 1989, 292–293). Once radio broadcasting had been developed into an expanding commercial enterprise, broadcasters became increasingly concerned about ASCAP's royalty demands. To counter these demands, the broadcasters brought the Justice Department's Antitrust Division into the fray, and it promptly filed an antitrust suit against ASCAP. Although the suit itself was unsuccessful, the broadcasters countered by forming their own association, Broadcast Music, Inc. (BMI). Nevertheless, ASCAP survived these so-called radio wars, and today is stronger than ever (Goldstein 1994, 73, 75). As the music industry matured, the copyright holders and the radio stations began to work together to expand the market for music. Although the development of frequency modulation (FM) radio fostered some disputes (the programming of whole albums allowed in publishers' eyes too great a temptation for home taping), only recently, in the face of a new threat focused on the digital duplication and reproduction of music, have intraindustry tensions risen again (Yu 2004).

The 1909 Copyright Act also incorporated the works-for-hire provisions that were initially intended to help encyclopedia publishers. Even though the motion picture industry had not been invited to participate in the copyright conferences that had developed the 1909 act, after some initial difficulties, the industry was able to exploit the new law to spectacular advantage. For film production companies, this new corporate copyright had the potential to underpin studios' control of content and its distribution as well as advertising and other derivative products (Vaidhyanathan 2001, 102). The Kalem Company made a movie of *Ben Hur* without bothering to obtain a license to use the book. Harper Brothers Publishers sued, and in 1911 the US Supreme Court decided the case in favor of Harper Brothers Publishers. The film company settled the suit for $25,000, but the industry was now made fully aware of the "problem" of copyright, and its lobbying efforts to further its specific interests started in earnest (Litman 2001, 41). These efforts quickly paid off when in 1912 the movie industry gained a legislative victory in the revisions to the copyright law to protect "motion picture photoplays" (Vaidhyanathan 2001, 99). The filmmaker D. W. Griffith ingeniously exploited these new provisions to retain control over every element of his films, including music scores. In Siva Vaidhyanathan's assessment, between 1909 and 1919 Griffiths had "moved from being someone interested in maintaining only minimal protection of others' works to someone who had a vested interest in encouraging maximum copyright protection for his own work. He had moved from being copyright-poor to copyright-rich" (Vaidhyanathan 2001, 105). This shift is similar to the pharmaceutical industry's shift in patent protection between 1919 and the interwar period. And, significantly, both D. W. Griffith's story and the story of ASCAP foreshadow the enormous late-twentieth-century power of both the motion picture and music industries in shaping global copyright policy.

Over time, the scope of subject matter eligible for copyright has broadened considerably. This has been particularly evident in the realm of high technology and computing. As William Cornish pointed out, "the major computer lobbyists in the United States pressed for computer programs to be protected by accretion, that is, by treating them as literary works within traditional norms of copyright; and they now have persuaded much of the world to adopt this approach" (Cornish 1993, 55). Under the TRIPs agreement, for example, computer programs are protected as "literary works." Although some users of copyrighted information have protested this expansion of copyright, the recent trend has been to protect more rather than less.[12] According to William Fisher, these extensions rest upon a foundation of "a strong interest group, largely unopposed in the lobbying process, able to draw effectively upon the labor-desert theory and the presumptive legitimacy of its members' 'property rights'" (Fisher 1999, 13). The manner in which the industry's interests in protection have been accommodated is different, however, for software and hardware.

The debate over semiconductor chip protection was hotly contested and clearly demonstrates how new technologies complicate the identification of what counts as intellectual property. In the early 1980s, American semiconductor chip manufacturers, faced with escalating competition from Japanese producers, sought to gain protection of the design structure (or "architecture") of semiconductor chips (mask works). Existing intellectual property regimes to protect their products were held to be inadequate by the industry: their chips often failed to meet the requisite standards of novelty and inventiveness for patent protection (Drahos 1997b). This situation prompted the chip manufacturers to seek protection by accretion into the broader copyright regime, but user groups, such as the American Association of Publishers (AAP), successfully resisted this effort. The AAP represented a broad group of industries that uniformly opposed copyright protection for semiconductor mask works on the basis that such protection would breach the fundamental principles underlying copyright (Doremus 1995, 159). Bowing to this political pressure, the semiconductor industry and its representatives abandoned its copyright initiative and instead devised a sui generis solution.

The Semiconductor Chip Protection Act of 1984 provided an entirely new form of intellectual property protection based in part on copyright and embodying reciprocity. The act protected both the mask works, which are fixed in semiconductor chips, and the chips themselves. It provided for a short-term, ten-year protection against copying the chip design and provided such protection only to those foreign nationals whose countries had adopted a similar law. Although this was a domestic law, the international ramifications were made quite clear at the outset. The United States broke new ground by extending protection to mask works and by incorporating extensive transition provisions to facilitate reciprocal protection by other countries (Sell 1998, 136). Although the TRIPS agreement also now includes this sui generis protection, the recourse to bilateral measures continues to play a central role in US international intellectual property policy and action more generally.

Another example of sui generis legislation is the 1996 European Community's Directive on the Legal Protection of Databases.[13] This sui generis regime radically departs from earlier intellectual property rights systems and presents new and difficult challenges to the public domain, open science, and national innovation systems (Reichman 2002, 464, 456). The European Union (EU) directive arose from the interest of the European Community (EC) Commission in promoting Europe's participation in the rapidly expanding world database market. By the late 1990s, data services had emerged as the sixth largest segment of the information industry, and service providers were earning over $100 billion annually—even without specific legal protection (Vaidhyanathan 2001, 163). The directive aimed to reduce uncertainty about legal protection and disharmony among various

European laws, in order to promote investment in databases (Samuelson 1997, 419–420). Like the Semiconductor Chip Protection Act, the EC directive built in the concept of reciprocity; it offered database protection only to those states that offered similar levels of database protection. It was designed to encourage as many states as possible to sign on.

The directive provides high levels of protection for databases. "The form of the selection or arrangement is protected by copyright. The content—the data in the database—is covered by *sui generis* protection" (Marlin-Bennett 2004, 114). The qualifications for getting such protection are minimal. All that a database owner must do to receive fifteen years of protection is to demonstrate that he or she "has made a substantial investment in preventing unauthorized use of the information" (Marlin-Bennett 2004, 114). This could be something as basic and simple as *maintaining* the database. With remarkably generous criteria for eligibility, database owners may renew their fifteen-year term. This sui generis right covering investments in and/or amendments to the database that can be renewed without end "breaks with the entire history of intellectual property law by allowing a property rule . . . to last in perpetuity" (Reichman 2002, 465).

The European database directive reflects a "sweat of the brow" conception of intellectual property protection in data, as expressed in the *Waterlow* and *Magill* cases. The "sweat of the brow" conception rewards database compilers for the work they did to collect the data (Goldstein 1994, 212). In the UK, in *Waterlow Directories Limited v. Reed Information Services Limited*, the British High Court upheld the sweat of the brow justification for copyright in data compilation (Marlin-Bennett 2004, 113). In 1995, the European Court of Justice case *Radio Telefis Eireann v. Magill* set a precedent for the European Union and ultimately supported rights to information property (Marlin-Bennett 2004, 114). The European approach goes beyond strict copyright principles by adding a tier of protection for a database's "underlying, uncopyrightable data"; it offers database owners fifteen years "against a competitor's 'unfair extraction' of data by rearrangement in different forms" (Goldstein 1994, 214).

This represents a sharp contrast to the 1991 US Supreme Court case *Feist Publications v. Rural Telephone Service*, in which the Court ruled that the Copyright Act and "the Constitution itself prohibited the use of copyright to protect the sweat of the brow invested in collecting data" (Goldstein 1994, 213). Sandra Day O'Connor supported the role of copyright as rewarding creativity; she wrote that although "it may seem unfortunate that much of the fruit of the compiler's labor may be used by others without compensation," the result "is neither unfair nor unfortunate. It is the means by which copyright advances the progress of science and art" (quoted in Goldstein 1994, 213). Indeed, critics of the European directive argue that it shrinks the information commons, omits fair use provisions to

balance the expanded rights of database owners, and contains the possibility of a limitless extension of sui generis protection (Marlin-Bennett 2004,
114). According to Reichman, the EC directive, in effect, "abolished the
concept of the public domain that had historically justified the grant of temporary exclusive rights in intangible creations from the start" (Reichman
2002, 466).

This clash between the European support for rewarding the sweat of
the brow and the US court's *Feist* ruling explicitly rejecting it reflected the
tension between private reward, on the one hand, and public-regarding
access to information, on the other. This contrast manifested itself in the
1996 deliberations at the World Intellectual Property Organization (WIPO).
The pressure of reciprocity under the European directive, combined with
the fact that the United States had no database protection (meaning that
Europeans could extract US data without penalty), prompted the US agenda
at WIPO (Samuelson 1997, 421). Certain interested private sector actors in
the United States worked closely with their European counterparts to press
for a strong multilateral agreement expanding database protection. Among
the champions of this high protectionist European approach were the New
York Stock Exchange, the American Medical Association, and realtors
(Reichman 2002, 467). The high protectionist agenda was disrupted by a
surge of opposition from a variety of actors, however, including the
National Academy of Sciences; the National Academy of Engineering; the
National Institute of Medicine; nongovernmental organizations such as the
United States Chamber of Commerce, the Digital Futures Coalition, and
the American Library Association; and executives from such companies as
Sun Microsystems and Netscape. These groups voiced concerns over the
potential for data costs to skyrocket under a high protectionist regime
(Reichman 2002, 467). Research scholars expressed concern that the proposed WIPO database treaty would sharply reduce access to scientific data
and "would have a deleterious long-term impact on our nation's research
capabilities" (Samuelson 1997, 424).

Database treaty opponents lobbied the US Congress, the Clinton
administration, various national delegations in Geneva, and WIPO-spon-
sored regional meetings and participated informally as observers and lobbyists in the negotiations. Their position revolved around the well-established legal norm of fair use, permitting limited uncompensated use of
copyrighted work for educational purposes or scientific research. As
Samuelson stated, "in the end, none of the original US-sponsored (high-
protectionist) digital agenda proposals emerged unscathed from the negotiation process, and . . . the proposed database treaty did not emerge at all"
(Samuelson 1997, 374–375). This can be interpreted as a strike against data
bottlenecks caused by overextending property rights in data. It is less of a
victory for the public-regarding position than a damage-limiting strategy

that succeeded in one particular round of deliberations at the multilateral level. (The European directive still stands.) The outcome reflected the spirit of the *Feist* decision, "that the constitutional purposes of copyright are promoted when second comers are free to extract and reuse data from one work in order to make another work" (Samuelson 1997, 438).

Owing to the huge market for data services, however, one can confidently expect continued pressure for expanded protection of databases. Trends in US courts and tensions remaining from the discrepancy between European and US approaches to database protection portend some expanded protection in any case. Since the mid-1990s, the philosophy underpinning the *Feist* decision has been under attack at the federal appellate level in US courts. A series of circuit court decisions has reflected judicial concerns about data compilers' abilities to appropriate returns from their investments, inducing them "to broaden copyright protection of low authorship compilations in ways that significantly deform both the spirit and letter of *Feist*" (Reichman and Uhlir 2003, 374).[14] The courts have stretched copyright law to cover such things as algorithms and aggregates of facts in ways that eradicate the ideas-expression dichotomy at the heart of copyright and extend new protection to facts per se (Reichman and Uhlir 2003, 375). Furthermore, given the reciprocity provisions of the EU directive and the asymmetrical legal regimes between the EU and the United States, pressure is building within the United States to adopt some form of database protection. Although in 1996 US high protectionist supporters and those resisting such protection stood poles apart, in recent years those resisting database protection regimes have yielded ground to the high protectionist agenda (Reichman and Uhlir 2003, 388–395; see also Reichman 2002, 470–478). As in times past, Reichman warned, the legislative process is at risk of being captured "by special interests and converted into a high-protectionist exercise with serious unintended consequences" (Reichman 2002, 481; see also Litman 1989, 275–361). Exclusive property rights in data threaten to shrink the public domain. As David and Foray suggested, "if that space becomes filled by a thicket of property rights, then . . . voyages of discovery will become more expensive to undertake . . . and the rate of expansion of the knowledge base is likely to slow" (David and Foray 2002, 16–17).

The quest for copyright expansion seems to be relentless. One particularly striking case pushed the notion of copyright to erode the idea versus expression boundary. In 1977 the Ninth Circuit in San Francisco heard a case brought by Sid and Marty Kroft against McDonald's fast food company.[15] The Krofts had created a children's television program, *H. R. Pufnstuf*, which portrayed a live-action fantasyland of talking trees and magical creatures. McDonald's approached the Krofts about basing some television advertisements on *H. R. Pufnstuf*. They did not agree to terms, but McDonald's went ahead and developed a series of commercials based in "McDonaldland" (complete with talking trees and magical creatures). Despite the fact that McDonald's had differentiated the expressions of the characters from *H. R. Pufnstuf* in its rendition, the court ruled against McDonald's and in favor of the Krofts. In so doing, the court "extended to the realm of visual and narrative entertainment a new principle of idea protection: 'total concept and feel'" (Vaidhyanathan 2001, 114). Vaidhyanathan suggested that this extension might well have a chilling effect on creative endeavors; "a concept as vague and subjective as 'total concept and feel' was bound to cause confusion among writers and artists, if not lawyers. Fear of infringing can be as effective a censor as an injunction" (Vaidhyanathan 2001, 114).

That the logic of US intellectual property law at the end of the twentieth century continued to privilege private rights over public-regarding limits to protection is illustrated by one of the most fraught arguments about copyright in the United States in recent years. The Sonny Bono Copyright Term Extension Act of 1998 is a classic example of what Lemley called "ex post" protection (Lemley 2004). The Walt Disney Corporation reputedly lobbied hard for this law because copyright protection for its character Mickey Mouse was about to expire. Lawrence Lessig has therefore dubbed this "the Mickey Mouse Protection Act" (Lessig 2001a, 1065), and Merges argued that this is a "classic instance of almost pure rent-seeking legislation" (Merges 2000, 2236). The law extends the copyright term from the life of the author plus fifty to the life of the author plus seventy or, in the case of works made for hire, from seventy-five to ninety-five years; retrospectively—in regard to works subsisting under copyright—it extends their term to a maximum of ninety-five years (Lessig 2001a, 1065). Publishers and users of public domain works challenged the act in the Supreme Court on the grounds that it violated the Constitution because Congress exceeded its powers by disregarding the "limited times" requirement under the copyright clause (Yu 2004, 923). The Court upheld the constitutionality of the act because, although quite lengthy, the time extension in the act is not *unlimited*. Several justices dissented, however, and even some of the seven who upheld its constitutionality expressed skepticism about the wisdom of the law (Yu 2004, 925). This reflects a dramatic institutionalization of romantic notions of authorship, where the continued protection of the authors' rights (even if held by another party) is regarded as sacrosanct, whatever claims might be mobilized on behalf of the public domain.

Although the corporate animator producing a work for hire is hardly the image of the lone artist with his quill in the garret, the romantic notion of authorship's natural rights has benefited the Walt Disney Corporation. As has historically been the case, once again intellectual property protection has been used to support the consolidation and control of important and valuable commercial assets. Lessig presented this as the outcome of a choice between a future in which "the most significant aspects of our culture remain perpetually in the control of a relatively small number of corporations—the publishers of our day" (Lessig 2001a, 1072) and one in which clear limits on such rights facilitate the circulation of knowledge, culture, and information. This choice is not one that is limited to the realm of US law, however; the influence of the current US commitment to protecting owners' rights has been one of the major moving forces behind the expansion and strengthening of the globalized protection of intellectual property.

Toward a Multilateral Settlement

In the 1980s US private sector actors led the charge for a new multilateral settlement embracing their expanded notions of property rights.[16] Just as in times past, leading industrialists (this time in the pharmaceutical, chemical, software, and entertainment sectors) lobbied for a reinvigorated approach to intellectual property protection at the international level that championed security over competition. Moreover, the perception of a new technological "revolution" linked to information and communications technologies (ICTs) had been an important stimulus to the heightened profile of intellectual property in policy circles. Popular and policy-related discussions of the information society were hardly novel (May 2002a, chap. 1), but the possibilities of a dynamic realm of globalized information flows had become an increasingly significant element of international policy discourse by the end of the 1980s. Only a decade earlier the Tokyo Round of GATT-related multilateral trade negotiations (1973–1979) had included no significant negotiations over intellectual property, partly because developing countries' governments had strongly resisted the expansion of the GATT disciplines into new areas. At the time of the launch of the Tokyo Round, ICTs were still typified by mainframe computing, and commercialized consumer applications of computing remained in their infancy.

By the time of the launch of the Uruguay Round in 1986, however, developed countries' governments and their negotiators had started to see that the issue of IPRs, their protection and use, was likely to become an increasingly important issue in future international trade relations (Primo Braga 1989, 245–246). The expanding possibilities for technical appropriation of knowledge or information, alongside widespread pirated reproduction and distribution of knowledge-based products, prompted rich countries' governments to act on behalf of their national corporate interests. Indeed, a major element in the political pressure to include the protection and enforcement of IPRs in the Uruguay Round originated in the response by the content industries to a series of ICT-related innovations. These enhanced both the possibilities of an international (commodity) trade in information- and knowledge-related goods *and* enlarged the possibilities of theft and piracy.

A group of US corporations formed the International Property Committee (IPC), which not only aimed to bring pressure to bear on the US government to get IPRs onto the agenda for negotiation but also provided considerable legal support to the negotiating team (Sell 2003, chap. 5). A crucial point was that the IPC's influence was not limited to US trade negotiators. The IPC also worked hard to convince industrial associations in Europe and Japan that a new governance regime for IPRs was possible and then mobilized them to support its quest to include intellectual property protection in the Uruguay Round. The IPC and the European and Japanese groups then worked together to produce a consensual document, rooted in industrialized countries' laws, on fundamental principles for a multilateral approach to intellectual property protection. This document was then presented to the GATT secretariat and Geneva-based representatives of numerous countries.

This process, in which industry played such a central role, was unprecedented for the GATT. Although the IPC derived its influence from the economic resources and power it represented in the US domestic economy, its (self)characterization as representing the crucial sectors of the new information-based economy helped it establish the negotiating framework for the TRIPs agreement. This was undoubtedly aided by the increasingly shrill proclamations of the imminent "new age" from think tanks and in the media (May 2002a). Supported by the United States, the IPC was able to get an intellectual property agreement that reflected most of its demands. The US government had begun to see the "information industries" as the competitive and crucial sectors for maintaining US economic strength, and the office of the US Trade Representative (USTR) took the IPC's demands very seriously. Furthermore, given the general perception of the specialized nature of intellectual property law, the IPC capitalized on the assumption that specialized knowledge was needed to "support" the negotiating teams. Thus, the IPC essentially drafted the TRIPs agreement, and the actual negotiations fine-tuned the text and made some concessions to developing countries' negotiators.

Trade negotiators themselves had already concluded that the complex of twenty-four multilateral treaties previously administered by WIPO produced too much rule diversity. Even within each agreement, there was considerable variance in the scope of protection offered. For instance, in 1988 a WIPO study for the TRIPs negotiating group had discovered that of the ninety-eight signatories to the Paris Convention for the Protection of Industrial Property, over forty excluded from their legislation pharmaceutical products, animal varieties, methods of treatment, plant varieties, and biological processes for producing animal and plant varieties; over thirty excluded food products and computer programs; and a further twenty-two excluded chemical products (Drahos 2002, 768). Making the problem more complex, it was not necessarily the same group of country-members excluding specific categories in each case. The USTR and developed countries' negotiators suggested, for the purposes of clarity in the international trade of IPR-related products, that a unified agreement would provide a clear benefit. This line of argument did little to stimulate the interest of developing countries' governments in including IPRs in multilateral trade negotiations.

To encourage a change of heart regarding the negotiation of the TRIPs agreement, the USTR threatened bilateral trade sanctions (under the Special 301 section of the Omnibus Trade and Tariff Act, 1988) and actually utilized these measures against a range of targets, including a majority of those developing countries whose governments had been active in opposing the position of the United States in the TRIPs negotiating group (Drahos 2002, 774–775; Matthews 2002, 31–33). This stick was combined with the carrot of a promise to open up agricultural markets and an offer to abolish the Multi-Fibre Arrangement that constrained developing countries' textile exports (May 2000, 88). The USTR also negotiated a number of bilateral trade and investment treaties with developing countries that included provisions that moved these countries toward a "TRIPs-model" of IPR protection. This lessened resistance to TRIPs compliance, as after concluding these agreements (and making the required legal changes) there was less legislative distance between domestic provisions and TRIPs-compliant legislation (Drahos and Braithwaite 2002, 134). Many developing countries lacked the expertise and resources to fully resist this firm bilateral pressure.

The divide-and-rule strategy of selectively withdrawing General System of Preference (GSP) market-access provisions also worked against the maintenance of a collective developing countries' negotiating bloc (Matthews 2002, 33). Although even in 1989 it was clear to many commentators and negotiators what the likely detrimental effects of an international trade agreement on IPRs would be (Gakunu 1989), this was not the same as being able to withstand the considerable political resources that the developed countries' negotiators brought to bear to secure TRIPs. The combination of political pressure and weakened resistance due to the complexity of the negotiations, relative to the limited resources that developing countries' governments could dedicate to them, ensured that when the developing countries joined the new WTO they had to accede (with some transitional arrangements to be sure) to the TRIPs agreement as well.[17]

Ironically, the original pressure to amend the international system governing intellectual property had not originated in the United States or other developed countries but with the Group of 77 some years before. During the 1960s and 1970s, developing countries' governments were worried about the problems of economic development and seized upon patent protection as one of the factors behind import monopolies and the failure to develop indigenous technologies (Sell 1998, chap. 4). The institution of intellectual property was perceived not as an organ of free trade, as it would be characterized in the TRIPs agreement, but as the tool of protection for the owners of IPRs in the rich and developed countries. Through IPRs the technology gap and uneven development (or underdevelopment) were maintained. This situation led developing countries' governments to be antagonistic toward demands that their national legislation should accord similar levels of protection to IPRs that were enjoyed in the United States, Europe, or Japan. Thus, during the 1960s and 1970s, the developing countries' governments and negotiators argued for a *dilution* of international intellectual property law, whereas the developed countries' governments merely supported the status quo.

The key distinction between the position of the Group of 77 and the developed countries rested on the purpose of patent (and other IPR) protection. For the developing countries' governments, the most important factor was their own countries' development and the narrowing of the technology gap. The rich countries' negotiating position, which in the end was consolidated by the TRIPs agreement, was that the rights belonging to owners, and therefore the sanctity of their property, was paramount. Only by ensuring that the property rights of innovators and entrepreneurs were protected from theft could any national economy hope to develop and support economic growth. The developing countries' governments, however, often used their national legislation to reduce the monopoly rights accorded to intellectual property. They received some support in this policy from the United Nations Conference on Trade and Development, most explicitly in the 1975 report *The International Patent System as an Instrument for National Development,* which was exclusively devoted to the question of revising the Paris convention, sharply criticizing existing arrangements and urging reforms to improve the situation of developing countries (Sell 1998, 116). Some diplomats suspected that developing countries' governments were using patents as a scapegoat for more difficult problems internal to their economies. Nevertheless, in 1980 the Diplomatic Conference for the Revision of the Paris Convention was convened. Unfortunately, the series of four conferences was deadlocked by the opposed views of the purpose of IPR protection, frustrating the attempts of the developing countries' negotiators to widen the public realm for intellectual property.

Having opened the Pandora's box of intellectual property revision, the developing countries' governments subsequently found themselves overtaken by events. Even though developing countries' governments still con-

sidered knowledge-based industries' intellectual property to be a development issue, for the developed countries' negotiators in the 1980s it was now
an invaluable and crucial resource linked to competitiveness and trade. This
viewpoint had already begun to radically shift domestic legislation, as
noted above, and it was not long before a similar dynamic was informing
international policy as well. The differences between the supporters or IPRs
and those more critical of their worth were clearly articulated during the
negotiations that led to the TRIPs agreement, although the developing
countries were ultimately unsuccessful in shifting the content of the agreement to any great degree. Conversely, many developing countries' negotiators also perceived some advantages to an agreement.

Certainly, the cross-issue linkage suggested that agreement on IPRs
could be used to leverage other trade benefits (of which market access in
textiles and agriculture was the most important). Many negotiators, seeing
the prospect of a growing bilateralism in IPRs, also regarded a multilateral
agreement (and hence TRIPs) as a better alternative. Furthermore, by the
last decade of the twentieth century, domestic businesses seeking some
form of IPR-related protection in specific sectors were lobbying some
developing countries' governments (Adede 2003, 32–34; Gutowski 1999,
754–757). Such protection could be attractive to domestic businesses generating their own intellectual property as well as to those seeking to gain
access to protected technology from abroad (Maskus and Reichman 2004,
287–290). Thus, although the negotiations may have been lopsided, the
governments of many developing countries could still see that there were
some national advantages to be gained.

Although at the beginning, the debate might have been characterized as
a North-South difference over the fundamentals of protecting IPRs, as the
negotiations gathered pace, the majority of meeting time was spent on trying to resolve the differences between the positions of the United States,
Europe, and Japan over the protection of IPRs, leaving the concerns of the
developing countries marginalized (Stewart 1993, 2287, 2313). In 1990 the
developing countries' negotiators were still expressing concern that the
negotiations continued to treat IPRs exclusively as a commercial matter
and that insufficient account was being taken of national development priorities (General Agreement on Tariffs and Trade 1990, 5). By this point the
battle had been lost, however, with only sectoral concessions left to hold
out for.

In the end the proposed staged dismantling of the Multi-Fibre
Arrangement, potentially benefiting a number of developing countries' textile and clothing sectors (by allowing market access to the previously protected markets of the developed countries), also played a role in securing
TRIPs. For smaller countries outside the various regional trade agreements,
there was also a clear political will to ensure that the multilateral agreement

did not fail, as this would have left them with severe market access problems (Sell 2003, 110). Finally, Lars Anell, the chairman of the TRIPs negotiating group, also utilized his position to shift the process toward conclusion, producing at a crucial moment a chairman's draft as a basis for further discussion, when five competing drafts were in circulation.[18] His consolidated text eventually resulted in the TRIPs text in the Uruguay Round final settlement. Therefore, a combination of "hardball" diplomacy, issue linkage, and a lack of appreciation regarding the possible future impact of undertakings regarding IPRs by some negotiators led to the achievement of the first global governance regime for IPRs as part of the new WTO.

TRIPs was the result of a political process, driven by specific industrial and national interests, not merely the consolidation of a set of legitimated regulatory provisions, with differences only regarding their implementation. Commenting on the successful conclusion of the trade negotiations, one private sector participant asserted that the private sector lobbyists got 95 percent of what they wanted.[19] As we will explore at more length in Chapter 7, the TRIPS agreement incorporates a notion of IPRs as a system of exclusion and protection rather than one of diffusion and competition. It extends rights holders' privileges and reduces their obligations. This far-reaching agreement has important implications for innovation, research and development, economic development, the future location of industry, and the global division of labor. Indeed, the dramatic expansion of the scope of intellectual property rights embodied in the agreement reduces the options available to future industrializers by blocking the route that earlier industrializers followed. It raises the price of information and technology by extending the monopoly privileges of rights-holders and requires states to play a much greater role in defending them.

As previous chapters have demonstrated, the industrialized countries built much of their economic prowess by appropriating others' intellectual property; with TRIPS this option is foreclosed to future industrializers. It is no longer possible for follower states to emulate the United States, Spain, Switzerland, or the Netherlands.[20] The agreement codifies the increasing commodification of the public domain and makes it unavailable to new and future innovators (Aoki 1996, 1336). As we will argue in Chapter 7, states and companies whose comparative advantage lies in imitation stand to lose under the new regime.

In the twentieth century intellectual property rights continued to evolve as a result of shifting conceptions of property rights, technological change, and institutionalization of legal settlements. Private actors played an important role in shaping these developments, but, as we have demonstrated, property owners have not *always* prevailed; rights of ownership are dynamic, contested, and socially constructed. As Lauren Edelman suggested: "Institutionalized ideas about what is rational develop at the societal level in concert with institutionalized ideas about what is fair, what is legal, what is legitimate, and even about what is scientifically or technically possible. These institutionalized ideas vary, of course, across social and geographical realms over time" (Edelman 2004, 186–187). Moreover, "social and political power affect bargaining strategies, who is even at the bargaining table, and most fundamentally, how actors assign value to actions" (Edelman 2004, 188). The privileging of "economic necessity" obscures the extent to which necessity itself is a highly contested social construction. What is deemed necessary depends on different countries' stages of development and the relative political and social power of various domestic sectors. As we related above, the US government resisted the nascent US pharmaceutical industry's pleas in 1919 to weaken patent protection in response to the German chemical cartels because other, more developed sectors, such as electrical equipment, were prospering under the existing intellectual property policies.

Indeed, as the foregoing historical examples have demonstrated, sometimes patent-based cartels are "necessary" or "rational," whereas at other times it is "rational" for the government to seize patents under compulsory licenses. These judgments are historically contingent, not a reflection of timeless laws or rights. During World War I, the US government used its compulsory licensing prerogatives to obtain access to the Wright brothers' aviation technology, and during World War II it resorted to compulsory licensing of process patents for desperately needed antibiotics. More recently, after the terrorist attacks on the United States of 11 September 2001, the October 2001 anthrax scare prompted the US secretary of health and human services, Tommy Thompson, to threaten to compulsorily license Bayer's Cipro. Without needing to follow through, the threat prompted Bayer drastically to reduce prices to ensure adequate supplies in the event of a large-scale attack.

Despite the rhetoric of efficiency, property rights are fundamentally about distributive policies, and history is rich with examples of policy driven by distributive norms. According to Terence Halliday, "distributive norms can weigh as heavily on the shoulders of political leaders as efficiency norms. And without a careful balancing of efficiency, equity, and stability, market construction may lead to social destruction" (Halliday, 2004, 216). When the Lancaster spinners prevailed over the patent holder, Richard Arkwright, it reflected the court's distributive focus on employment and British economic hegemony as opposed to private reward. A similar distributive logic informed the US reluctance to weaken patent protection in 1919, despite the pharmaceutical industry lobby, while the patent-based and internationally strong US electrical equipment industry prospered. Yet distributive norms also inspired Thompson's threat of compulsory licensing of Cipro. Each new round of contestation and settlement produces new winners and losers. Depending upon how well-mobilized and badly threatened the losers are, they can rise up to challenge the settlement.

Sometimes they prevail and help to redress egregious imbalances, and sometimes, as is currently the case for US copyright law, they fail. Nevertheless, history provides some hope for a more balanced future for intellectual property rights, and it is to the current global settlement and its future that we now turn.

Notes

1. Facing similar competition from the Germans, in 1919 the British amended their patent laws to prohibit patents for chemical compounds (Braithwaite and Drahos 2002, 462). See also the discussion of the Swiss law in Chapter 5.

2. *Standard Oil Co. (Ind.) v. United States,* 283 U.S. 163, 167–168 (1931).

3. This section is based on Sell (2003, 66–67).

4. *Mercoid,* 320 US 661; *Mercoid Corp. v. Minneapolis-Honeywell Regulator Co.*, 320 US 680 (1944) (sustaining antitrust liability); and *Mercoid* 320 US at 669.

5. 314 US 488 (1942).

6. 448 US 176 (1980).

7. *Henry v. A .B. Dick & Co.,* 244 US 1 (1912). The Court ruled that a patentee "could extract whatever price or other concession he chose as a consideration for granting a patent license" (quoted in Kastriner 1991, 6).

8. This section is drawn from Sell (2003, 68–72).

9. The quote is from the decision in *Smith International v. Hughes Tool* (1983).

10. This paragraph substantially draws from Sell (2003, 74).

11. This paragraph draws from Sell (2003, 63).

12. For an exception to the trend toward more protection, see the discussion of the victories of the interoperable developers, such as Sun Microsystems, over the advocates of highly protective norms, such as IBM and Microsoft, in Band and Katoh (1995). For the position of advocates of high protectionist norms, see Clapes (1993).

13. Directive 96/9/EC of the European Parliament and of the European Union Council of 11 March 1996.

14. For example, *CDN, Inc. v. Kapes*, 197 F.3d 1256, 1259–1260 (9th Cir. 1999); *CCC Info. Servs., Inc. v. Maclean Hunter Mkt. Reports, Inc.*, 44 F.3d 61, 65 (2d Cir. 1994); *Warren Publ'g Inc. v. Microdos Data Corp.*, 115 F.3d 1509, 1518–1519 (11th Cir. 1997); *Bellsouth Adver. & Publ'g Corp. v. Donnelley Info. Publ'g Inc.*, 999 F.2d 1436, 1446 (11th Cir. 1993).

15. Summary based on Vaidhyanathan (2001, 112–114).

16. Where not explicitly noted, this section draws on our previous work, notably May (2000) and Sell (1998; 2003).

17. Extended discussions of the negotiations that led to TRIPs can be found in Matthews (2002, chap. 2) and Stewart (1993, 2245–2333).

18. Drahos and Braithwaite (2002, 139–143) make a convincing case for the importance of Anell's stewardship of the final stages of the negotiations.

19. Interview with Jacques Gorlin, adviser to the Intellectual Property Committee, 22 January 1996, Washington, D.C.

20. The same comment applies to more recent successful follower states in East Asia. See Kumar (2003).

7

The Twenty-First Century: TRIPs and Beyond

IN THE LAST decade of the twentieth century, international trade diplomacy finally established a global regime for the governance of intellectual property rights: the Agreement on Trade Related Aspects of Intellectual Property Rights (TRIPs). Rather than being the final achievement of a natural global order of rights for creators and innovators, TRIPs is merely the most recent stage of a long and contested history. Since the World Trade Organization (WTO) was finally established with TRIPs as one of its central elements, it has become clear that rather than being a final settlement that left only technical issues of implementation to be resolved, the TRIPs agreement is being challenged from two directions. On one hand, a strategy of bilateralism by the developed countries' governments (most obviously the United States) has attempted to further enhance and extend the global reach of intellectual property rights (IPRs). On the other, a widening and increasingly powerful global political movement has questioned a number of claims regarding intellectual property, not least the claimed relationship between IPRs and economic development. The political forces that pushed for the TRIPs regime seem therefore to have stimulated a response that no longer accepts intellectual property as a technical and arcane matter outside the realm of global politics.

In many ways TRIPs, like much of the previous history of the governance of IPRs, was a response to technological changes. TRIPs was also part of a more general agreement among the crucial regional trading blocs, in the wake of the end of the cold war, that the governance of international trade should move from the relatively weak General Agreement on Tariffs and Trade (GATT) to a new and more robust governance regime. The inclusion of TRIPs, alongside the General Agreement on Trade in Services (GATS) and a number of other agreements (ranging from investment to antidumping), into the final settlement of the Uruguay Round of multilateral trade negotiations was the culmination of a general strategy on behalf of

161

the US government and the European Union (EU) to force developing countries to adopt multilateral agreements in sectors that they had hitherto resisted (Steinberg 2002). By withdrawing from their previous commitments under GATT 1947, and therefore terminating any obligations under that agreement, the United States and EU forced developing countries to accede to a wide-ranging agreement under the WTO if they wished to regain the trade arrangements with which they had started the Uruguay Round.

TRIPs

TRIPs presents WTO members with a single framework for dealing with the diverse aspects of intellectual property. It brings the fragmented set of treaties and sectoral agreements previously overseen by the World Intellectual Property Organization (WIPO) into a single framework.[1] It is not a model piece of legislation that can be incorporated directly into national law but rather sets the minimum standards to be established by all WTO members. National legislatures are required to ensure that IPRs are protected, but the method for this protection is only important as regards its consequences, not its form; the agreement is concerned with ends, not means. The agreement also is explicitly reciprocal, although reciprocity as a principle does little in itself to change the character of the intellectual property governance regime. As Rajan Dhanjee and Laurence Boisson de Chazournes (1993, 9–10) have stressed, the principle of nonreciprocity in the intellectual property agreements administered by WIPO was already significantly eroded by the adoption and adaptation of sui generis legislation common to many signatories and stimulated by bilateral political pressures prior to 1995.

Unlike the WIPO's stewardship of the conventions, governing IPRs through the WTO offers a considerably more robust enforcement mechanism for countries' governments to appeal to when the laws of a particular country are seen to impede the rights of other nationals. This "juridification" of disputes removes much of the potential for political maneuvering over the agreement's provisions and articles. Indeed, Joseph Weiler has argued that this shift to governance by norms and the practices of the "rule of law" is at "odds with the ethos of diplomacy" previously evident in the realm of global economic relations (Weiler 2000, 8). TRIPs is a clear attempt to remove IPRs from the realm of global politics and to (re)define them as only subject to arcane and technical legal debate.

The previous governance structure for intellectual property had included 135 states as members of WIPO, although of the eighteen conventions administered, even the Paris convention, with the most signatories, had been ratified by only 108 countries. With the exception of the Bern convention (95 signatories), other agreements overseen by WIPO only had between 20 and 50 signatories. Thus, the inclusion of IPRs in the WTO immediately widened the scope of intellectual property governance to all of its over 140 members. The agreement also set up the TRIPs Council to scrutinize members' compliance with the agreement's various undertakings. Members notify the council of their progress toward full implementation, not least of all as most new members of the WTO are required to be TRIPs compliant from the date of accession. Furthermore, the TRIPs Council is empowered to seek answers to questions regarding a particular member's compliance forwarded to it by any other WTO member.[2]

It is crucial that, unlike other aspects of WTO members' undertakings, TRIPs is a set of requirements for *positive* legislative action to establish the rights and protections mandated by its various articles, rather than merely requiring states to refrain from certain actions or practices. This had led Ruth Okediji to argue that these compliance demands, in light of the robust dispute settlement mechanism, mean the agreement "turns the traditional national/international paradigm upside down; it appears to contemplate a substitution of domestic processes that have produced a competitive balance in the domestic setting with an international process that presumes that the domestic balance should be renegotiated in the light of obligations in TRIPs" (Okediji 2003, 915). The history of domestic political deliberation that has produced varied and locally determined solutions to the question of making knowledge and information property is not merely undermined by the agreement, it is explicitly replaced by a set of standards that have (for most countries) been developed elsewhere.

In the preamble to TRIPs, the recognition that IPRs are "private rights" is partly balanced by an explicit allowance of the need for "public policy objectives" to be accorded some weight in regard to both developmental and technological objectives. The agreement clearly focuses, however, on extending owners' rights. Indeed, Kurt Burch contended that this expansion of ownership rights "promotes the vocabulary of rights and property and the liberal conceptual framework they help define" (Burch 1995, 215). For knowledge and information, this leads to the emphasis on *individualized* rights to reward for effort, alongside the practical organization of production through alienable property. Furthermore, Samuel Oddi argued that the use of a natural *rights* discourse is intended to establish that

> these rights are so important that individual [WTO] member welfare should not stand in the way of their being protected as an entitlement of the creators. This invokes a counter-instrumentalist policy that members, regardless of their state of industrialization, should sacrifice their national interests in favor of the posited higher order of international trade. (Oddi 1996, 440)

Although TRIPs includes instrumentalist justifications alongside the more rights-oriented language, throughout the text the agreement systematically privileges the rights side of any balance between individual rights and public development benefits.

The widespread use of the term *piracy* by negotiators before and after the TRIPs negotiations is symbolic of this set of naturalized claims, implying that infringers should be thought of like the pirates, slave traders, and torturers of the past (Murumba 1998, 444; Halbert 1999, 85–94). This is a rhetorical attempt to establish the parallel with (the more violent) assaults on human rights, despite the fact, as Howard Anawalt noted, that IPRs "lack the compelling necessity of human rights covenants or rules on the use of force" (Anawalt 2003, 401). The "rights" rhetoric continues to be a powerful aspect of the agreement's normative commitments, however.

TRIPs itself is a complex and wide-ranging set of requirements on signatories, divided into seven sections that we will briefly set out here.[3] The main text of TRIPs commences with eight articles setting out the general provisions and basic principles of the agreement. Article 1 establishes that (as noted above) TRIPs is a set of obligations and not a piece of model legislation, that implementation of these obligations is a matter for national legislation, and that the agreement is not intended to harmonize national laws (although neither does it preclude such harmonization). The first two articles also establish the agreement's links with previous treaties and conventions that covered intellectual property (the Paris, Bern, and Rome conventions and the Treaty on Intellectual Property in Respect of Integrated Circuits) and require members of the WTO to treat all members' nationals on the basis that their countries are also signatories of these conventions.

By bringing intellectual property into the governance mechanisms for international trade, TRIPs requires the application to intellectual property of the principles that are central to the WTO (like the GATT before it): national treatment (Article 3) and most-favored-nation (MFN) treatment (Article 4). Introducing MFN and national treatment ensures that favoritism accorded domestic inventors or prospective owners of IPRs relative to non-nationals is rendered illegal, as is the favorable treatment of IPR owners from specific trading partners. This is an important shift because in the past many national IPR systems, including the US system, favored domestic owners either through legislative or procedural means.

Therefore, although the character of intellectual property, what is actually to be protected, is modified to some extent by TRIPs (especially for computer programs), one of the main areas of discontinuity with prior practice is in the national protection of IPRs. Further, Article 41 of the agreement stipulates that "procedures shall be applied in such a manner as to avoid the creation of barriers to legitimate trade" and makes this undertaking central to national intellectual property law (General Agreement on

Tariffs and Trade 1994, sec. A1C, 19). If only nationals are protected, this acts as a barrier to nonnationals who receive no protection for the IPR-related goods or services they wish to export to that jurisdiction. TRIPs requires that nondiscrimination must be explicitly part of clear, open, and fair procedures for the protection of IPRs. Article 5 carves out an exception from the requirements for MFN and national treatment, however, for agreements concluded by the WIPO.

One of the areas where it proved impossible to conclude an agreement during the Uruguay Round of negotiations was regarding the exhaustion of rights (Article 6), not least as the EU negotiating team was unprepared to accept the extension of national exhaustion of rights (Matthews 2002, 48). The international exhaustion of rights is when the first sale of an item anywhere in the world exhausts the rights encompassed (it then becomes secondhand and not subject to the same limitations of sale), whereas the national exhaustion of rights is when only a sale in the jurisdiction in which the rights are claimed exhausts them. Essentially, the latter halts parallel imports, whereas the former allows them. Owing to the lack of agreement, TRIPs leaves the choice over exhaustion of rights to national legislatures.

The final two articles in the first section of the agreement set out the objectives (Article 7) and principles (Article 8) of the agreement. The first, reflecting the interests and concerns of the developing countries' negotiators (Watal 2003, 387), declares that the protection and enforcement of IPRs "should contribute to the promotion of technological innovation and to the transfer and dissemination of technology, to the mutual advantage of producers and users of technological knowledge and in the manner conducive to social and economic welfare, and to a balance of rights and obligations" (General Agreement on Tariffs and Trade 1994, sec. A1C, 5). The second allows members to adopt measures to protect public health and to promote the public interest in sectors of vital national importance, alongside provisions for halting abuses of IPRs by rights holders, explicitly including problems with the transfer of technology. As we will discuss later in the chapter, these principles have been relatively ineffectual in the face of bilateral and other political pressures.

The next section of the agreement sets out WTO members' obligations across various forms of intellectual property. Articles 9 through 14 cover the protections that TRIPs established for copyright, defined in accordance with common usage as "expressions not ideas, procedures, methods of operation or mathematical concepts as such" (General Agreement on Tariffs and Trade 1994, sec. A1C, 6). A significant reflection of the US domination of the negotiations is that, although requiring members to comply with Articles 1–21 and the appendix of the Bern convention (1971), the agreement explicitly excludes members from the obligations under Bern's article 6*bis* to respect authors'/creators' moral rights. Thus, the agreement focuses on economic rights (which remain fully alienable) rather than on nontransferable moral rights in copyrighted products, which remained controversial in the United States.

In another area that has proved controversial and has been frequently raised in public debates, Article 10 makes it clear that "computer programs, whether in source or object code, shall be protected as literary works under the Berne Convention" (General Agreement on Tariffs and Trade 1994, sec. A1C, 6). This article not only extends the Bern convention itself but also allows computer programs to be covered by the longest period of protection available under the agreement. Computer programs are also, therefore, subject to considerably less stringent conditions of recognition as intellectual property than other sorts of manufacturing/industrial processes (or tools) covered by patents. Given the importance of information and communication technologies (ICTs) and other forms of knowledge resources in the global economy, this raises profound concerns about technology transfer as it favors owners over possible users. The second clause of Article 10 also explicitly includes "compilations of data or other material, whether in machine readable or other form, which by reason of selection or arrangement of their contents constitute intellectual creations," although such protection "shall not extend to the data or material itself" (General Agreement on Tariffs and Trade 1994, sec. A1C, 6). Thus, databases, directories, and other electronically stored public knowledge shall be protected by copyright and as such brought into the intellectual property regime, at least in their particular patterning (or structure of compilation).[4]

Powerful lobbying by representatives of the music industry also managed to introduce into the agreement's text the recognition not only of performers' rights in sound recordings but also the "neighboring rights" of producers and broadcasters (Article 14). Here, the discourse of piracy and theft played a major role in consolidating the rights that performers, producers, and broadcasters can expect in respect of their works. The article's text established the right for performers to authorize or prohibit the "fixing" of works that have not previously been fixed into a medium for reproduction (Article 14.1) and to halt "bootlegging" of live performances or broadcasts; the rights of producers of "phonograms" to authorize or prohibit the reproduction of their products (Article 14.2) to halt pirated copies of music recordings; and the rights of broadcasters to authorize or prohibit the fixation, reproduction, or rebroadcasting of their broadcasts. As Article 14.6 makes clear, these obligations reflect rights initially set out in the Rome convention (1961). As with the rental right below, rentals are allowed provided they do not lead to extensive copying (Article 14.4) and the terms of protection are set at fifty years for nonbroadcast rights and twenty years for broadcasts (Article 14.5). These provisions clearly reflect the growing consensus among content industry corporations in the early

1990s that piracy and counterfeiting were a growing problem, stimulated and extended through digitization.

The agreement extends a right of copyright holders to authorize or prohibit the rental of their works (Article 11), although, through French insistence, an exclusion to this right was inserted that holds except when there is a clear demonstration that rentals have led to widespread copying (Matthews 2002, 52). The term of copyright protection is held at fifty years, either from the death of the author or (where no single author can be identified) fifty years from the end of the calendar year in which authorized publication took place (Article 12). This, of course, is a minimum that has been extended in the United States, and elsewhere has been subject to extensive lobbying for extension. Exceptions to all the provisions noted are limited by Article 13 to special cases that neither conflict with normal exploitation nor unreasonably prejudice the legitimate interests of the rights' holder.

Articles 15 through 21 set out WTO members' obligations in the realm of trademarks. The agreement presents a relatively standard definition of trademarks (Article 15.1), although it also establishes a right to refuse a mark, on a number of grounds drawn from the Paris convention (1967); for instance, that a mark would be contrary to public morality or might deceive the public (Matthews 2002, 54). Recognizing the divergence of conditions for registration across members, the other three paragraphs of Article 15 allow, but do not require, questions of prior use to be taken into consideration and provide for an appeal process to be instituted by members, but again does not make this mandatory. Article 16 is concerned to confer exclusive rights and, again drawing explicitly from the Paris convention (1967), seeks to establish the protection against similar or confusing marks, what is usually termed "passing off," including the possibility of such protection for as yet unregistered foreign marks that are "well known" in a WTO member's jurisdiction. Although the WIPO has drafted nonbinding advice on how a mark might be recognized as well-known, many developing *and* developed countries seem unlikely and unwilling to extend protection to (nationally) unregistered marks (Watal 2003, 261).

TRIPs maintains exceptions to applying for marks for signs, terms, and other marks that are already in the public domain (Article 17); establishes a term of protection of at least seven years, renewable indefinitely (Article 18); and unless there are obstacles to use, allows marks to be cancelled after an uninterrupted period of three years of nonuse (Article 19). Finally, the ability of national laws to require conditions on use (such as requiring use with another trademark) is limited (Article 20), and the agreement explicitly grants the mark owner the exclusive right to assign the trademark, and thus prohibits compulsory licensing. This is not the only area where compulsory licensing has been constrained or halted in TRIPs, and as such the new arrangements differ from the flexibility on this issue that developing countries' negotiators proposed for this and other forms of intellectual property. Although the protection of trademarks was a major concern for the developed and industrialized countries' negotiators, for the developing countries the question of trademarks was more an area for "horse-trading" than for serious antagonism between negotiating groups (Maskus 2000, 63).

A number of members of the EU as well as Switzerland were instrumental in establishing an agreement on geographical indicators (GIs) as part of TRIPs (Maskus 2000, 20), and these are covered in Articles 22 through 24. French negotiators were particularly anxious to protect "appellations of origin," most particularly for wine-making regions. As a result, wines and spirits enjoy a separate Article (23) setting out the provisions of TRIPs as relates to these products. Article 23 seeks to address cases in which geographical indicators have become more generic terms for forms of wine or spirits (the key example being champagne), and therefore even the use of such modifiers as *style, kind, type,* or *imitation* is curtailed This produces a considerably more forthright protection of GIs for these beverages than for other products. The general provisions under Article 22 seek to constrain uses of GIs that would produce unfair competition or would mislead the public as regards the origin of the goods concerned (including those uses that although "literately true" still misrepresent the origins of goods), although there is a significant list of "fair use" and "good faith" exceptions to these provisions.

Because the extended protection (available for wine and spirits) is not extended to non-European products such as Basmati rice or Darjeeling tea (Maskus 2000, 239), for many developing countries this extra protection has been particularly contentious. As Jayashree Watal pointed out:

> Developing countries will have to persuade their legislatures to accept a higher level of protection for wines and spirits, mainly of European origin, without having the benefit of reciprocal protection on their [own] geographical indicators. . . . Worse still, many of the indications that they are forced to protect are already termed as "generic" or "semi-generic" in some important developed countries. (Watal 2003, 273)

In other words, as elsewhere in the governance of IPRs, the developing countries effectively are being required to uphold standards of protection that are higher than those in the richer, developed country members of the WTO.

Two short articles follow on industrial designs. An important provision is that of Article 25.2, which extends the provision of protection for textile designs and notes that the administration of the grant of rights must not impair the opportunity to seek protection. This reflects the recognition of concerns from developing country negotiators in this area, that the mandated protection of ten years (Article 26.3) should be available to indigenous textile designs, most specifically in the protection against unauthorized making, selling, or importing for sale of articles that copy either all or a substantial part of the design (Article 26.1).

The protection of patent rights as set out in TRIPs' Articles 27 through 34 has been one of the areas that has generated the most political debate and conflict since the agreement entered into force in 1995. Although TRIPs carries the normal provisions regarding the criteria for patenting forward (newness, usefulness, and applicability under Article 27.1) and sets the term of protection at a slightly longer period than in some jurisdictions, at twenty years (Article 33), it expressly does not preclude a considerable expansion of "patentable subject matter." This extension is produced through the provisions of Article 27, which allow that members *may* exclude from patent provisions a number of classes of goods and materials such as diagnostic, therapeutic, and surgical methods as well as plants and animals and the "essentially" biological processes for their production (Articles 27.2 and 27.3). These classes of objects and processes may be excluded,[5] but they are not *required* to be outside patent regimes, and certainly in the last decade industrialized countries have deployed considerable bilateral pressure to ensure that developing countries' new TRIPs-compliant legislation covers certain new "products."

It is more important that, in order to ensure that patents on genes and biotechnological materials are covered in all member states, these exceptions expressly do not include microorganisms, nonbiological and microbiological processes of plant and animal production, or pharmaceutical products. In addition, members "shall provide for the protection of plant varieties either by patents or by an effective *sui generis* system or by any combination thereof" (General Agreement on Tariffs and Trade 1994, sec. A1C, 13). These biotechnological provisions ensure that although plant varieties may be treated differently, they will also be brought into the system of IPRs, even while responding to the requirements of the International Convention for the Protection of New Varieties of Plants (UPOV [the acronym is for the French name for the convention]). For the purposes of clarity, the GATT always tried to reduce nontariff barriers, even if this merely meant transforming them into actual tariffs. Here, the same logic is being applied: the reduction of differences in institutionalized treatment to a variation in the same broad legislative method.

The rights holder's exclusive rights, under the above conditions, are set out in Article 28, and Article 29 sets out the requirement for sufficient disclosure within patent applications to allow a person "skilled in the art" to be able to utilize the innovation. The following three articles concerning exceptions to rights held (Article 30), other use without authorization of the right holder (Article 31), and revocation/forfeiture (Article 32) have generated considerable dispute, however. As for trademarks, these articles effectively constrain the compulsory licensing of innovations.

In the past, developing countries have argued that the refusal to grant patent licenses for particular innovations, or the failure to work them in a national economy (relying on imports for the fulfillment of demand), has impeded technology transfer. Some economists have found that patents *can* facilitate technology transfer to more affluent developing countries (Smith 2001; Maskus and Penubarti 1995), although there appear to be clear threshold effects in market-based technology licensing (Maskus and Reichman 2004, 289). Therefore, although some of the literature is more optimistic about a positive relationship between intellectual property protection and technology transfer to middle-income developing countries, even Maskus and Smith are very pessimistic when it comes to poorer developing countries (Smith 2001; Maskus 2000).

The manner in which the majority of patents have been used in sub-Saharan Africa is illustrative of the problem for many developing countries. Rather than facilitating the importation of new technologies for production (or service fulfillment), patents have historically been used to maintain import monopolies (Kongolo 2000, 275). They have not been "worked" and therefore do precisely the opposite of what TRIPS rhetoric and its supporters promise. The patent holder is protected from any copying or competition regarding its technology while also gaining new markets through imports. In such cases, local production either by the patent holder or by imitators is foreclosed, ensuring no real economic developmental benefits (apart from the direct consumption of the product).

In the past, governments could respond to the nonworking of important patents by issuing compulsory licenses for domestic producers. Governments seldom used these mechanisms, however, because patent documents often did not provide sufficient information about the related know-how needed to deploy the technology even if a compulsory license were secured. Indeed, compulsory licensing is by no means a panacea. Local producers may lack adequate manufacturing capacity or may be inefficient producers. The most effective use of the policy instrument has been to *threaten* to seize a patent, as Brazil has done in its quest for affordable human immunodeficiency virus/acquired immunodeficiency syndrome (HIV/AIDS) drugs, and then to *negotiate* better terms of transfer or sharply reduced costs.[6] Nevertheless, compulsory licenses remained a potential policy response to problems related to technological (non)transfer (not least, as a policy bargaining chip). TRIPs strengthens the position of the patent holder who wishes merely to ship finished goods (but have them protected by a national patent). Indeed, with the specific inclusion in Articles 27 and 28 of imports, the importation of a patented technology effectively has been equated with "working" the patent (Dhar and Rao 1996, 321; Verma 1996, 355). In TRIPs, although it proved impossible to render compulsory licenses completely illegal,[7] the developed countries' negotiators did manage to put significant limits on the legal recourse to compulsory patent as regards nonworking and also in cases of national emergencies.

Therefore, under the various subclauses of Article 31, the circumstances under which WTO members can consider and utilize compulsory licenses are circumscribed. A compulsory license can no longer cover a whole field of technology (Article 31.a), and although Article 31.b provides a national emergency exception (including issues of public health), this has proved remarkably difficult to enact as the debates and conflicts around the Doha Declaration on the TRIPs Agreement and Public Health revealed. Furthermore, any compulsory license issued under TRIPs provisions must be limited to a specific purpose (Article 31.c); must be nonexclusive (Article 31.d), nontransferable, nonassignable (Article 31.e); must only be used to supply a domestic market (Article 31.f); must include "adequate remuneration" to the rights holder (Article 31.h); and must be subject to the prospect of judicial review (Article 31.i). These measures taken as a whole, even though stopping short of actually rendering compulsory licenses illegal under TRIPs, so limit the circumstances in which they can be utilized, as well as effectively limiting the uses to which such licensed technologies can be put, that the governments of developing countries (and indeed of developed countries) have seen this policy strategy effectively removed from their hands.[8]

Perhaps emblematic of the whole agreement, under Article 34, in the area of process patents, the burden of proof has been switched from the plaintiff (the owner of the patent) to the defendant (Dhar and Rao 1996, 315–317). If a product has been produced that is new, or it is likely that it has been produced by the patented process, it is up to the defendant to prove that the patented process has *not* been used. Thus, if the manufacturer is to prove that no infringement has occurred in circumstances where the patent's "owner has been unable to determine the process actually used," the details of manufacture will be forced into the public domain (General Agreement on Tariffs and Trade 1994, sec. A1C, 16). And although the agreement provides for the "legitimate interests of the defendant in protecting his manufacturing and business secrets [to] be taken into account," the balance of rights has shifted quite significantly to the owner of the original process patent (Verma 1996, 345–346). It is easy to imagine that when a new process for a particular product is developed in a particular jurisdiction, the patent holder of the previous process will find it possible through the courts to push its competitor into revealing the new process. When reverse engineering has failed, there is now legal recourse to force competitors to reveal how they are competing. Although apparently no one has filed such a suit, if they do, the historical legal notion that defendants might be innocent until proven guilty has been eradicated where the interests of corporate intellectual property holders deem it obstructive to the benefits that they enjoy from their property.

Despite the deadlock that had precluded Japan and the United States from signing the 1989 Washington Treaty on Intellectual Property in Respect of Integrated Circuits, these two countries, home to the two largest chip fabrication industries, acquiesced in having integrated circuits included in the TRIPs agreement. Leaving aside the previous arguments about the term of protection, with some strengthening of the provisions of the Washington treaty, it was incorporated into TRIPs under Articles 35 through 38, on the basis of the developing countries' argument that it represented an emerging pre–Uruguay Round international consensus (Matthews 2002, 63). Article 35 sets out this incorporation; Article 36 establishes the levels of protection for importing and selling of infringing (that is, copied) circuit boards.

Although under Article 37.2 the same limitations on compulsory licensing that are set out in Article 31 (see above) are invoked, Article 37.1 allows an exception due to ignorance that a circuit design is in infringement of a specific grant (although once revealed, such infringements must generate royalty payments to the rights holder). Resolving the earlier dispute, the Washington treaty's term of protection is extended from eight years to the ten years (from the date of filing an application for a grant) that Japan and the United States required, although the term of protection *may* be limited to fifteen years from creation of the lay-out should members so wish (Article 38.3). Some business representatives have suggested that this is a "third world draft" despite the strengthening from the Washington treaty (Matthews 2002, 63), but this may merely reveal that here the balance between conflicting interests has been better mediated than elsewhere in the agreement.

For the first time in international public law, TRIPs recognizes the protection of trade secrets (Article 39), mainly on the basis of unfair competition. The most important aspect of this measure is the use, and abuse, of commercially sensitive pharmaceutical test data (Maskus 2000, 22–23). Although limits are placed on the "unfair commercialization" of data and other "undisclosed information," the lack of a consensual position even among developed countries meant that the provisions have remained voluntary. The question of "fairness" is also raised by the final article of this section that seeks, on the basis of demands by developing countries' negotiators, to establish the control of anticompetitive practices in contractual licenses (Article 40). In light of these demands, Article 40.1 recognizes this problem and the rest of the paragraphs set out the manner in which such disputes can be resolved, including the prevention of certain licensing practices (Article 40.2) and mechanisms for international negotiation and mediation.

Having set out the standards and scope of protection of IPRs established by TRIPs, the next section moves on to the issue of enforcement of these rights. As the failure of previous conventions to provide enforceable protection was one of the key stimuli to negotiating the TRIPs agreement, it should be no surprise that this section presents a robust set of measures to ensure that IPRs will now be protected throughout the WTO membership. The articles set out the requirement for fair and equitable procedures (Article 42) and the evidence of proof required (Article 43). In another significant departure from previous international legislation, TRIPs adopts precedents developed in British law to grant applicants access to the premises of a defendant to seize and discover materials that might *potentially* represent an IPR infringement (Blakeney 1996, 126). Based on the 1976 *Anton Piller v. Manufacturing Processes* case under the Court of Appeal in Britain, the ability to act prior to an act of infringement of rights (the legal acceptance of the likelihood of infringement) had previously been available in only a small minority of jurisdictions.

Articles 44 through 49 set out further obligations as regards the procedures that rights holders can expect for remedies for infringement, even where such remedies are administrative (Article 49). These cover injunctions (Article 44), the expectation of damages when infringement occurs (Article 45), and other remedies such as disposal (where this does not compromise the rights holder's legitimate commercial interests) (Article 46). Infringers are also required to inform the authorities about third parties to the infringing actions (Article 47) and to pay defendants' expenses (Article 48). Under Article 61, the more serious offenses are required to be dealt with under criminal law, to allow for custodial sentences and sufficiently large fines to ensure a deterrence function. Article 62 ensures that the formalities in claiming the rights set out in TRIPs are both reasonable and prompt, to ensure that protection can be realistically claimed.

Furthermore, under Article 50 provisional measures are set out that were intended to ensure that the protections available under TRIPs would be available in advance of any legislative changes required to bring national laws into compliance with the agreement. In addition, because the TRIPs agreement focuses on the regulation of trade, a significant number of its provisions (Articles 51 through 60) deal with the powers of and requirements for border-related enforcement in each member's jurisdiction. Despite the impossibility of concluding a formal agreement on the exhaustion of rights, Article 51 does mandate clear limits to the importation of unauthorized goods from other jurisdictions. Under TRIPs this covers not only trademarked goods but also "pirated copyright goods . . . [and] goods which involve other infringements" of IPRs (General Agreement on Tariffs and Trade 1994, sec. A1C, 23). This reflects the centrality of the rhetoric of international intellectual property theft that permeated the negotiations that led to the agreement.

The most obvious, and politically contentious, effect of this aspect of TRIPs was to render the importation of pirated generic pharmaceuticals illegal for any WTO member, even if the health emergency provisions of the agreement had been enacted (as reasserted within the Doha ministerial declaration). There have been some moves to modify this aspect of TRIPs through the workings of the TRIPs Council. Nevertheless, with the inclusion of the requirement for border-control authorities to be responsible for policing IPR-related trade, the protection to IPR holders is strengthened both inside particular national legislatures, where before protection had been weak or ineffective, and between national jurisdictions, where many of the problems for consumer goods manufacturers lie (most obviously the problem of parallel imports).

To aid the management of TRIPs itself, and more generally the global governance of IPRs, Article 63 sets up the TRIPs Council (Article 63.2) in the interests of transparency in the realm of further negotiation, implementation, and interpretation of the agreement's requirements. This builds on a requirement for the publication by all members of judicial rulings and administrative decisions relating to IPRs (Article 63.1) and provides for requests for information by other WTO members (Article 63.3), although confidential and commercially sensitive information may be held back (Article 63.4). There is a real danger that this scrutiny may develop into a major administrative load, especially for underresourced developing country members of the WTO (Matthews 2002, 83), not least of all as it is already clear that many requests for information are duplications (or perhaps worse, not quite duplications and therefore requiring the drafting of "new" answers). This information can become vitally important as (of course) the new robust dispute mechanism at the WTO is explicitly empowered to deal with IPR-related, TRIPs-related, disputes (Article 64).

Finally TRIPs included some transitional arrangements (Articles 65 and 66) that with the exception of the Doha extension for pharmaceuticals have now lapsed and, perhaps more important, the provision of technical assistance (Article 67), which we deal with below. The final provisions included the formal establishment of the TRIPs Council (Article 68), a declaratory statement that members agreed to cooperate to eliminate the trade in infringing goods (Article 69), a requirement for review by the TRIPs Council (Article 71.1), the acknowledgment that no member wishing to take advantage of reservations in the agreement need seek formal consent from other members (Article 72), and a national security exemption (Article 73).

It is interesting, but not surprising, that although Article 71.2 sets out a mechanism for amending the TRIPs agreement in light of an agreement to raise the standards of protection, it has no provisions should WTO members seek to lower the levels of protection (indeed, measures for reducing protection are absent from the entire agreement) (Matthews 2002, 76). This leaves one final article: Article 70 sets out how TRIPs relates to previous sets of protections and confirms that the agreement does not give rise to obligations in respect of acts that occurred before the application of the agreement (Article 70.1) unless specifically set out in the previous articles (Article 70.2). Thus various paragraphs ensure that there is no need to retroactively remove items from the public domain. This position has led to some claims by multinational pharmaceutical companies that pipeline protection is included in the agreement (Matthews 2002, 75), despite only the more limited establishment of "mailbox" arrangements for developing countries (Article 70.8). This is linked to the provision of exclusive marketing rights (where a patent system is yet to be established) (Article 70.9), but certainly does not establish pipeline protection for pharmaceuticals under development but not yet in commercial production.

To conclude this discussion of TRIPs' various provisions, we can see that TRIPs widened and entrenched a particular perspective regarding IPRs that had previously been part of the much weaker governance regime overseen by WIPO. The agreement changes a number of aspects of the previous agreements. Its most significant elements have been, however, (1) to bring all members of the WTO under the same set of principles and minimum standards for the recognition and protection of IPRs; (2) to give this governance regime "teeth" by applying the WTO's dispute settlement mechanism to any international disputes regarding the undertakings within TRIPs; and (3) by linking IPRs to the wider issues of international trade at the WTO, to make significant inroads into the hitherto sovereign ability of countries to establish, govern, and regulate intellectual property in response to perceived national political economic priorities.

At the core of TRIPs is a particular set of norms regarding the treatment of knowledge as property. These norms underpin the entire agreement and are based on the notion that the private ownership of knowledge as property is a major spur to continued economic development and social welfare. They further emphasize the development of knowledge as an individualized endeavor and the legitimate reward of such individualized effort. It is most obvious that this includes a robust norm of commodification of knowledge and information. Although the agreement is potentially quite flexible, as evidenced by the negotiations over the Doha ministerial declaration on public health, the forces that support a particular reading of the agreement are difficult to overcome. The Doha declaration itself, despite extensive negotiations, *only* reasserted the broad thrust of the original text's invocation of health emergencies as legitimate reasons for the compulsory license of pharmaceuticals.

The TRIPs agreement represents a major watershed in the international history of intellectual property, but the establishment (finally) of a globalized regime of governance has also revealed some serious problems and disputes. Although a significant and important moment in the governance of IPRs, TRIPs, as has been the case throughout history, has engendered considerable contestation, and the (global) politics of IPRs have become more fraught in the last decade since the agreement became international law with the establishment of the WTO. We now move to this most recent period.

After TRIPs: Contestation, Bilateralism, and Problems of Legitimacy

Since the adoption of TRIPs the issue of intellectual property has continued to move up on the global political agenda; governments of many countries have become worried about the impact of TRIPs compliance on other political priorities (such as economic development, public health, and technology transfer); various nongovernmental groups (sometimes grouped together as civil society) have worked hard to publicize the social costs of recognizing strong owners' rights in the realm of knowledge and information (most successfully as regards pharmaceutical patents); and technological changes, especially digitization, have caused companies in some industrial sectors to become increasingly concerned about the ability of even TRIPs-compliant legislation to protect their business models (here the music industry is emblematic). Rather than finally settling the governance of IPRs at the global level, TRIPs paradoxically has revealed the numerous political problems with recognizing and enforcing IPRs. These problems, as we have indicated, are hardly new; their current global manifestation, however, has revealed them to a wider (political) audience than at any time in the past. In this sense, the new millennium may see the emergence of a new global politics of knowledge.

One of the key elements of IPRs has always been the political attempt to balance the private rights to rewards accorded owners with the public (and social) benefits of information access and availability. Although hardly plausible in the current negotiating climate, the opt-in model of obligations utilized by the GATS, even if not perfect, might have been more appropriate for TRIPs, as Constantine Michalopoulos has suggested (Michalopoulos 2003, 20). This would have allowed the establishment of *special and differential* treatment for the developing countries in a more robust and defensible manner than the exceptions-driven logic of their accession to TRIPs. Certainly, political pressure has driven the extension of the transition period for some developing countries, but only relating to pharmaceuticals, back to 2016. At a global level, extending special and differential treatment would allow the balance between the private rights of developed country–based multinationals and the public-regarding welfare aspects in poorer developing countries to be restructured.

To a great extent this balancing, at the global level, has been skewed by the manner in which rights and obligations were set out in TRIPs' text. The developing countries' obligations (to renew their national legislation) and the developed countries rights (as regards their nationals' IPRs) are enforceable through the WTO's dispute settlement mechanism and are clearly expressed in the text of TRIPs. As Robert Wade pointed out, for the complementary set of rights and obligations this is less true, however. The developing countries' rights (to economic development) and the developed countries' obligations (to aid technology transfer to underpin that right) are much less enforceable. These are only set out in general terms in TRIPs' text and are much more difficult and expensive to litigate (Wade 2003, 624). All rights seem to reside with the owners, whereas all duties reside with the users of intellectual property. In one area the developed countries *are* to some extent fulfilling their obligations; Article 67 obliges developed countries to provide technical cooperation to the WTO's developing country members.[9]

Under Article 67 the developed countries have organized a major program of capacity building to support the establishment of TRIPs compliance by developing countries. From Geneva, WIPO runs the Cooperation for Development Program, providing support and training, and in Munich the European Patent Office offers various programs (from awareness raising to model legislation). The World Bank has also included IPRs in its own wider legal training program and aids countries to develop TRIPs-compliant legislation and practices. Other organizations, ranging from the WTO itself and the United Nations Conference on Trade and Development (UNCTAD) to nongovernmental organizations (NGOs), also provide various forms of support. In the realm of bilateral aid, the US Agency for International Development (USAID) now spends around a quarter of its annual budget on legal and regulatory training, including technical assistance from the US Patent and Trademark Office (USPTO), to help bring domestic legislation into compliance with TRIPs, including assessments of draft laws and recommendations regarding existing laws.

Most developing countries are likely to be dependent on this assistance to establish the mechanisms and legal infrastructure required by their TRIPs obligations because such political-legal transformations require considerable resources and investment. Although TRIPs does not actually mandate the forms of law that any member may adopt, Michael Finger and Philip Schuler have concluded that "moving away from established standards may be particularly difficult in the area of intellectual property rights. They are, after all, an existential matter of legal definition, not a scientific matter of empirical estimation . . . [Thus] the benefit of the doubt will rest with systems presently in place in the industrialized countries" (Finger and Schuler 1999, 20).

Capacity building and technical assistance programs seldom support novel or different solutions to the problems of IPR protection. Indeed, capacity building seems to have a clear object: it aims to ensure that developing countries do not exploit fully the flexibilities for national legislation (Austin 2002; Reichman 1997). Rather, national solutions are only supported when this does not conflict with TRIPs' invocation of required legal effect and, more important, when it dovetails with the "best practice" acknowledged by the various agencies involved in technical assistance. These programs represent a form of socialization for WTO members, and as such present the form of IPRs constituted in TRIPs as a technical solution to a set of problems regarding a posited "market failure" in knowledge and information utilization.

This strategy does not self-evidently serve many developing countries' immediate best interests. Indeed, in an attempt to ensure that their clients are not caught up in costly IPR-related trade disputes with developed country members of the WTO, the staff of WIPO have often encouraged developing countries to adopt legislation that goes beyond the formal requirements of the TRIPs agreement (Drahos 2002, 777). In any case, and in the wake of bilateral trade agreements with the United States and the EU, a number of developing countries have found themselves needing "TRIPs-plus" legislation, which again reinforces this dynamic within the assistance program at WIPO. Thus, in trying to help developing countries avoid trade disputes, assistance programs themselves have often undermined the possibilities of diplomatic (and democratic) critical engagement with the agreement itself.

TRIPs has also engendered a political response, especially in those developing countries where significant groups remain skeptical of the appropriateness of the TRIPs model (of which the farmers' rights movement in India is perhaps the best-known example). Recent debates have ranged across a number of sectors, sometimes focusing on perceptions of biopiracy (Shiva 2001, 49–68), elsewhere concerned with pharmaceutical products, or software piracy, and the "theft" of traditional knowledge (Gervais 2002). These debates directly affect the legitimacy of the intellectual property norms that are being imported into developing countries through technical assistance. As Peter Drahos and John Braithwaite pointed out, however, whatever critiques may be mobilized against these norms of propertization, the global regime governing IPRs sets "strong limits on a state's capacity to define territorial property rights in ways that enhance national welfare" (Drahos and Braithwaite 2002, 75). It is these welfare effects in developing countries that are the central problem in the global governance of IPRs, but welfare is seldom given the weight in international trade law that it is in other areas of international law.

Of course, as always, the reality is more complex than this might suggest. As in the case of the US electrical industry (led by Edison and championing strong intellectual property protection) versus the fledgling US pharmaceutical industry (seeking weak intellectual property rights to curb German predominance) in 1919, sharp divisions of interests and preferences exist within each country. In addition, as countries "move up" the ladder of innovation and economic success, they become more amenable to intellectual property rights for their own welfare (versus coercion or foreign imposition). For example, countries such as India and China possess some strong sectors clamoring for increased intellectual property rights. Even within sectors, preferences for property rights often vary between large enterprises and small and medium-sized businesses. As this suggests, national developmental strategies in the realm of intellectual property law are likely to vary widely in accordance with local circumstances. This complexity is not unique to the national level, however.

The relationship between WTO law and the rest of international law is more complex than attempts to privilege the WTO's rules might imply. Joost Pauwelyn has argued at some length that the law that can be applied in WTO dispute panels and in the Appellate Body is not limited to *intra*-WTO law. Rather, by virtue of the place of the WTO's legal regime within the complex of international law, "a defendant should be allowed to invoke non-WTO rules as justification for breach of WTO rules, even if the WTO treaty itself does not offer such justification (say, with respect to human rights) . . . [and more important] non-WTO rules may actually apply before a WTO panel and overrule WTO rules" (Pauwelyn 2001, 577). The automatic assumption that WTO law should be privileged is a misconception of the WTO's relationship with the general body of international law. Certainly it is a complex and dynamic relationship; the privileging of other agreements over WTO treaty undertakings cannot be assumed one way or the other. For IPRs, however, the effects of full TRIPs compliance must be assessed in relation to other multilateral undertakings and a political case made for which treaty's undertakings should take precedence.

The problem is that at the same time that the rights rhetoric is mobilized to justify IPRs within TRIPs, the practical organization of international rights has been effectively depoliticized through the juridical systems of enforcement and appeal. By removing conflicts regarding the protection and enforcement of IPRs from the political/diplomatic realm and placing them in the legal realm, the TRIPs agreement reduces international disputes to the question of whether specific legislation is TRIPs compliant; it depoliticizes subsequent disputes. Political engagement between the parties has been legalized, and in the process previous "wiggle room," flexibility, or gray areas within the governance regime for IPRs have been removed (Weiler 2000). If the TRIPs agreement is perceived as essentially legitimate, then this strategy would allow the governance regime to do its intended work, but it is far from clear that TRIPs *is* regarded as legitimate throughout the membership of the WTO.

As Daya Shanker has argued at some length, quite apart from the legitimacy problems that the effects of TRIPs have engendered, the agreement's legitimacy is also undermined by the way it has been deployed by the more powerful members of the WTO (Shanker 2003). Not only were the negotiations themselves fraught with dispute, the decisions of the Appellate Body have shifted the demands on developing countries as regards the manner in which their legislation can achieve TRIPs compliance. For instance, although the Appellate Body has been willing to accept administrative (rather than legislative) undertakings regarding patenting practice by the United States, this has not been the case for India and Brazil, among others, whose practices closely match those of the United States in the area of parallel importation (Shanker 2003, 177). Furthermore, despite the formal mechanisms for establishing TRIPs compliance, the United States and the EU have also deployed bilateral pressure to force developing countries to rework their legislation in the manner that undermines the multilateral legal status of TRIPs and the Appellate Body. The bilateral use of sanctions to enforce GATT/WTO-linked law has been rendered illegal unless sanctioned by the Appellate Court, but this has not halted their continued use by the US Trade Representative (USTR) as regards IPRs (Sen 2003, 128; Shanker 2003, 186). Although the question of formal legal legitimacy matters, however, the *social* impact of TRIPs has stimulated a widespread and growing political reaction.

As we noted in Chapter 1, the high profile disputes over access to AIDS-related pharmaceuticals through compulsory licensing for generic producers established for many political organizations the importance of TRIPs. In areas ranging from the music industry to biotechnology, however, the question of IPRs owners' rights has become the subject of significant political debates. We have chosen four specific issues to explore that we regard as good examples of the contemporary political economy of IPRs in the global realm. There are many other issues that we could have selected, but we have chosen issues intended to illustrate specific and important trends in the politics of IPRs. This certainly should not be regarded as an exhaustive list of looming problems.

Digital Rights Management and Fair Use

In the last few years the legal recognition and protection of digital rights management (DRM) software has been included in regional (EU) and national (US, UK) legislation.[10] These moves were prompted by the 1996 WIPO Copyright Treaty that many developing countries are also under pressure to adopt alongside their TRIPs commitments. The WIPO treaty, which we discuss in Chapter 8, includes under Articles 11 and 12 significant legal measures supporting the introduction of DRM technologies into the realm of intellectual property, although like TRIPs compliance, the form of implementation of these requirements remains a national concern.

The US Congress passed the Digital Millennium Copyright Act (DMCA) in 1998, which was the enabling legislation for the WIPO copyright treaty. The software and entertainment industry, music and film associations, lobbied very hard for protection of works disseminated on the Internet (Yu 2004, 910). They prevailed over the vociferous opposition of public interest advocates such as librarians, law professors, and electronic civil liberties activists (Vaidhyanathan 2001, 175). As Merges pointed out, "given the potential economic stakes and Congress's desire to please the new media industries, the end result surprised no one: strong legal recognition of technical protection schemes" (Merges 2000, 2201).

The DMCA offers broad protection for digital works. It prohibits circumvention of any technological protection against copying and prevents the production of any device or provision of any service designed to defeat protection mechanisms. By directly prohibiting the use of specific technologies, "the protection of expression" is now "achieved through the regulation of devices" (Merges 2000, 2202). As Vaidhyanathan argued, for the first time the law "puts the power to regulate copying in the hands of engineers and the companies that employ them. It takes the decision-making power away from Congress, courts, librarians, writers, artists, and researchers" (Vaidhyanathan 2001, 174). Critics have charged that these provisions go too far and constrict activities that were once considered to be fair use. For instance, a professor can use copyrighted material for educational purposes under the doctrine of fair use. Since the DMCA, professors may not incorporate copyrighted material into a PowerPoint presentation because "the music and motion picture industries are using copy protection to prevent such duplication. The DMCA makes any attempt to circumvent copy protection a criminal offense, even if the ultimate goal is considered fair use" (Marlin-Bennett 2004, 86). Industry has used the DMCA to prevent the dissemination of information about circumventing encryption technologies; for example, "Professor Edward Felten of Princeton University was asked to withdraw his paper from a scholarly conference, lest he be prosecuted under the DMCA" (Yu 2004, 911–912). Therefore, according to critics, free speech and academic freedom are also at risk under this law. By contrast, content providers praise this expanded protection, although they complain that it is difficult to enforce (Marlin-Bennett 2004, 85).

As the debates over the DMCA in the United States have demonstrated, the use of DRM, and its legal enforcement, can represent a major challenge for previous practices (and precedents) regarding fair use or, in European terms, fair dealing.[11] It seems likely that the deployment of DRM technologies will consolidate (or even worsen) the uneven distribution of information and knowledge across the so-called digital divide. This is most obvious in the collapse of the generally accepted social norms of content usage. On one side, content users have utilized technology they have purchased legally to "infringe" on the rights of content owners (MP3 technologies being the best-known example); on the other, content owners have actually expanded the potential scope of their rights (relative to previous settlements). As Reichman and Uhlir pointed out:

> In effect, the DMCA allows copyright owners to surround their collections of data with technological fences and electronic identity marks buttressed by encryption and other digital controls that force would-be users to enter the system through an electronic gateway. To pass through the gateway, users must accede to nonnegotiable electronic contracts, which impose the copyright owner's terms and conditions without regard to the traditional defenses and statutory immunities of copyright law. (Reichman and Uhlir 2003, 378)

Therefore, one of the key elements of the problem of DRM is the solidification of aspects of copyright law that have hitherto been indeterminate at the margins, with areas of legal grayness amenable to politics and diplomacy circumscribed or removed. Previously the assertion of rivalrousness had been effectively managed through its incompleteness and the recognition of certain fair use of rights-bearing works. Rather than construct a sharp division between owners' rights and theft, in the twentieth century an area at the edge of the realm of IPRs' coverage, which has been de facto unenforced as regards owners' rights but within the realm of de jure protection owners might expect, was developed. For most industries this led to a tacit acceptance of "piracy" or "leakage" while it was of relatively minor extent. Digitalization has transformed the terrain on which this settlement rested, however.

Digitalization has removed the quality/copy trade-off, by allowing generational copies to be, for all intents and purposes, exact copies of the original digital artifact, and thus the monopoly on high quality reproduction has been removed from authorized distribution channels. A "frictionless environment" for content, where successive copies do not degrade (Scott 2001), immediately raises the potential threat that once a digital good is distributed, unauthorized copies can compete throughout its market for consumer use. And whereas in the past the users of copied goods would receive an inferior product, and thus the price discrimination between authorized and unauthorized copies was clearly reflected in the quality of product, digital copies have removed this distinction. The speed of this technological advance "forced" the content industries to respond (Kim 2003, 97), but this also means that the previously legitimated political process for (re)balancing private and public rights/benefits has been left behind in the scramble for protection. Reichman and Uhlir found this state of affairs troubling insofar as the DMCA grants new powers to "owners of copyrightable collections of facts to contractually limit online access to the pre-existing public domain in ways that contrast drastically with the traditional availability of factual contents in printed words" (Reichman and Uhlir 2003, 379).

Digital rights management technologies were intended to shore up private rights and finally establish the rights that, it was claimed, had been promised for years in IPR laws. This also made the constriction of the public realm more obvious, however, by removing the mediated area that older technologies had left as a buffer zone between contending interests over knowledge and information usage. This raises two problems: first, the assumption underlying DRM is that private rights are privileged, leaving public access as the gift of the owner, a policy that represents a significant denial of the historic role of the public domain (but reflects TRIPs' privileging of private interests/rights); second, by making use requests explicit and user driven, owners may be swamped by requests (producing delays), and users may be dissuaded at the margins from using certain informational resources owing to the process of requesting permissions (Kim 2003, 112). More generally there may be a "chilling" effect on the use of copyrighted materials.

As Jessica Litman has argued, copyright laws "never gave copyright owners rights as expansive as those they have recently argued were their due" during debates around the "copyright problem" online (Litman 2001, 114). Indeed, the move to enact measures such as the DMCA has not reflected the balance of interests that copyright laws slowly established over their political history. Rather, this is another attempt, facilitated by technological advances, to expand the rights of one specific interest, the owners, with little regard for the diminution of the other interests accorded weight by copyright in the past: the public or social good of access. The report by the Commission on Intellectual Property Rights (commissioned by the British Department for International Development) concluded that for developing countries, "where Internet connectivity is limited and subscriptions to on-line resources unaffordable, [DRM technologies] may exclude access to these materials altogether and impose a heavy burden that will delay the participation of those countries in the global knowledge-based society' (Commission on Intellectual Property Rights 2002, 106). The extra controls that subscription online services and copy-protected products allow content owners dissipate the hard-won compromises for users that have been encapsulated by previous understandings of fair use or fair dealing.

Lawrence Lessig has argued that DRM and other linked control technologies may allow powerful industries to "leverage" their control of "real" markets into a control of "virtual" markets on the Internet (Lessig 2001b, 200 passim). This is not to say that Lessig is necessarily arguing against copyright or other forms of IPRs; rather, he is concerned about the likely reorientation of IPRs' balance between private rights and public goods. As he noted, recently IPR regimes have expanded beyond their initial justification (as encapsulated in law): "the restrictions [IPR law] imposes are artificial . . . they simply benefit one person at the expense of another. . . . [But] if they limit the range of creativity by virtue of the system of control they erect, why do we have them?" (Lessig 2001b, 217). Indeed, this normative problem reveals that the questions around DRM technologies are not questions of technical efficacy and cost, but rather the problem of mediating clashing interests in a relatively new technological realm.

The legitimization of IPRs, as laid out in the extensively used narratives of justification we discussed at the beginning of this book, assumes that property rights in knowledge serve a set of social goods. Chief among these is that social advance is served by the innovation and creation that copyright, patents, and other forms of IPRs support. Although these justifications stress private rights, they also imply a "knowledge commons" that is enlarged by the temporary enclosure of knowledge to encourage further intellectual activity. The globalization of the control of content that DRM allows produces two clear problems for global society as regards the enforcement of IPRs: a disjuncture between the society in which rights are protected and the society in which users' costs are evident; and the breakdown of the mediated settlement over IPRs, leading to a "blowback" that is already evident in the music industry. The desire of owners to enact monopoly controls has led content users to become more cynical about perceived profiteering, and hence the rhetoric of responsible consumption (allied to the narratives of private rewards) has started to crumble (May 2003). These problems represent a breakdown in the social, or normative, bargain that had previously underpinned the recognition, use, and acceptance of IPRs.

In many national jurisdictions there remains a chance that public and/or political opinion can be mobilized either to restrain the actual enforcement of rights and their scope or to (re)establish fair use through legal means as a recognition of the continued needs of the public realm. Furthermore, in national jurisdictions, the bargain between private rights and public access has an easily discernible pay-off: the society involved reaps the benefits of innovation and creativity. In the global realm, given the extremes of economic inequality, alongside necessarily diffused user communities, the rewards flow to a relatively closed group, and the social advantages of advances may be limited by the constrictions put on use of content goods.

Where poor groups are excluded from use, access to ascertain any fair use demands may not be possible (that is, they may not be able to discover what specific content-goods might serve their needs without first paying for them). This has led Ruth Okediji (2000) to argue that although there are some aspects of fair use that can still be discovered within TRIPs, such provisions are fragmented and unsatisfactory. She has argued that an "international fair use doctrine" is required that would better reflect the explicit objective of Article 7 of TRIPs, expressing the agreement's support for national legislation that balances rights *and* obligations. The case of DRM demonstrates once again the power of technological innovations to disrupt the legal settlements around IPRs, and certainly as with other innovations in content distribution from print to video recording, there is likely to be a period where the previous balance between private rights and public benefits (or social use) remains disrupted before political process produces, through a series of explicit and implicit negotiations, a newly legitimated balance. In the post-TRIPs world, however, the political process and deliberation (at the WTO or elsewhere) may seriously be truncated owing to the wholesale shift in the balance of rights and obligations and to the tension between global regulation and national political deliberative processes.

Economic Development and Technology Transfer

Another crucial set of debates about the contemporary realm of IPRs involves technology transfer and national economic development. The previous chapters have demonstrated that from Venice onward, the legal recognition of IPRs was dependent on *national* registration or national production to serve explicit mercantile interests. More recently, the privileging of trade interests in IPR protection has almost completely obscured these development aspects. Developed countries' trade negotiators and governments now suggest that economic development is best served by the commodification of knowledge. For many developing countries, the more pressing need is to access information and knowledge that will support their further economic development cheaply or at no cost. In a very real sense the two sides are talking past one another (Bawa 1997, 96). This might suggest that the location of the global governance of IPRs in the

WTO (at least for the developing countries) is itself the most pressing problem because it foregrounds the trade-related aspects of IPRs.

In the experience of the newly industrialized countries (NICs) of East Asia, the tension between trade and development issues becomes clear. The reliance on weak (or nonexistent) IPR protection in the early stages of development was instrumental in the NICs' success. Surveying a number of studies, Nagesh Kumar concluded that

> the east Asian countries, viz., Japan, Korea and Taiwan have absorbed substantial amount[s] of technological learning under weak IPR protection regime[s] during the early phases [of economic development]. These patent regimes facilitated the absorption of innovation and knowledge generated abroad by their indigenous firms. They have also encouraged minor adaptations and incremental innovations on the foreign inventions by domestic enterprises. (Kumar 2003, 216)

Certainly when local industries themselves started to innovate, then a stronger regime of protection was established, *but only then*. Here, the character of national laws (only recognizing national invention or creation) supported the appropriation of foreign knowledge and information, as it did when the United States, and before that Britain, were developing countries.

As Dru Brenner-Beck pointed out in his extensive study of countries that had utilized the nonrecognition of IPRs as a development strategy, "former pirate activities strongly contributed to the development of the infrastructure and technical capacity necessary to ensure that the touted advantages of intellectual property protection actually materialize" (Brenner-Beck 1992, 115). The protection of IPRs only makes policy sense once a certain level of technological momentum has been achieved. This threshold requires developing countries to have developed the social infrastructure that can allow the posited benefits of IPRs to be captured by domestic societies; such benefits were characterized by Brenner-Beck as including "an educated workforce, a basic industrial capacity, domestic entrepreneurial ability, and domestic capital mobilization" (Brenner-Beck 1992, 103). The development of these factors is supported in its early stages by the ability to obtain new technologies without the costs associated with patents. In today's climate, even though some studies show a positive correlation between strong intellectual property laws and higher volumes of international technology transfer, there is a trade-off in terms of costs—that is, "increased payments per unit of technology" (Maskus and Reichman 2004, 290).

Furthermore, given the current debates regarding pharmaceutical patents, it is as well to recall that France, Germany, Japan, and Switzerland, among others, only extended patent protection into this sector in the 1960s and 1970s, by which time their industries had matured. Indeed, as we have established, since the fifteenth century the national restrictions on who was granted patents represented a strategic development policy to encourage the importation of innovation by domestic companies (and before them artisans). It is ironic that having reached the heights of economic development, the governments of the most developed countries now argue in multilateral negotiations that the very protection they ignored in their years of speedy expansion will actually aid and support the economic development of other countries.

The costs to the developing countries of protecting IPRs are high: the World Bank has estimated annual "net patent rents" on full implementation of the TRIPs agreement (in 2000 US dollars), revealing a very clear tendency for funds to flow away from developing countries and to developed countries' patent holders. These figures suggested that the United States in 2002 received annualized payments of around $19 billion, whereas the Republic of Korea (being at the forefront of TRIPs compliance and a model of economic development for many) experienced a net outflow of more than $15 billion. Although some developed countries gained rents (the UK, nearly $3 billion; Germany, $6.768 billion), and some experienced outward flows (New Zealand, just over $2 billion; Canada, $574 million net outflows), most noteworthy were the annual outflows from the developing countries listed (Brazil, $530 million; China, $5.121 billion; India, $903 million) (World Bank 2002, 133, table 5.1). Phillip McCalman concluded that these "transfers significantly alter the perceived distribution of benefits from the Uruguay Round trade liberalization measures" (McCalman 2001, 163). Using figures similar to those of the World Bank, although not completely in agreement with them, McCalman suggested that only six countries stand to gain from patent harmonization (the United States, Germany, France, Italy, Sweden, and Switzerland), with all other countries experiencing various levels of net loss (McCalman 2001, 178). Significant rent-seeking behavior predominates, rather than the posited encouragement of technological transfer.

To take just one case, the demand for fees itself can be used to stifle development and reinforce technological monopolies. As part of its obligations under the Montreal Protocol to phase out chlorofluorocarbons (CFCs) and other substances that contribute to the degradation of the ozone layer, the Indian government needed to have the Indian manufacturers of components that were used in refrigerators and air conditioners change their production processes. The manufacturers' preferred alternative was to utilize a less environmentally damaging substitute chemical called hydrofluorocarbon (HFC) 134a. The patent holder, when approached by one Indian company for an international license, quoted the price of US$25 million. Knowing that this was beyond the Indian company's resources, the corporation proposed that either the company could ensure that none of the products using the patented technology were exported from India (limiting the company's access to global markets) or, in a move reminiscent of Thomas Edison's dealings with James Swan, that they set up a joint venture in which the patent-holding corporation, not the Indian company, would hold the majority stake (thereby gaining access to both the market and the local technical knowledge the company deployed domestically). Neither alternative was acceptable, especially as independent analysts had set the cost of the license at a more affordable US$6–8 million (Khor 2002, 206–207). Here a patent was used to maintain (and even expand) the power of the patent's owner, constraining the transfer of technology unless the Indians acceded to a relationship of economic domination. Although technology transfer may be offered, the terms of that transfer can be abusive.

Another method of control is the use of patent grants to maintain import monopolies. As we have noted, considerable efforts were mobilized in the negotiations that led to TRIPs to ensure that the nonworking of patents was diminished as a justification for compulsory license. Generally, the possibilities of compulsory licensing appear under Article 31 "Other Use Without Authorization of the Right Holder" (General Agreement on Tariffs and Trade 1994, sec. A1C, 14–15), although the usual terminology of compulsory license is conspicuous by its absence here and elsewhere in the agreement (although it *does* reappear in the Doha Ministerial Declaration on Public Health). Rather than harmonizing previous arrangements, Article 31 adds restrictions (specifically on prelicense efforts at agreement with the patent holder and the limitation of scope of use of the compulsory license) that did not appear in Article 5A of the Paris convention that it replaces (Oddi 1996, 456). Various US-based industry organizations had expressed displeasure with the 1960s revisions of Article 5A that could allow governments to appropriate property in the public interest (Reichman and Hasenzahl 2002, 6–8) and lobbied heavily to change these "concessions."[12] Thus, it is no accident that Article 31 of TRIPs quite severely circumscribes the use of compulsory licenses.[13]

It is difficult to see how to ameliorate these problems within the TRIPs governance regime as it currently stands. As Kumar noted, these changes constrict "an important contributor to growth that has been variously described as imitative duplication, reverse engineering or knowledge spillovers from abroad" (Kumar 2003, 221). Expanded patent and copyright protections may serve to "prohibit reverse engineering by honest means" (Maskus and Reichman, 2004, 297). But attitudes regarding the usefulness or value of enforcing IPRs may change with increased development. As Rafik Bawa suggested, "while the ideological conception of attaching property rights to products of the mind may be novel to [developing countries], it is novel primarily because the conception runs counter to their developmental objectives rather than because of any inherent moral objection to the concept in and of itself" (Bawa 1997, 111). Once the social interest shifts from the widest possible dissemination of useful ideas to the support of indigenous innovation, then policymakers' perceptions regarding IPRs may well change.[14] Countries such as India, the Republic of Korea, and China now have some important sectors in which enterprises are eager for intellectual property protection. Given that even under TRIPs, IPR legislation is still a domestic matter (albeit subject to the discipline of the WTO), differences in levels of development and political economic circumstances continue to lead different countries' governments to assess their needs from IPR-related legislation quite differently (Austin 2002). The problem is that the unevenness of the global political economy is not well enough recognized within TRIPs' required undertakings. A one-size-fits-all approach cannot fully reflect the diversity of the WTO's membership's needs and capabilities.

It is not so much that the transfer of technology is explicitly obstructed by TRIPs but rather that this purpose has been subsumed beneath the protection of individualized rights. This contrasts with the historical deployment of IPR legislation in the (now) developed countries and has been increasingly seen as a major iniquity within the WTO/TRIPs system. Indeed, rather than enhance free trade, the IPR system consolidates the competitive advantage of high-tech companies in the developed world at the cost of technological backwardness in the developing economies. As Jerome Reichman put it, "oligopolists in developed countries seek to make it harder for firms in developing countries to gain access to the most valuable technologies or otherwise to catch up with the leaders in the global market for higher-tech products" (Reichman 1997, 22). Referring to these oligopolists as a "knowledge cartel," Maskus and Reichman more recently argued that since "they depend on sales of existing innovation, they push their governments to regulate the global market in ways that lock in temporary advantages without necessarily advancing the global public interest in innovation, competition, or the provision of complementary public goods" (Maskus and Reichman 2004, 295). These practices are reminiscent of General Electric and the electric light cartels and of the antibiotics cartel discussed earlier. Insofar as the "knowledge cartel" was the driving force behind TRIPs and shaped its provisions to its liking, TRIPs seems to be more a mechanism for retarding development than any stimulus to technology transfer. In this context, compulsory licensing, patent misuse doctrines, and vigorous competition (antitrust) policies are essential to protect against abusive and anticompetitive business practices.

Biotechnology, Biopiracy, and the "New Imperialism"?

A third prominent set of debates in the discussion of IPRs has been the development of new biotechnologies. Biotechnology itself builds on centuries of husbandry, the accumulation of knowledge about the manner in which the "building blocks" of nature work together, and a period of extensive public-sector support for science since 1945. The development during the 1970s and into the 1980s of sophisticated methods for cutting and splicing deoxyribonucleic acid (DNA) coincided with a plateau in the chemical development of pharmaceuticals. Searching for new compounds to commercialize, and new or innovative products, companies working in agriculture, food, medicines, and more generally chemicals saw in the biotechnology revolution a new set of resources to exploit and further develop. Although the accelerating biotechnology sector, in the first instance, hardly relied on IPRs (not least as many innovations were produced in public laboratories), industrial interests required exclusive control of these new resources to exploit them profitably (Drahos and Braithwaite 2002, 154). Hence, industry's increasing recognition of biotechnology's commercial potential touched off a patent "gold rush."

In the wake of the US Supreme Court's decision in *Diamond v. Chakrabarty* in 1980, by a five to four majority, that genetically *modified* organisms could be patented, it is not surprising that the rate of patent applications further accelerated. Although the USPTO had originally rejected Chakrabarty's application for a patent covering a genetically engineered bacterium (that would be used to break up crude oil), the Supreme Court's decision went on to have a global significance. Previously, in 1969, both the Australian and the German patent offices had reached this conclusion, but it was only the US decision that really established the legal grounds for the emergence of a strongly IPRs-oriented biotechnology sector, not least of all as most of the key players were based in the United States (Drahos and Braithwaite 2002, 158–159). Although the Supreme Court may have intended this decision to be read narrowly, the outcome has been that since 1980 the scope of patentable materials has widened considerably to encompass much that might have previously been regarded as natural, and hence outside the realm of intellectual property.

In this issue area, TRIPs is not the only governance mechanism: the Convention on Bio-Diversity (CBD) and the UPOV convention also have some impact on how biological matter of various forms is rendered as (intellectual) property.

Article 27 of TRIPs concerns patentable subject matter and lays out the standard criteria for granting patents (newness, nonobviousness, and usefulness) in paragraph one. The second and third paragraphs then establish allowable exclusions from patentability. Paragraph two establishes a moral or "order public" exception to "protect human, animal or plant life or health or to avoid serious prejudice to the environment, provided such exclusion is not made merely because the exploitation is prohibited by domestic law" (General Agreement on Tariffs and Trade 1994, sec. A1C, 13). Further important exceptions to patentability are contained in paragraph three:

Members may also exclude from patentability:
(a) diagnostic, therapeutic and surgical methods for the treatment of humans or animals;
(b) plants and animals other than microorganisms, and essentially biological processes for the production of plants or animals other than non-biological and microbiological processes. However, Members shall provide for the protection of plant varieties either by patents or by an effective *sui generis* system or by any combination thereof. (General Agreement on Tariffs and Trade 1994, sec. A1C, 13)

These possible exclusions from patentability reflected the domestic law of many developing countries that hitherto had extended no protection to living organisms and also the political disquiet in European countries about "patents on life" (Matthews 2002, 58; Sell 2003, 111–112). Thus, paragraph 27.3(b) allows plants and animals, as well as "essentially biological processes," to be excluded from patentability but does require some form of protection for plant varieties. This marks the intersection of TRIPs, UPOV convention, and the CBD.

Being permissive rather than introducing a mandatory limitation on patentability, this exclusion immediately suggests that bilateral pressure can be brought to bear on developing countries to extend the scope of patents in their domestic law. Many developing countries' governments are critical of patents in the area of biological resources, partly because of their own (varied) national histories of community ownership of biological resources and partly because patenting has become a central mechanism for the capture (and exploitation by developed country–based corporations) of natural resources and their genetic materials. Thus, Jeanne Zoundjihekpon noted that because IPRs encompass neither farmers' rights, "even though these are recognized by the Food and Agriculture Organization (FAO), nor the local community rights highlighted in Article 8(j) of the CBD, a conflict arises between biodiversity and the world trade rules" (Zoundjihekpon 2003, 110). Indeed, the multilateralism (and legal harmonization) envisaged by TRIPs is in direct contrast with the sovereign rights countries enjoy over their natural resources that the CBD explicitly recognizes.

Unlike TRIPs, Article 8j of the CBD recognizes the idea of communal knowledge; such knowledge is not assignable to an individual, who can then enjoy rights of ownership. This article of the CBD concerns the need to respect and preserve communal knowledge resources, partly to ensure the sanctity of traditional practices and lifestyles but also "to promote their wider application with the approval and involvement of the holders of such knowledge, innovation and utilization of such knowledge, innovations and practices" (cited in Sell 2003, 144–145). Implicitly this suggests that assigning ownership rights to individuals would constrain the dissemination and further development of these communal techniques and practices.

Article 16 of the CBD recognizes the utility of biotechnology patenting, however, and the convention fails to explicitly protect bioresources from commodification, although it does allow more latitude than TRIPs to national legislatures to limit patenting of genetically modified biological organisms on the basis of their environmental impact.[15] The CBD also focuses on national sovereignty as regards the use and exploitation of these resources, in direct contrast to the universal or global perspective encapsulated in TRIPs. Although the relationship between these agreements has been revisited by the TRIPs Council (having again been raised during the Doha ministerial), like other aspects of the global governance of IPRs under review, the political tensions between WTO members in this area have deadlocked the council. It has not been able to resolve or redirect the political disputes over the relationship between bioresources and intellectual property.

One of the major worries for peasant farmers in sub-Saharan Africa and elsewhere has been the impact of IPRs on the informal systems of seed distribution and (re)use. Although many countries operate more formal systems, much subsistence farming (and even low-level commercial agriculture) is patterned by informal networks of seed exchange, where quality control is a function of local and community knowledge (and, of course, communal trust relations). For more than three decades the Consultative Group on International Agricultural Research (CGIAR) has not only organized agricultural research within (and for) these communities (initially in support of the "green revolution") but has also held a germplasm collection explicitly "in trust for the benefit of the international community, in particular the developing countries" (cited in Blakeney 2002, 108). When these collections were launched, however, IPRs were not yet so politically prominent.

Michael Blakeney suggested that there are three issues that the CGIAR system must address in light of TRIPs. First, there have been a number of attempts to patent material held in CGIAR's public collections (funded by the UN's Food and Agricultural Organization, the World Bank, and other public or nongovernmental organizations). This raises the issue of "prior art" as regards specific claims but also questions the ownership of germplasm resources where work on these has been conducted for research purposes. Second, and leading directly from this issue, is the increased potential value that CGIAR's stocks may now represent, with partial privatization now an independent funding opportunity for CGIAR itself. Patent patterns also reveal the failure by applicants to notify CGIAR that they are seeking patents on (valuable) material possibly held in its various locations. Third, where material is required for specific research, there are problems of access and/or limitations on use as well as raised costs that are already having a deleterious effect on CGIAR's ability to organize research for developing countries' agricultural sectors (Blakeney 2002). Currently, the private sector plays very little part in the distribution and use of seeds in most developing countries, but the experiences of CGIAR suggest that the introduction of IPRs into these networks might well disrupt previous practices.

If the modes of privatization and control of IPRs that have patterned other areas of technology take hold in the agriculture sector, there is a very real danger that small agriculture communities will find themselves living under the threat of litigation from the new rights holders to particular genetic resources they continue to utilize. Much of the critical commentary as regards agricultural patents (see, for instance, Shiva 2001) has taken this position, noting cases such as RiceTec Inc.'s patent on Texmati, a variant on the Indian staple basmati rice; Monsanto's soya and maize patents; and W. R. Grace's patent on the neem seed and its linked medical and agricultural uses.

The retention and exchange of seed directly contravenes the legal constrictions on use of patented varieties, and thus, considerable ongoing discussions at the WTO and elsewhere among developing countries (from sub-Saharan Africa and Asia especially) have centered on developing a new sui generis system that fulfills their TRIPs obligations to provide an "effective" system while retaining the traditional methods of farming that breeders' rights previously recognized (Matthews 2002, 132; Shiva 2001, 121–128). Developing countries' negotiators have adopted the position that effectiveness does not require a specific level of protection, but rather is more a process-related concern (Rangnekar 2003, 93–96). Given the different traditional practices that particular governments wish to recognize as communal knowledge, there is a good argument that there is no single sui generis system that can be imposed instead of a stringent IPR system. Such potential flexibility, however, as in other areas, is being buried beneath the pressures brought to bear through bilateral negotiations. While political maneuvering continues, many developed countries' agrobusiness and pharmaceutical multinationals have been voraciously patenting whole and partial genetic sequences from living organisms (including the race to identify and patent elements of the human genome). Patents have been applied for and granted to rich countries' companies on genetic materials (sometimes modified) that are already in wide use across developing countries' subsistence and small-scale agricultural communities.

Court challenges of politically problematic patents are distinctly possible, but this is both an expensive and time-consuming process. In 1997, for instance, the Indian government spent over US$200,000 fighting the RiceTec patent on basmati (Texmati), settling the case when a compromise, although not outright cancellation, was mediated between the litigants. This was merely one rice-related grant among many (in 2000 alone, over 500 patents were granted relating to rice), however, and the cost of fighting each questionable grant is prohibitively expensive. The Indian government's Ministry of Commerce reportedly told campaigners in 2003 that there was no money available to fight further cases whatever their merits (Ramesh 2004). Less-wealthy developing countries will no doubt come to the same decision, and those campaigners in other areas (from software to pharmaceuticals) who seek to challenge patents on their own account will need to raise large amounts of money without any real confidence of mounting a successful challenge.

The real problem is that patent examination is not as stringent as it should be for balancing a public-regarding interest with the grant of private rights. When, in patents' early history, the question of monopoly was at the forefront of governments' concerns, early forms of examination were developed and deployed to ensure that the grants were justified by measure of specific public-regarding policy ends. As the policy focus has increasingly shifted toward the individual, such examination seems to have become less important than enhancing the private rights of applicants. Thus, most patent offices see it as their job to issue patents (and in many cases the fees from doing so generate income for their operations); they are not overly concerned with any particular grant's relationship to the public realm. Critics have cited business method patents as particularly egregious examples of ill-conceived and misguided patent grants (Gleick 2000). As any grant *can* be challenged in court, patent office personnel seem to have accepted, at least implicitly, that their "mistakes" can be tidied up through a judicial process without considering that the expense of this process severely limits its effectiveness as a mechanism for protecting the social interest in maintaining any limitations to the scope of patent.

The Commodification of Traditional Knowledge?

Debates over so-called traditional knowledge have ranged widely and addressed such diverse issues as biopiracy, medicines, biodiversity, traditional agriculture, music, textiles, and the very definition of what constitutes property. Additional issues concern the fit between Western conceptions of innovation and ownership that underpin copyright and patent protection and traditional knowledge. Traditional knowledge is "knowledge that has been developed on the traditions of a certain community or nation" (Weeraworawit 2003, 159). WIPO has gone so far as to establish an Intergovernmental Committee on Intellectual Property and Genetic Resources, Traditional Knowledge, and Folklore. The issues embedded in the notion of traditional knowledge resurrect age-old historical debates about innovation, ownership, and the distribution of rewards. A number of nations are experimenting with new forms of regulation and protection of traditional knowledge, but the legal status of such knowledge remains uncertain.

The traditional knowledge debates highlight a recurrent theme in our history. Property rights are always socially constructed, and they are repeatedly contested. The discussion about the legal status of traditional knowledge as property underscores how people come to decide what is to be deemed "property." Critics of so-called biopiracy have highlighted this dynamic quite sharply. Biopiracy is seen as a new form of Western imperialism in which global seed and pharmaceutical corporations plunder the biodiversity and traditional knowledge of the developing world. Biopiracy is the unauthorized and uncompensated expropriation of genetic resources and traditional knowledge. According to this argument, corporations alter these "discoveries" with science, patent them, then resell the derived products or processes at exorbitant rates to the very people from whom they stole them in the first place. This turns the discourse of piracy, as bandied about in arguments about TRIPS and proceedings under section 301 of the US 1988 trade act (which covers intellectual property), upside down. A number of activists seek to demonstrate that, rhetoric to the contrary notwithstanding, the global corporations of the United States are the biggest "pirates" on the planet (Shiva 1997).

Two Indian examples catalyzed opposition to these practices and animated a quest for more formal recognition of traditional knowledge. In the turmeric and neem tree cases, US researchers and foreign corporations respectively were granted patents on what Indians considered to be traditional uses for these substances. These cases raised the larger question of the status of traditional methods and practices passed down orally, sometimes referred to as "folklore." Many so-called scientific discoveries are nothing more (or less) than folklore that researchers may stumble upon or seek out among indigenous peoples, farmers, shamans, and healers. Western patent systems have no protections for this type of innovation. They only recognize "individual innovations which were 'scientifically' achieved[;] the typically communal 'folk' knowledge of developing countries [is] excluded" (Marden 1999, 292). The arbitrariness of this conception becomes clear insofar as under TRIPs, as Grethel Aguilar noted, "we are accepting that the only form of knowledge deserving of legal protection is that generated in laboratories" (Aguilar 2003, 181). By contrast, traditional knowledge continues to be treated as part of the public domain (Sahai 2003, 168).

The terms of the debate are reminiscent of the controversies that preceded the Diplomatic Conference for the Revision of the Paris Convention and continued in its aftermath (Sell 1998). At that time developing countries were pressing for scientific and technological knowledge, as possessed by industrialized countries, to be redefined not as property but rather as the "common heritage of mankind." This notion underpinned the developing countries' quest for resource and technology transfers from North to South. In more recent years, in the environmental context, industrialized countries have sought to define biodiversity as the "common heritage of mankind" to get the holders of major biodiversity resources in developing countries to preserve them. Developing countries have responded by asserting their sovereign rights to their natural resources, reserving the right to control access to territorially limited resources such as rainforests (Sell 1996). In a similar fashion, in the traditional knowledge context, "countries endowed with genetic resources, traditional knowledge and folklore seek to secure protection for such resources, while the user countries are bound to be reluctant to submit to additional restraints on innovating and creating in ways that conform to existing intellectual property agreements" (Weeraworawit 2003, 163).

The politics are relatively straightforward. According to Dutfield, countries from Latin America and Africa favor new legal norms protecting traditional knowledge, whereas countries such as the United States and Canada oppose them (Dutfield 2003, 221). These latter countries would prefer that solutions be found within existing intellectual property frameworks and "while willing to contemplate additional legal obligations, would prefer these to be non-binding" (Dutfield 2003, 221).

In the copyright context, traditional knowledge and folklore concerns often arise in music production. Sound recordings often use traditional music as a basis, but then alter the product in a sufficiently original way as to earn copyright protection for the finished product. As Gervais suggested:

> Many creators of folklore find this situation doubly unacceptable: while they are unable to benefit from their creative efforts, others are "using" the intellectual property system not only gainfully, but in fact, against the original folklore creators who may be prevented from using their own material if, as it evolves, it comes to resemble the derivative work. To traditional knowledge holders, this is a perverse, if unintended, result. (Gervais 2002, 958–959)

The current intellectual property system effectively excludes traditional knowledge and folklore creators at the same time that it allows nontraditional knowledge holders to acquire intellectual property rights that block the original creators from their preexisting rights (Gervais 2002, 960).

To what extent do current intellectual property systems apply to traditional knowledge and folklore? The current system is based on Western notions of individualism, and the ability to identify "owners" to reward. Critics of the current system argue that applying patent and copyright protection to traditional knowledge will not work "because of the inherent mismatch between the protection that was created for finite, inanimate objects coming out of industrial activity, and the flowing, mutable and variable properties of biological materials and associated indigenous knowledge" (Sahai 2003, 173). For example, oral traditions are not covered by patenting, which relies on extensive published specifications. Copyright is difficult to assign for creations such as kente cloth that are continuously and communally created and improved upon. The very question of identifying an "owner" of such resources bedevils the current system. As Gervais asked:

> Should intellectual property be defined by the common characteristics of current forms of intellectual property, namely (a) identifiable authors or inventors, (b) an identifiable work or invention or other object, and (c) defined restricted acts in relation to the set object without the authorization of the rightsholders? Or are these historical accidents, as it were, of the nineteenth century world in which these forms of intellectual property emerged? And yet, even if that is the case, how can one protect amorphous objects or categories of objects and grant exclusive rights to an ill-defined (and ill-definable) community or group of people? (Gervais 2002, 966)

We have argued that current forms of intellectual property protection have been socially constructed and are contingent products of historical circumstances. The traditional knowledge debates provide an opportunity for a new construction of the meaning of property rights. In response to concerns about biopiracy in particular, a number of countries are experimenting with new forms of protection for traditional knowledge and folklore. Costa Rica has controlled access to its biodiversity and succeeded in gaining resource transfers to underwrite its bioprospecting efforts (Sell 1996). The Indian government is developing a digital database of public domain traditional knowledge related to medicinal plants that it will make available to patent offices worldwide "so that examiners are aware of the prior art relating to a particular medicinal plant" (Sahai 2003, 172). This is to help prevent the improper awarding of patents, such as occurred in the turmeric and neem tree cases. In Colombia, a private institute is coordinating efforts with local nongovernmental organizations representing indigenous communities and a plant pharmacology laboratory to develop benefit-sharing mechanisms (Salgar 2003, 184). One of the core features of this framework is that the pharmacology lab may not seek intellectual property protection for its research results without obtaining prior consent (in writing) from the chiefs of the indigenous communities belonging to the association. Further, the laboratory must provide a proposal for benefit sharing and an explicit recognition of the moral rights of the association as provider of the knowledge (Salgar 2003, 186). Prior informed consent and benefit sharing are the core principles underlying the increasing documentation of indigenous

communities' resources (Utkarsh 2003, 190). These principles are informing WIPO's work documenting traditional knowledge and developing features of a model for sui generis protection for traditional knowledge and
folklore (Dutfield 2003, 221).

*   *   *

The current era is characterized by extensive property rights and economic concentration in leading industrial sectors. To be a member of the
WTO, follower countries must abide by TRIPS strictures that sharply
reduce their policymaking autonomy. This is evocative of the late nineteenth and early twentieth centuries when countries began to accept some
uniformity and consolidation in international intellectual property policy.
Under intense bilateral economic pressure, and desperate for foreign investment, many developing countries have signed bilateral investment agreements that require them to offer much higher standards of protection than
are incorporated in TRIPS, despite no proven linkage between intellectual
property protection and incentives to invest (Drahos 2001, 791–808). The
global governance regime for IPRs itself is in no sense stable, however, and
TRIPs does not represent some final settlement in the (global) governance
of IPRs. As we have seen in the past, new groups have mobilized to protest
the extension of property rights into new areas. Although this movement
has been most pronounced in connection with access to HIV/AIDS drugs in
sub-Saharan Africa, throwing into sharp relief the trade-offs inherent in
IPRs, these problems resonate in other policy areas as well.

Although patterns of settlement and contestation have been evident
throughout the long history of intellectual property, it is also clear that in
recent years the baseline for property rights has moved significantly in the
direction of private reward over public access. Rights, which used to be
thought of as privileges and exceptions, have superseded obligations and/or
duties; the balance must be restored, and our history clearly suggests that it
can be. Highlighting this imbalance, and characterizing it as a "one-way
ratchet," Rochelle Cooper Dreyfuss has proposed the incorporation into
TRIPS of a bill of rights for users (Dreyfuss 2004). Such a crucial change
could revisit the possibility of reinstating into the global governance of
IPRs some of the important instruments that nearly all countries used in the
past, such as working requirements, compulsory licensing, and differential
treatment for foreigners.

It is most important to realize that a legitimate international intellectual
property rights regime *must* recognize the variegated constellation of interests and capabilities within *and* between countries. A one-size-fits-all
approach makes no sense in light of the historical record of economic
development: only differential treatment can effectively allow countries'

governments to reclaim their autonomy to craft policies appropriate to their levels of economic development and comparative advantages in innovation and imitation. The fundamental mismatch between TRIPS as a blanket form of global governance and the diverse patchwork it purports to address has already caused—and is destined to continue to cause—political, economic, and social difficulties.

When the debates about patents and copyrights became politicized in the view of the USTR and others, negotiations to further strengthen the international regulation and global governance of IPRs were shifted back to WIPO, as we relate in Chapter 8. The problem for developing countries has been that even though their trade negotiators have started to appreciate the political economic issues that IPRs raise, developing countries' representatives at WIPO are much more likely to be legal professionals (often having been trained in some part under WIPO programs) who only perceive technical implementation problems in the governance of IPRs. The WIPO negotiations have already revealed a continuing desire by developed countries' negotiators to sidestep the political problems raised by TRIPs and to continue a globalized program of asserting and expanding owners' rights relative to any recognition of a public-regarding realm of nonownership, or commons. TRIPs has not ended the arguments over what the global governance of IPRs should encompass. The harmonization of IPRs is not acceptable or legitimate given the vast disparities of political and economic development across the WTO membership (and beyond).

At its simplest, we are arguing that either the global governance of IPRs needs to more resemble the previous national regimes of governance, or states' governments need to reassert their sovereignty over certain aspects of the governance of IPRs. Countries need to have flexibility to incorporate intellectual property rights into an integrated national system of innovation appropriate to their stage of economic and technological development and in response to the varied needs of their particular economic sectors. Whether such flexibility can be achieved within the multilateral regime remains to be seen. Indeed, it may be the case that, when the issues become so politically charged, the notion of an emergent global polity collapses under the weight, returning the politics of IPRs to the national level. Here many governments feel the need to respond to a domestic polity whose interests are likely to be somewhat different from the global class of knowledge owners.

Notes

1. Where not explicitly noted, this section draws on our previous work, notably May (2000) and Sell (1998; 2003).

2. Matthews (2002, 78–83) contains a full discussion of the TRIPs Council's function and activities.

3. Further detailed accounts of TRIPs' numerous sections can be found in Maskus (2000, chap. 2), which offers a good concise summary of the agreement, as does Matthews (2002, chap. 3). Blakeney (1996) provides a useful and well-laid-out discussion of the whole agreement, and readers requiring an extended clause-by-clause treatment of the TRIPs agreement will find his account illuminating.

4. The European Community Database Directive takes protection of information even further than is required under Article 10 and as such has engendered significant comment and criticism. See Ginsburg (2001) on arguments in the United States and Europe over this possible "overprotection" of database rights.

5. Although there has been some concern that these exceptions might be extended to pharmaceuticals in certain circumstances (Matthews 2002, 59), subsequent disputes have revealed that this is far from evident, even for those countries who might *want* to exclude pharmaceuticals.

6. A notable occasion was in October 2001, when—feeling threatened by an anthrax attack that killed several US postal and media workers—both the United States and Canada threatened Bayer with compulsory licensing in a successful effort to obtain Cipro at reduced cost and to ensure adequate supplies of the drug.

7. Bénédicte Callan noted: "Many US companies are also disappointed that TRIPs still permits some compulsory licensing of intellectual property" (Callan 1997, 23).

8. One could argue that compulsory licensing is still available as a policy tool under TRIPs, citing the Paris convention's Article 5A, for example, as well as TRIPs Articles 8 and 40. One certainly could invoke these articles, finding legal language that would make local working available as a policy option. In our view, however, the legal language does not solve the problem of huge power disparities and heavy-handed tactics that are employed to ensure that developing countries do *not* avail themselves of options under TRIPs. Although it is true that the United States withdrew its WTO complaint against Brazil when Brazil challenged the United States on this point (Brazil had retained a local working provision in its domestic legislation that the United States declared was inconsistent with TRIPs insofar as importation constitutes working), the United States did not back down because it was persuaded of the legal and technical merits of Brazil's position but rather because of the horrifying negative publicity about US tactics in the South African case generated by the advocates of access to medicines. Politically it was too costly to pursue the case against Brazil, the one country that successfully and boldly was tackling its HIV/AIDS crisis (Rosenberg 2001; Sell and Prakash 2004).

9. This discussion of technical assistance draws on a longer analysis in May (2004).

10. A comprehensive guide to the legislative changes made by the EU, Australia, Japan, and the United States in response to the WIPO treaty can be found in Kim (2003), which rather optimistically concludes, however: "Hopefully, in the future, with decreased transaction costs and an efficient way to deal with access to works, there will be fewer problems [regarding 'fair use' access]" (Kim 2003, 119). We are not so sure.

11. Although the UK Copyright Designs and Patents Act of 1988 would seem to offer similar protection to DRM technologies, this has been subject to considerably less comment, which may tell us something about the dominance of US-related issues on the Internet!

12. The displeasure of US industries with Article 5A of the Paris convention is documented in Sell (1998).

13. For the impact of Intel and other members of the Semiconductor Industry Association on Article 31 of TRIPs, see Drahos and Braithwaite (2002, 148–149).

14. Of course for those with more principled objections to IPRs, the possibility of their acceptance in this way merely reveals the domination of the capitalist economic model, rather than any acceptable value in making knowledge or information property.

15. We are grateful to Aykut Çoban for making this point.

8

Forgetting History
Is Not an Option

THE TRADE Related Aspects of Intellectual Property Rights (TRIPs) agreement was included as part of the "single undertaking" required of all members of the World Trade Organization (WTO). As we have noted, TRIPs is not a set of laws that can merely be written into national law; rather, it is a set of requirements for the *effects* of law. In theory at least, how these requirements are legislated is a sovereign issue for the WTO's member states. Frequently the technical assistance mandated under Article 67 of the agreement is so closely focused and directed, however, that there is little effective national autonomy. With the additional use by the United States and the European Union (EU) of bilateral trade agreements and diplomatic pressure, there is little chance for WTO members to develop different ways of enacting laws to establish TRIPs compliance (Drahos 2001).

For intellectual property (as well as for antidumping and countervailing duties, government procurement laws, sanitary and phytosanitary measures, and competition law) the WTO is seeking to harmonize national laws (Reich 2004). Whereas the General Agreement on Tariffs and Trade (GATT) clearly focused on trade issues as related to national borders, the Uruguay Round and subsequently the WTO have widened this brief to focus on measures *within* national jurisdictions that might distort international trade. Although intellectual property is not the only area where this expanded reach is evident, it is most developed here. In this last chapter, we consolidate our argument regarding the importance of history for the contemporary global politics of intellectual property and then move to examine the resurgence in the last few years of the World Intellectual Property Organization (WIPO). Finally, we offer an overview of the contemporary dynamics of the (global) political economy of intellectual property.

The Importance of History:
The Global Politics of Intellectual Property Today

The key argument we draw from our study is that the history of intellectual property was not (and is still not) a neutral, functionally driven set of improvements towards an "optimal" legal settlement that is naturally just. Rather, as we have demonstrated at length, the history of intellectual property has been a *political economic* history: intellectual property has been the policy battleground among contending economic interests, politically driven governments, and contrasting philosophical traditions. Into this complex sociopolitical environment, technological changes have introduced successive opportunities to rejoin battle over the issues of making property from ideas, information, and knowledge. The recourse to arguments from natural law, or from the economics of efficiency, have been mobilized by various groups to mask interest and the political processes behind the development of specific legal structures. We need to understand the history of the legal institution of intellectual property, alongside the history of technology and the philosophical debates about ownership and knowledge, if for no other reason than to understand the current political conflicts over the global governance of intellectual property. At its most basic, our argument has been that history matters and that we must not ignore it.

We are certainly not alone in recognizing the importance of the complexities and variances in the historical development of intellectual property law. Perhaps the most obvious issue that has prompted historical comparisons is the link between the protection of intellectual property and economic development. Here Eric Schiff's seminal study of "industrialization without national patents" in the Netherlands and Switzerland during the second half of the nineteenth and into the first decade of the twentieth century has become a much-cited source (Schiff 1971). Indeed, recent work by Ha-Joon Chang (2001), Ikechi Mgbeoji (2003), Dominique Ritter (2004), and Graham Dutfield and Uma Suthersanen (2004), among others, has made explicit the implied skepticism in Schiff's monograph about the posited causal link between prior institutionalization of intellectual property rights (IPRs) and subsequent economic development or industrialization. Arguing for further comparative research in IPR-related law, Thomas Meshbesher has suggested that "the most important role of history in the use of the comparative method is to keep the focus of comparative study from wandering too far from the concerns of economics and public policy which gave [intellectual property] law its first and most enduring surge of vitality" (Meshbesher 1996, 614). Like us, he urges those examining IPRs (and their global governance) never to forget their origins in (and the continuing influence of) mercantilist policy ends.

Our history of IPRs problematizes the assertion of a direct relationship between the protection of IPRs and the early acceleration of economic development or industrialization. For different countries with different mixes of industries and/or services, alongside differing structural positions in relation to the global economy, there are multiple answers to the question of when do IPRs start to serve the policy goals of our country? What is becoming clear to many writers and analysts, however, is that there *is* a threshold, and thus much recent work has focused on examining in specific instances when such a threshold might be crossed and how this can be linked to the future economic development of poorer and under-, or undeveloped, countries in the global system.

For Dru Brenner-Beck, only when countries recognize that it is in their interest to adopt specific IPR-related legislation will workable laws be deployed (even under TRIPs) (Brenner-Beck 1992). For instance, the successes of Japan, Korea, and Taiwan all follow a similar pattern with the absorption and copying of important technologies pushing industrial development forward, until the point is reached when domestic companies start to seek protection for their *own* ideas and innovations. Only then did these countries start to develop stronger protection of IPRs (Kumar 2003). In a review of historical lessons for the UK's Department for International Development's Commission on Intellectual Property Rights, Zorina Khan concluded that

> the major lesson that one derives from [the international] aspect of the economic history of Europe and America is that intellectual property rights best promoted the progress of science and the arts when they evolved in tandem with other institutions and in accordance with the needs and interests of social and economic development in each nation. . . . [A]ppropriate policies towards intellectual property are not independent of the level of development nor of the overall institutional environment. (Khan 2002, 58)

This immediately raises the questions of periods of transition and, perhaps most important, how best to judge when countries have reached a level of development when they should be required to become TRIPs compliant. It also, by implication, poses the political problem of which institution or body should be empowered to make, and enforce, this judgment.

Although it may be difficult to fix exactly the point of change in domestic politics (indeed it may take place at different times for different sectors), as with the developed countries' governments in the past, the newly industrialized countries only adopted the policies and laws (now mandated by TRIPs) once they become clearly beneficial to domestic industry. Synthesizing his typology from a number of different studies of threshold criteria, Rafik Bawa has suggested there are three possible thresholds above which the protection of IPRs might be politically expedient:

> First, [a developing country] needs a literate work force and the existence of trained scientific and technical personnel to attract foreign investment, utilize transferred technology, and implement and sustain domestic inventive ability. Second, a level of industrialization and industrial infrastructure sufficient to support an IP regime is essential. Thirdly, base levels of domestic capital mobilization rates and levels of entrepreneurship must be in existence. These factors enable domestic enterprises to participate in and gain from the incentives provided by IP protection. (Bawa 1997, 108–109 [footnotes omitted])

To this we would add a fourth: there is also a clear requirement to construct a widespread social consensus that the protection of IPRs is legitimate. Any immediate costs of transition need to be ameliorated through governmental action, and longer-term costs can be dealt with via mechanisms to balance the private rights introduced into the system with a recognition of public-regarding issues and, most important, social welfare.

Although questions of development certainly are central to our analysis of intellectual property, this is not strictly a North-South issue. Indeed, new questions have arisen about the expansion of intellectual property rights within industrialized countries as well. The ratcheting up of domestic and global intellectual property rights has been driven by members of the so-called knowledge cartel, large globally active firms that "control the distribution of a disproportionately large share of existing technologies without necessarily being particularly innovative themselves" (Maskus and Reichman 2004, 295). A key question in this regard is how much extra innovation do the strong intellectual property rights that corporations press for actually provide? Or, rather, does this system stifle follow-on innovation and lead to abuses of market power?

Maskus and Reichman suggested that overly strong protection hurts small and medium-sized enterprises that have been leaders in important innovation in the past. To the extent that current levels of protection shrink the research commons, expand and multiply exclusive and overlapping rights, increase barriers to entry, constrict reverse-engineering and other procompetitive strategies built around value-adding applications of new technologies, this impact of protection threatens to undermine the purpose of intellectual property rights as an incentive for innovation (Maskus and Reichman 2004, 310). Changes in companion institutions have increased the dangers that too many rights for too many things will have negative effects *everywhere*.

In the past, innovation in the United States was built upon competition (supported by vigorous antitrust policies and enforcement), patent misuse doctrines, easy availability of government-generated data and a rich research commons, mechanisms to foster exchange of technical know-how, and the preservation of the right to reverse-engineer routine innovations in order to improve upon them (Maskus and Reichman 2004, 311). This regulatory balancing act, in recent years, has given way to a lopsided system in which exclusive property rights tend to trump these other concerns and assail these core elements that fueled innovation in the past. Indeed, if the current system is dangerous even for the most innovative agents within countries such as the United States, it makes no sense to export this system to others.

The question of transition between previous legal institutions and those that are required for TRIPs compliance has been one of the key areas of political conflict at the WTO as well as in academia and the advocacy community of nongovernmental organizations (NGOs). As Ritter pointed out, "had the TRIPs agreement been signed in 1883 instead of the Paris Convention, Switzerland never would have met the requirements within the limited transition period, of one, five or even eleven years" (Ritter 2004, 492). Certainly, as our history demonstrates, the period of development enjoyed by the now rich and developed countries was very long. Even with the technical assistance provided, the transition times for the developing country members of the WTO are unprecedentedly short, at between five and ten years (or sometimes less, under bilateral pressure). Ituku Elangi Botoy made this point powerfully:

> As the level of protection of IPRs similar to that of the TRIPs agreement was reached in industrialized countries only in the mid-1980s, it can be calculated that from the Paris Convention to 1985, it took one hundred and two years, and from 1985 to 1995, it took ten more years. If industrialized countries have benefited from one hundred and twelve years (plus one year for transition according to Article 65(1) TRIPs), why grant only five or ten years to other countries [to achieve] . . . what industrialized countries took over one hundred years to achieve? (Elangi Botoy 2004, 129)

Indeed, if one further examines where many developing countries' legal starting point is, the actual lead time may be even longer when directly compared to the historical development of IPRs in Europe and the United States. Or, as Chang put it, "it seems unfair to ask modern-day developing countries to behave to a standard that was not even remotely observed when the now-advanced countries were at the similar, or even more advanced, stages of development" (Chang 2001, 293). The point that all these authors stress is that there is more than a trace of hypocrisy on display in light of the historical record of those countries clamoring loudest for developing countries to become TRIPs compliant.

Such hypocrisy is hardly recent. At the close of the nineteenth century, the United States was adamant that other countries needed to enhance and improve the protection of patents in their territories in the run-up to ratification of the Paris convention, even though at the same time showing a flagrant disregard for foreign copyrights (and, of course, remaining outside the Bern convention until the last quarter of the twentieth century). Likewise, at the same time that Germany was putting pressure on Switzerland to introduce a patent law to protect German intellectual property, German manufacturers were happily violating British trademarks and producing what would now be regarded as pirated goods (Chang 2001, 303). Indeed, the rhetoric of "pirates" has been deployed extensively by the office of the US Trade Representative (USTR) and others; for instance, Bénédicte Callan titled her discussion of the "Asian challenge" to high technology industries *Pirates on the High Seas* (Callan 1997). The behavior that is now being labeled piracy, however, is exactly the development strategy adopted by the now-developed countries at an earlier stage in their history.

Rather than a response to natural rights, or justice for creators and innovators, the establishment of TRIPs was driven by a policy of protectionism and mercantilism by the developed countries' trade negotiators and governments, as it was in the past (even if this is often obscured by rhetoric). Indeed, even when IPRs' role in technology transfer approximates the rhetoric, the price charged for licenses or the terms for use that are set by the owners frequently dissipate any real advantage to developing countries' economies. Furthermore, even if licenses are secured, high prices may make exports utilizing these processes or techniques uncompetitive in a global market. And, of course, license requests themselves may just be refused (Maskus and Reichman 2004, 309). Thus, for developing countries the IPRs owners' "withholding" power is frequently encountered as a block to deployment and profitable utilization of up-to-date techniques and technology in the current system.

Despite the largely negative impact of TRIPs on developing countries, however, it is also necessary to recall that (especially in the realm of copyrights) many developing countries have for some time protected certain aspects of IPRs and thus have already achieved partial TRIPs compliance on their own terms. Laws introduced when some countries were still colonial possessions of developed states are in line with TRIPs-compliant modes of enforcement; other countries had joined both the Bern and Paris conventions during their period of decolonization, and their laws for certain IPRs were close to what TRIPs requires. But, as we noted previously, one of the driving forces behind the establishment of TRIPs was the variety of national strategies that were accommodated within the international governance regime overseen by WIPO. Hence, we emphasize, in some cases it is not an outright rejection of the notion and logic of intellectual property that has caused political tensions between members of the WTO, but rather it is the specific TRIPs-mandated settlement's replacement of the "variable geometry" of the previous period that has caused problems.

The return to a variable geometry of protection would also allow the recognition that the protection of IPRs is not equally supported by all political systems or philosophies. In our discussion, although we self-avowedly concentrated on the European and US political economic history because these were the most influential in the contemporary institutional arrangements, we have at a number of points acknowledged very different traditions of thought about the possibility of property in knowledge. Indeed, for a number of authors this is an important further reason why harmonization is not only difficult but unwelcome. Howard Anawalt (2003) and Rafik Bawa (1997), as well as others, have identified different approaches to (and dismissals of) the notion of IPRs, based on cultural and social mores of non-Western societies. For countries whose cultures cannot encompass conceiving of knowledge as property, whatever the flexibilities allowed in TRIPs, any approach to compliance will involve a cultural and political disjuncture that governments may be unwilling to contemplate.

Nevertheless, although TRIPs continues to mark a significant and robust minimum standard for IPRs, further harmonization at a higher level is now being negotiated elsewhere in Geneva. In the same way that in response to the perceived shortcomings of WIPO's stewardship of the previous IPR treaties, the United States and the EU successfully shifted the forum for the governance to the new WTO during the Uruguay Round of trade negotiations, now these countries have decided that their best interests are served by returning the debates about further harmonization to WIPO.

The Resurgence of the World Intellectual Property Organization

Although there are still many issues to be resolved at the WTO, a core group of developed countries has moved to negotiate further IPR-related treaties at WIPO. This was at least partly a result of a sustained campaign by WIPO to return the organization to the center of global IPR policymaking, as well as illustrating a case of "forum shopping." Having been sidelined in the negotiation of TRIPs, in 1994 and 1995 the General Assembly of WIPO passed two resolutions to attempt to reestablish its importance as regards the global governance of intellectual property. The first required the organization's International Bureau to assist WIPO members in relation to their obligations under TRIPs. The second expanded this obligation to offer support in establishing TRIPs compliance to WTO members that are not WIPO members, as part of a formal agreement over the coordination of technical assistance and other matters with the WTO (Drahos 2002, 776). As we noted in Chapter 7, the technical assistance offered through this arrangement is hardly neutral or without problems. Aside from this capacity building, however, WIPO has also been active in the establishment of an expansive agenda of harmonization intended to raise the global standards of protection (and enforcement) of IPRs above those set by TRIPs.

In 1996, WIPO adopted the WIPO Copyright Treaty (WCT) that, most significantly, introduced the anticircumvention principle into the multilateral governance of IPRs (Drahos and Braithwaite 2002, 184). As we have discussed, the introduction of digital rights management is intended to privilege the rights of intellectual property owners, and recognizing that technological fixes are seldom permanent, the WCT sought to establish a further legal layer of protection for these technologies. This legal innovation subsequently was enacted in the US Digital Millennium Copyright Act (DMCA) and the EU Copyright Directive. The WCT and the WIPO Performances and Phonograms Treaty (WPPT), adopted in the same year, further extended the rights of IPR owners, even as the TRIPs agreement started to attract significant criticism. Both the WCT and WPPT responded to a similar set of demands for the control of content that we identified as leading to the expansion of the work-for-hire elements of copyright in the United States. These agreements were not developed with the interest of performers or creative people in mind but rather were intended to ensure that copyright owners could both consolidate and expand their rights in the realm of Internet-mediated communication.

The renewed vigor of policymaking at the WIPO also led to the development of the WIPO Patent Agenda and the subsequent process of consultation (World Intellectual Property Organisation 2002). At the center of this agenda is the perceived need to develop a "universal patent," a fully globalized and harmonized patent regime, building on the international application procedure already existing under the Patent Cooperation Treaty. The process of discussing the agenda has revealed some very clear areas of tension between developed country and developing country members of WIPO, as well as among the developed countries themselves. The agenda aims to remove those areas of national self-determination regarding patents that remain in the minimum standards set by TRIPs, but this now confronts differences among the developed countries themselves.

The 2002 report by the UK Commission on IPRs presented the problem in this area as being between a policy focusing on quantity of patents versus one that would focus on the *quality* of patent grants:

> The ever-expanding demand for patents is regarded as a right which has to be met by increasing the productivity of the granting process at the expense of a possible further reduction in quality. [The Commissioners] believe that policy makers in both developed and developing countries should seek to tip the balance away from quantity and back towards quality. Fewer and better patents, which retain their validity in the courts, would in the longer term be the most efficacious way of reducing the burden on the major patent offices and, more importantly, securing widespread support for the patent system. (Commission on Intellectual Property Rights 2002, 133)

It is this last issue that continues to represent the most severe Achilles heel for the global governance of IPRs. Without some generalized legitimacy, enforcing and protecting IPRs remains a difficult if not impossible task. The Patent Agenda seems to many critics to be interested only in the system's legitimacy among its users, however (which is to say, the corporations that patent most widely), rather than any other interested parties.

Reflecting the Patent Agenda's "quantity" focus, two significant treaties regarding patents have emerged from WIPO-facilitated negotiations since 1998: the Patent Law Treaty (PLT), which defines a single set of rules for preparing, filing, and managing patents in signatory countries, and the Substantive Patent Law Treaty (SPLT), which has yet to be finalized but is intended to encompass rules regarding the scope of patent (their subject matter), exclusions, and rules for deciding between competing claims. The most important aspect of the PLT is the relaxation of requirements for the submission of patent applications, allowing early and partial submission of applications and in addition explicitly shifting the burden of proof as regards fraud or procedural shortcomings to the complaining party (Correa and Musungu 2002, 6–7). These new practices are intended to raise the throughput of patent applications and grants by reducing the procedures that applications must undergo. Deploying the commission's distinction, it seems unlikely that the relaxation of procedures at the heart of the PLT will do much to *raise* the quality of patents (indeed, it is more likely to expand the number of problematic and contentious patents).

The key elements that are to be harmonized by the SPLT (if an agreement can be reached) are (1) the establishment of patentability (to limit or remove national interpretations of the criteria for recognizing a qualifying invention), (2) the determination of the characteristics of an "invention" for the purpose of patenting (to remove the technical aspect, and by doing so to expand the scope of patents to include, for instance, "business methods," software, and "research tools" such as Expressed Sequence Tags in genomics), and (3) the scope of patent protection (to reduce the possibility of using environmental or public health criteria for limiting grants otherwise covered by patent criteria). This goes well beyond TRIPs and in so doing seeks to remove national determination of these issues and also aims to harmonize the doctrine of equivalents (governing what is regarded as an infringement). Even more important, the SPLT includes a provision to prohibit contracting parties from establishing any further conditions for patenting apart from those explicitly laid out in the treaty (Correa and Musungu 2002, 15–22). The political project behind the draft agreement is to remove the remaining flexibility that, although difficult to operationalize, has so far remained within the TRIPs-mandated system of governance.

The SPLT sets a clear limit on any further limitations that national legislatures might regard as a political response to local problems and issues. If the SPLT were to be ratified, for those states that signed on (and if it gets to this stage, significant bilateral pressure surely will be applied to ensure accession), governments' ability to shape their patent law to their specific circumstances would be further circumscribed. These changes are required if the universal global patent is to become a reality and would make the balance between public and private benefits, at the center of the law of IPRs since their original legislative emergence, a global matter. As we have already argued, however, there are few, if any, mechanisms that allow the social or public interest to be fully articulated at this global level.

Conversely, the evident difficulty of finalizing a text of the SPLT itself may indicate that the high-water mark for the global governance of IPRs has been reached and that without further normative (re)construction, it is unlikely that the SPLT will become law. This is not because the developed countries recognize the problems that other WIPO members might encounter in signing on to the SPLT, but rather because the remaining differences among the United States, the EU, and Japan are more difficult to resolve. Although TRIPs harmonized those aspects of the IPR system that were already essentially the same across the leading "trilateral" countries, the SPLT requires that these major players also have to compromise in areas of their national practice, making agreement that much harder to reach now that they may need to compromise *their* autonomy.

Therefore, apart from these formalized instruments, WIPO also has attempted to adopt a "soft law" approach for other forms of IPRs, most obviously trademarks. In 1999 the Assembly of WIPO adopted a Resolution Concerning Provisions on the Protection of Well-Known Marks and the following year approved a Recommendation Concerning Trademark Licenses. Then in 2001, a Recommendation Concerning Provisions on the Protection of Marks and Other Industrial Property Rights in Signs on the Internet was adopted. These three agreements, although not formal treaties, were intended to work toward establishing specific norms regarding the protection of trademarks as part of a "soft law initiative" at WIPO. Indeed, Edward Kwakwa suggested that there is "evidence that the

Resolution and Recommendations passed to date are already exercising a real influence on national law and practice" (Kwakwa 2001, 193).

The clearest example of working to reproduce specific requirements was WIPO's role in the adoption by the Internet Corporation for Assigned Names and Numbers (ICANN) of the Uniform Domain Name Dispute Resolution Policy (UDRP). This policy mediates disputes regarding ownership of trade names when used as Internet addresses, ensuring that in the future trademarked names will be correctly assigned. Adoption of this policy was a response to a number of cases where individuals or companies with no trademark rights had registered specific named domains and then offered them for sale to the trademark owners. Although in some respects a rather ambiguous policy process, Graeme Dinwoodie argued that essentially WIPO "acted at the request of a single member state (the United States) to produce a report that, by virtue of delegation of de facto control of the domain name registration process from the single government, could be implemented by ICANN as substantive law without the usual airings found in intergovernmental lawmaking of which WIPO is a part" (Dinwoodie 2002, 1001 [footnotes omitted]). Although WIPO did circulate the proposals for comments, because this was outside their standard intergovernmental practice and also because the UDRP can be contradicted in national courts, it does not suggest a major move away from previous policy. Conversely, it does suggest that WIPO does not merely operate on the basis of the clearly articulated interest of a *majority* of its members.

Peter Drahos has argued that one of the key political problems of this revival of WIPO as the site of IPR-related policymaking is that most developing countries send representatives from their intellectual property offices to WIPO meetings. Even though these individuals may have good technical knowledge (itself often derived from WIPO training schemes), they have little interest in, or knowledge of, the public policy aspects of IPRs as regards regulation or economic development. Hence, although the Africa Group has been quite effective at the TRIPs Council, there is no equivalent counterpart among developing country representatives at WIPO (Drahos 2002, 785). Here, the characterization of WIPO as a technical organization pays a dividend for those developed countries wishing to push the harmonization agenda forward, raising standards of protection and enforcement. *Political* issues are sidelined; discussions are merely about the refinement of the relevant international treaties. Indeed, technical assistance, as a socialization mechanism that "educates" patent office personnel across the developing countries into the TRIPs mindset, not only produces advocates for IPRs but also encourages their acceptance of the WIPO Patent Agenda when they are negotiating on behalf of their governments in Geneva.

Therefore, utilizing soft law methods as well as training and technical assistance, the WIPO secretariat has demonstrated a clear understanding of the centrality of norms in the politics of establishing IPR-related legislation. Indeed, as we have argued throughout, the normative realm has been one of the key elements of the history of intellectual property. Thus, WIPO's actions and practices can be firmly located within this historical narrative. As in previous periods, the development of IPR-related laws (now at the global level) has been pushed by specific sets of interests, articulating narratives of (natural) rights and efficiency. In this role of normative advocate, however, the practices of WIPO are somewhat problematic.

Although it is clear that the political agenda at WIPO is not driven by development concerns but rather by the "logic" of the benefits of establishing IPRs across the global system, as Sisule Musungu and Graham Dutfield have pointed out, this position sits in direct contrast to a wider reading of WIPO's mandate and purpose based on the agreement that the organization made with the United Nations in 1974. Since 17 December 1974, WIPO has been a specialized agency of the UN. Musungu and Dutfield noted that

> The Agreement clearly states that WIPO's role is subject to the competence and responsibilities of the UN and its organs. . . . Therefore, while WIPO has a specialized competence on matters of intellectual property, the intention was clearly that its mandate should be constructed in the context of the development objectives of the specified UN agencies as well as the broader objectives of achieving international co-operation in solving problems of an economic, social, cultural and humanitarian character, and in promoting and encouraging respect for human rights and fundamental freedoms. (Musungu and Dutfield 2003, 19)

The key point is that for an organization to become (and continue to be) a specialized agency of the UN, its purposes must be compatible with those of the UN and its agencies.

Yet we remain skeptical of WIPO's ability fully to embrace a development agenda. WIPO ultimately is constrained by its dependence on users of the Patent Cooperation Treaty for the bulk of its funding. About 85 percent of WIPO's income comes from user fees for its services in administering its various treaties.[1] The majority of these users are globally active firms that drove the TRIPs agenda and promote ratcheted-up intellectual property rights. It is hard to imagine that these firms will sit by idly as WIPO takes steps directly against their stated interests. Further, given the fact that WIPO has worked hard to reassert its importance to the Organization for Economic Cooperation and Development (OECD) (after the United States shifted to GATT to address intellectual property policy for the Uruguay Round), it seems unlikely that WIPO would be keen to jeopardize this work by directly challenging the high protectionist agenda.

The United Nations Conference on Trade and Development (UNC-

TAD), the agency with the most claim to competence in this area and one that has been the locus of much debate and policy discussion among developing countries, has, however, been effectively marginalized within WIPO. Furthermore, other UN agencies with significant interests in IPRs, from the United Nations Educational, Scientific, and Cultural Organization (UNESCO) to the United Nations Development Programme (UNDP), have also been effectively excluded from the policy deliberations at WIPO. This suggests that one potential solution to the question of (re)establishing a public-regarding aspect to global policymaking in the realm of IPRs would be to hold WIPO to the undertakings it made when it was originally recognized as a specialized agency of the UN. Thus, at the same time that the move to reestablish WIPO as the focus of global policymaking for IPRs represents an attempt to further advance and strengthen the private interest in IPRs, it also potentially establishes a mechanism to once again balance these private interests with some nascent notion of a (global) *public interest*. Our history would suggest that once again at the moment of seeming consolidation of private rights, there is also the possibility of a contrary movement.

Political Implications

One of the key themes we have explored is the importance of norms in the construction and maintenance of legal institutions; specifically, in our case, the commodification of knowledge and information through the institution of intellectual property. Given the law's often counterintuitive demands, we have argued, like Tom Tyler, that IPRs "require the creation of an appropriate moral climate" to ensure that the laws related to intellectual property do not have to be constantly enforced (Tyler 1997, 229). Without a basic legitimacy, the law becomes little more than the actions of the powerful; for the rule of law to function easily in any society (from local to global), there has to be a significant level of acceptance of its legitimacy. For products and services covered by IPR-related laws, this is most especially the case, as often infringement is a private activity that is difficult to police. As we have noted above, however, the attempt to establish the legitimacy of the (now global) governance of IPRs has been a long, difficult, and continuing political project.

Our central argument has been that the politics of the global governance of IPRs cannot be understood without having some developed cognizance of the history of their protection and enforcement. Only by understanding the long history of intellectual property can the problems of its contemporary global governance be properly assessed. The prevailing arrangement still emphasizes the territoriality of rights, the few regional arrangements (such as the European Patent Office) aside, leaving the state as the key locus of rights enforcement and protection. As noted above, the WTO may be moving into the realm of legal harmonization but is still dependent on national legislation and action to finally institutionalize IPRs. Samuel Murumba argued, however, that IPRs' relative "success in the domestic sphere, far from predicting its effectiveness at the universal level, augurs ill for universality since both law's domestic success and its floundering at the universal level may be due to the common feature of embeddedness" (Murumba 1998, 448). What has been too often forgotten about the rule of law at the global level is that in national jurisdictions it is always embedded in a sociopolitical set of processes and institutions that are not (at least currently) evident at the global level. Furthermore, the state continues to be the central mechanism through which the political processes of legitimization of law operate to underpin governance and regulation of socioeconomic affairs. In the realm of intellectual property this is especially clear.

Lifting the mask of supposed universalism, for good or ill we still can see the central role of the state. Recognizing this situation, during the closing stages of the Uruguay Round, Paul David observed that "discussions of the 'correct' international system for protecting intellectual property are more likely than not to degenerate into rhetorical efforts to impose institutional arrangements that may well be adapted to the national purposes and legal contexts of one country (or several similar countries) on societies that are quite different in those respects" (David 1993, 55). These remarks now seem remarkably prescient and have been echoed more recently by Carlos Correa and Sisule Musungu of the South Center in Geneva (Correa and Musungu 2002, 22–23). Likewise, Murumba suggested that "these rules are simply national ones shorn of their domestic socio-ethical roots—disembodied norms orbiting in global space" (Murumba 1998, 443). The continuing reliance on the state for enforcement and legislative enactment has meant that the domestic legal roots of IPRs are never far from the surface of debates.

We also have noted that there is little evidence that a shift to higher standards in IPRs is necessarily of economic benefit at all levels of economic development; indeed, there is convincing evidence that there is a profoundly detrimental effect on poorer, lesser-developed countries. There is too much unevenness in the global system, especially as related to economic development, for there to be an effective one-size-fits-all policy. Furthermore, as our history has demonstrated, the broad developed-country position as regards the worth of strong IPRs contradicts these countries' own historical experience. Contemporary structures that have grown as a response to various stages of economic development are treated as the final establishment of a neutral and ahistorical solution for making markets in knowledge and information. The issues that so trouble the US government and the interests it represents, however, are not those that are worrisome elsewhere in the global system.

Peter Drahos argued that as the evidence for the advantage of moving to robust protection of IPRs in currently developing countries has largely been absent, the onus is on those who wish to continue strengthening the global governance of IPRs to substantiate their claims (Drahos 1997a, 57). The argument that the claimed benefits of global governance should clearly be demonstrated does not seem outlandish. The past ten years of governance since 1995 have demonstrated, however, that many of these claimed advantages to developing countries are, at the very least, difficult to substantiate. This is the case both for the direct benefits of ratcheting up the protection of IPRs and for the indirect, diplomatic benefits of horse trading during the Uruguay Round of trade negotiations. Specifically, there has until recently been very slow progress on opening international agriculture markets by removing subsidies (and other support) in the United States and EU, although developed countries have continued to force the pace of TRIPs compliance. Any structure of global governance can only be legitimate if it takes into account the various levels (or stages) of development achieved by various countries across the global system. The attempt to argue that there is some universal policy interest in intellectual property seems to us to be profoundly mistaken.

Again, as we have demonstrated, there is certainly a great deal to be said for recognizing what Chang has termed "historical justice" (Chang 2001, 304): the need to recognize the manner in which the now rich and developed countries treated intellectual property when they were developing, as a solvent of hypocrisy as regards the claimed timeless worth of IPRs. Although some supporters of IPRs may argue that the developing countries should learn the lessons of the past and institutionalize IPRs early to support and enhance innovation, we suggest that the real lessons of history are closer to the argument of those who, although accepting that IPRs certainly serve a purpose for some economic actors at certain levels of economic development, suggest that such socioeconomic benefits cannot be universalized. The history of IPRs suggests that there is a threshold moment when disadvantage is finally outweighed by the advantages of protecting IPRs. Few developing countries are at this point for all their commercial sectors, however, and thus for historical justice to be served, a return to a more varied diet of global legal protection of IPRs is required.

For Murumba, therefore, what is needed at the global level is a "justice-constituency" for IPRs' governance. This constituency would face two challenges: first, it should articulate "what the public purpose is at the global level, instead of simply transposing ready-made purposes and rules from national jurisdictions"; second, it would need to "formulate rules, norms and concepts that are carefully calibrated to achieve that public purpose" (Murumba 1998, 459). This constituency would need to be able to resist (or to offer help in resisting) the continuing bilateral pressure to ratchet up the standards of protection of IPRs, expressed both within the WIPO's Patent

Agenda and by the office of the USTR and the EU trade negotiators, among others.

Although mechanisms exist at the national level to ameliorate problems that the conflict between private rewards and public benefits might produce, similar mechanisms still remain difficult to enact at the global level. There are few ways for developing countries to meaningfully factor in the national social costs of strong IPR laws into the global political process at the WTO or WIPO. Whereas in national political debates those groups shouldering the immediate social costs may (potentially) have a number of political avenues through which countermeasures can be mobilized, there is much less scope for such mediation at the global level, with the exception of breaking international agreements. Thus, although there are considerable organizational structures for the global governance of IPRs, any mechanisms for the realization of a global polity or community interest within these interactions are currently severely underdeveloped.

If the political economy of intellectual property rights tells us one thing, it is that the world is far too insufficiently globalized for the imposition of a global legal settlement that does not allow for the divergent social developmental interests of all countries to be recognized (and acted upon). Not only is greater historical sensitivity required as regards the manner in which intellectual property rights have been governed in the past, an explicit recognition of the social bargain that lies at the center of the justification of intellectual property is also required. Political campaigners and critics should look to the history of the governance of intellectual property rights for political sustenance. Our explicit intent in this history has been to lay out the historical context of contemporary debates about intellectual property rights in order to provide an intellectual armory for those arguing that further harmonization of intellectual property rights at the global level is not only premature but is unlikely to be just, until the wide disparities of wealth in our global society have been greatly reduced. As we have demonstrated at some length, the history of intellectual property has been driven by a volatile and changing interaction among technological change, rhetorical argument, legal precedent, and political maneuvering. Today is no different, and therefore the politics of intellectual property remain indeterminate and open to continuing political struggle. Embedding the political debates around the (global) governance of intellectual property rights in their historical context will, we hope, eventually produce a more just political economy of intellectual property.

Note

1. See http://www.wipo.int/documents/en/document/govbody/budget/2002_03/rev/pdf/pbc4_2.pdf.

Acronyms

AAP	American Association of Publishers
AIDS	acquired immunodeficiency syndrome
ASCAP	American Society of Composers, Authors, and Publishers
BMI	Broadcast Music, Inc.
CAFC	Court of Appeals for the Federal Circuit
CBD	Convention on Bio-Diversity
CFC	chlorofluorocarbon
CGIAR	Consultative Group on International Agricultural Research
DMCA	Digital Millennium Copyright Act
DNA	deoxyribonucleic acid
DRM	digital rights management
EC	European Community
EU	European Union
FM	frequency modulation
GATS	General Agreement on Trade in Services
GATT	General Agreement on Tariffs and Trade
GE	General Electric
GI	geographical indicator
GSP	General System of Preference
HFC	hydrofluorocarbon
HIV	human immunodeficiency virus
ICANN	Internet Corporation for Assigned Names and Numbers
ICT	information and communications technology
IPC	International Property Committee
IPR	intellectual property right
MFN	most-favored-nation
NGO	nongovernmental organization
NIC	newly industrialized country
OECD	Organization for Economic Cooperation and Development

PLT	Patent Law Treaty
SPLT	Substantive Patent Law Treaty
TLA	Tungsten Lamp Association
TRIPs	[Agreement on] Trade Related Aspects of Intellectual Property Rights
UDRP	Uniform Domain Name Dispute Resolution Policy
UNCTAD	United Nations Conference on Trade and Development
UNDP	United Nations Development Programme
UNESCO	United Nations Educational, Scientific, and Cultural Organization
UPOV	Convention for the Protection of New Varieties of Plants
USAID	US Agency for International Development
USPTO	US Patent and Trademark Office
USTR	US Trade Representative
WCT	WIPO Copyright Treaty
WIPO	World Intellectual Property Organization
WPPT	WIPO Performances and Phonograms Treaty
WTO	World Trade Organization

Bibliography

Abel, Paul. 1967. "Copyright from the International Viewpoint." *Journal of World Trade Law* 1, no. 3: 399–433.

Abrams, Howard B. 1983. "The Historical Foundation of American Copyright Law: Exploding the Myth of Common Law Copyright." *Wayne Law Review* 29, no. 3 (Spring): 1119–1191.

Adede, Adronico Oduogo. 2003. "Origins and History of the TRIPs Negotiations." In C. Bellmann, G. Dutfield, and R. Meléndez-Ortiz, eds., *Trading in Knowledge: Development Perspectives on TRIPs, Trade, and Sustainability,* 23–35. London: Earthscan.

Aguilar, Grethel. 2003. "Access to Genetic Resources and Protection of Traditional Knowledge in Indigenous Territories." In C. Bellmann, G. Dutfield, and R. Meléndez-Ortiz, eds., *Trading in Knowledge: Development Perspectives on TRIPs, Trade, and Sustainability,* 175–183. London: Earthscan.

Alford, William P. 1995. *To Steal a Book Is an Elegant Offence. Intellectual Property Law in Chinese Civilisation.* Stanford, CA: Stanford University Press.

Allen, P. S. 1913. "Erasmus' Relations with His Printers." *Transactions of the Bibliographic Society* 13: 297–321.

Anawalt, Howard C. 2003. "International Intellectual Property, Progress, and the Rule of Law." *Santa Clara Computer and High Technology Law Journal* 19, no. 2: 383–405.

Aoki, Keith. 1996. "(Intellectual) Property and Sovereignty: Notes Towards a Cultural Geography of Authorship." *Stanford Law Review* 48, no. 5 (May): 1293–1357.

Arblaster, Paul. 2001. "Policy and Publishing in the Hapsburg Netherlands, 1585–1690." In B. Dooley and S. Baron, eds., *The Politics of Information in Early Modern Europe,* 179–198. London: Routledge.

Archer, Margaret. 1982. "Morphogenesis Versus Structuration: On Combining Structure and Action." *British Journal of Sociology* 33, no. 4: 455–483.

———. 1995. *Realist Social Theory: The Morphogenetic Approach.* Cambridge: Cambridge University Press.

Arrow, Kenneth. 1996. "The Economics of Information: An Exposition." *Empirica* 23, no. 2: 119–128.

Austin, Graeme W. 2002. "Valuing 'Domestic Self-Determination' in International

Intellectual Property Jurisprudence." *Chicago Kent Law Review* 77, no. 3: 1155–1211.

Azmi, Ida Madieha., Spyros M. Maniatis, and Bankole Sodipo. 1997. "Distinctive Signs and Early Markets: Europe, Africa, and Islam." In A. Firth. ed., *The Prehistory and Development of Intellectual Property Systems*. Perspectives on Intellectual Property Series 1, 123–159. London: Sweet and Maxwell.

Band, Jonathan, and M. Katoh. 1995. *Interfaces on Trial: Intellectual Property and Interoperability in the Global Software Industry*. Boulder, CO: Westview Press.

Barfe, Louis. 2004. *Where Have All the Good Times Gone? The Rise and Fall of the Record Industry*. London: Atlantic Books.

Barron, Brian. 1991. "Chinese Patent Legislation in Cultural and Historical Perspective." *Intellectual Property Journal* 6 (September): 313–339.

Batzel, Victor M. 1980. "Legal Monopoly in Liberal England: The Patent Controversy in the Mid-Nineteenth Century." *Business History* 22, no. 2: 189–202.

Bawa, Rafik. 1997. "The North-South Debate over the Protection of Intellectual Property." *Dalhousie Journal of Legal Studies* 6: 77–119.

Beatty, Edward. 2002. "Patents and Technological Change in Late Industrialization: Nineteenth-Century Mexico in Comparative Context." *History of Technology* 24: 121–150.

Bettig, Ronald V. 1992. "Critical Perspectives on the History and Philosophy of Copyright." *Critical Studies in Mass Communication* 9, no. 2 (June): 131–155.

Bhagwati, Jagdish. 1998. *A Stream of Windows: Unsettling Reflections on Trade, Immigration, and Democracy*. Cambridge, MA: MIT Press.

Birn, Raymond. 1971. "The Profit of Ideas: *Privilèges en librairie* in Eighteenth-Century France." *Eighteenth Century Studies* 4, no. 2: 131–168.

Birrell, Augustine. [1899] 1971. *Seven Lectures on the Law and History of Copyright in Books*. South Hackensack, NJ: Rothman Reprints.

Black, Donald. 1976. *The Behaviour of the Law*. New York: Academic Press.

Blakeney, Michael. 1996. *Trade Related Aspects of Intellectual Property Rights: A Concise Guide to the TRIPS Agreement*. London: Sweet and Maxwell.

———. 2002. "Agricultural Research: Intellectual Property and the CGIAR System." In P. Drahos and R. Mayne, eds., *Global Intellectual Property Rights: Knowledge, Access, and Development*, 108–124. Basingstoke, UK: Palgrave Macmillan/Oxfam.

Blank, David L. 1985. "Socrates Versus Sophists on Payment for Teaching." *Classical Antiquity* 4, no. 1 (April): 1–49.

Boseley, Sarah. 2000. "Glaxo Stops Africans Buying Cheap Aids Drugs." *The Guardian*, 2 December, 25.

Bouckaert, Boudewijn. 1990. "What Is Property?" *Harvard Journal of Public Policy* 13, no. 3: 775–816.

Bourdieu, Pierre. 1987. "The Force of Law: Toward a Sociology of the Juridical Field." *Hastings Law Journal* 38 (July): 805–853.

Bowrey, Kathy. 1996. "Who's Writing Copyright's History?" *European Intellectual Property Review* 18, no. 6 (June): 322–329.

Boyle, James. 1992. "A Theory of Law and Information: Copyright, Spleens, Blackmail, and Insider Trading." *California Law Review* 80: 1415–1540.

———. 1996. *Shamans, Software, and Spleens. Law and the Construction of the Information Society*. Cambridge, MA: Harvard University Press.

———. 1997. "A Politics of Intellectual Property: Environmentalism for the Net?" *Duke Law Journal* 47, no. 1: 87–116.

———. 2001. "The Second Enclosure Movement and the Construction of the Public Domain." <http://www.james-boyle.com> (accessed 24 January 2002).

Brady, Robert. 1943. *Business as a System of Power.* New York: Columbia University Press.

Braithwaite, John. 1984. *Corporate Crime in the Pharmaceutical Industry.* London: Routledge and Kegan Paul.

Braithwaite, John, and Peter Drahos. 2002. "Intellectual Property, Corporate Strategy, Globalisation: TRIPS in Context." *Wisconsin International Law Journal* 20: 451–480.

Braudel, Fernand. 1981. *The Structures of Everyday Life. The Limits of the Possible.* Vol. 1 of *Civilisation and Capitalism. 15th–18th Century.* London: Collins.

Brenner-Beck, Dru. 1992. "Do As I Say, Not As I Did." *UCLA–Pacific Basin Law Journal* 11: 84–118.

Brown, W. F. Wyndham. 1908. "The Origin and Growth of Copyright." *Law Magazine and Review* 34: 54–65.

Bugbee, Bruce W. 1967. *Genesis of American Patent and Copyright Law.* Washington, DC: Public Affairs Press.

Burch, Kurt. 1995. "Intellectual Property Rights and the Culture of Global Liberalism." *Science Communication* 17, no. 2 (December): 214–232.

———. 1998. *"Property" and the Making of the International System.* Boulder, CO: Lynne Rienner.

Burckhardt, Jacob. [1860] 1944. *The Civilisation of the Renaissance in Italy.* Oxford: Phaidon Press.

Burkitt, Daniel. 2001. "Copyrighting Culture—The History and Cultural Specificity of the Western Model of Copyright." *Intellectual Property Quarterly* 2001, no. 2: 146–186.

Burrell, Robert. 1998. "A Case Study in Cultural Imperialism: The Imposition of Copyright on China by the West." In L. Bently and S. M. Maniatis, eds., *Intellectual Property and Ethics.* Perspectives on Intellectual Property Series 4, 195–224. London: Sweet and Maxwell.

Callan, Bénédicte. 1997. *Pirates on the High Seas: The United States and Global Intellectual Property Rights.* Washington, DC: Council on Foreign Relations Study Group on American Intellectual Property Rights Policy.

Carrier, Michael. 2003. "Resolving the Patent-Antitrust Paradox Through Tripartite Innovation." *Vanderbilt Law Review* 56: 1047–1089.

Carson, Anne. 1999. *Economy of the Unlost.* Princeton, NJ: Princeton University Press.

Chandler, Alfred D. 1977. *The Visible Hand. The Managerial Revolution in American Business.* Cambridge, MA: Belknap Press/Harvard University Press.

Chang, Ha-Joon. 2001. "Intellectual Property Rights and Economic Development: Historical Lessons and Emerging Issues." *Journal of Human Development* 2, no. 2: 287–309.

Chavasse, Ruth. 1986. "The First Known Author's Copyright, September 1486, in the Context of a Humanist Career." *Bulletin of John Rylands Library* 69: 11–37.

Clapes, Anthony. 1993. *Softwars: The Legal Battles for Control of the Global Software Industry.* Westport, CT: Quorum Books.

Clark, Aubert. 1960. *The Movement for International Copyright in Nineteenth Century America.* Westport, CT: Greenwood Press.

Collins, A. S. 1926. "Some Aspects of Copyright from 1700 to 1780." *Transactions of the Bibliographical Society* 7: 67–81.

Commission on Intellectual Property Rights [CIPR]. 2002. *Integrating Intellectual Property Rights and Development Policy.* London: CIPR/Department for International Development.

Commons, John R. [1924] 1959. *Legal Foundation of Capitalism.* Madison: University of Wisconsin Press.

Cornish, William R. 1993. "The International Relations of Intellectual Property." *Cambridge Law Journal* 52, no. 1 (March): 6–63.

Correa, Carlos M., and Sisule F. Musungu. 2002. *The WIPO Patent Agenda: The Risks for Developing Countries.* T.R.A.D.E. working paper no. 12. Geneva: South Centre.

Coulter, Moureen. 1991. *Property in Ideas: The Patent Question in Mid-Victorian Britain.* Kirksville, MS: Thomas Jefferson University Press.

Cox, Robert W. 1996. *Approaches to World Order.* Cambridge: Cambridge University Press.

Cribbet, John Edward. 1986. "Concepts in Transition: The Search for a New Definition of Property." *University of Illinois Law Review* 1: 1–42.

Cullis, Roger. 2004. "Fiat Lex: The Role of Law in the Early Development of the Electric Light Industry." Paper prepared for ESRC Research Seminar Series, "Intellectual Property Rights, Economic Development, and Social Welfare: What Does History Tell Us?" Ironbridge Gorge Museum, Coalbrookdale, UK, 26 April.

David, Paul A. 1993. "Intellectual Property Institutions and the Panda's Thumb: Patents, Copyrights, and Trade Secrets in Economic Theory and History." In M. B. Wallerstein, M. E. Mogee, and R. A. Schoen, eds., *Global Dimensions of Intellectual Property Rights in Science and Technology,* 19–61. Washington, DC: National Academy Press.

———. 1994. "The Evolution of Intellectual Property Institutions." In A. Aganbegyan, O. Bogomolov, and M. Kaiser, eds., *Economics in a Changing World,* 126–149. Basingstoke, UK: Macmillan.

———. 2000. *A Tragedy of the Public Knowledge "Commons."* Oxford IPR Research Centre Working Paper WP04/00. Oxford: Oxford Intellectual Property Rights Research Centre. <http://www.oipc.ox.ac.uk/ejindex.html> (accessed 15 August 2001).

David, Paul, and Dominque Foray. 2002. "Economic Fundamentals of the Knowledge Society." Stanford Institute for Economic and Policy Research Discussion Paper no. 01-14, 2002. <http://siepr.stanford.edu/papers/pdf/01-14.html> (accessed 4 September 2004).

Davies, D. Seaborne. 1932. "Further Light on the Case of Monopolies." *Law Quarterly Review* 48, no. 191 (July): 394–414.

———. 1934. "The Early History of the Patent Specification." *Law Quarterly Review* 50, no. 198 (April): 260–274.

Davies, Gillian. 2002. *Copyright and the Public Interest.* London: Sweet and Maxwell.

Demsetz, Harold. 1967. "Toward a Theory of Property Rights." *American Economic Review* 57, no. 2 (May): 347–359.

Dhanjee, Rajan, and Laurence Boisson de Chazournes. 1993. "Trade Related Aspects of Intellectual Property Rights (TRIPs): Objectives, Approaches, and

Basic Principles of the GATT and of the Intellectual Property Conventions." *Journal of World Trade* 24: 5–15.

Dhar, Biswajit, and C. Nianjan Rao. 1996. "Trade Relatedness of Intellectual Property Rights." *Science Communication* 17, no. 3 (March): 304–325.

Dinwoodie, Graeme B. 2001. "The Development and Incorporation of International Norms in the Formation of Copyright Law." *Ohio State Law Journal* 62, no. 2: 733–782.

———. 2002. "The Architecture of the International Intellectual Property System." *Chicago-Kent Law Review* 77, no. 3: 993–1014.

Dolza, Luisa, and Liliane Hilaire-Pérez. 2002. "Inventions and Privileges in the Eighteenth Century: Norms and Practices. A Comparison Between France and Piedmont." *History of Technology* 24: 21–44.

Doremus, Paul. 1995. "The Externalisation of Domestic Regulation: Intellectual Property Rights Reform in a Global Era." *Science Communication* 17, no. 2 (December): 137–162.

Drahos, Peter. 1995. "Global Property Rights in Information: The Story of TRIPS at the GATT." *Prometheus* 13, no. 1 (June): 6–19.

———. 1996. *A Philosophy of Intellectual Property*. Aldershot, UK: Dartmouth.

———. 1997a. "States and Intellectual Property: The Past, the Present, and the Future." In D. Saunders and B. Sherman, eds., *From Berne to Geneva: Recent Developments in International Copyright and Neighbouring Rights*, 47–70. Nathan, Queensland: Australian Key Centre for Culture and Media Policy.

———. 1997b. "Thinking Strategically About Intellectual Property Rights." *Telecommunications Policy* 21, no. 3: 201–211.

———. 2001. "BITS and BIPS: Bilateralism in Intellectual Property." *Journal of World Intellectual Property* 4, no. 6 (November): 791–808.

———. 2002. "Developing Countries and Intellectual Property Standard-Setting." *Journal of World Intellectual Property* 5, no. 5: 765–789.

Drahos, Peter, and John Braithwaite. 2002. *Information Feudalism: Who Owns the Knowledge Economy?* London: Earthscan Publications.

Dreyfuss, Rochelle Cooper. 1989. "The Federal Circuit: A Case Study in Specialized Courts." *New York University Law Review* 64, no. 1 (April): 1–77.

———. 2004. "TRIPS–Round II: Should Users Strike Back?" Special issue, Colloquium on Intellectual Property, *University of Chicago Law Review* 71, no. 1 (Winter): 21–35.

Dutfield, Graham. 2003. *Intellectual Property and the Life Sciences Industries: A Twentieth Century History*. Aldershot, UK: Dartmouth Publishing.

Dutfield, Graham, and Uma Suthersanen. 2004. "Intellectual Property and Development: What Does History Tell Us?" Introductory paper for the ESRC Research Seminar Series, "Intellectual Property Rights, Economic Development, and Social Welfare: What Does History Tell Us?" Ironbridge Gorge Museum, Coalbrookdale, UK, 26 April.

Earle, Edward. 1991. "The Effect of Romanticism on the 19th Century Development of Copyright Law." *Intellectual Property Journal* 6 (September): 269–290.

Edelman, Lauren. 2004. "Presidential Address: Rivers of Law and Contested Terrain: A Law and Society Approach to Economic Rationality." *Law and Society Review* 38 (June): 181–194.

Eden, Kathy. 2001. "Intellectual Property and the *Adages* of Erasmus: *Coenobium v. Ercto non cito.*" In V. Khan and L. Hutson, eds., *Rhetoric and Law in Early Modern Europe*. New Haven: Yale University Press.

Eisenstein, Elizabeth L. 1980. *The Printing Press as an Agent of Change*. Combined paperback volume. Cambridge: Cambridge University Press.

Elangi Botoy, Ituku. 2004. "From The Paris Convention to the TRIPs Agreement: A One-Hundred-and-Twelve Year Transitional Period for the Industrialised Countries." *Journal of World Intellectual Property* 7, no. 1: 115–130.

Eugui, David. 2003. "Requiring the Disclosure of Genetic Resources and Traditional Knowledge: The Current Debate and Possible Legal Alternatives." In C. Bellmann, G. Dutfield, and R. Meléndez-Ortiz, eds., *Trading in Knowledge: Development Perspectives on TRIPS, Trade, and Sustainability*, 196–206. London: Earthscan.

Feather, John. 1980. "The Book Trade in Politics: The Making of the Copyright Act of 1710." *Publishing History* 8: 19–44.

———. 1987. "The Publishers and the Pirates: British Copyright Law in Theory and Practice, 1710–1775." *Publishing History* 22: 5–32.

———. 1994a. "From Rights in Copies to Copyright: The Recognition of Authors' Rights in English Law and Practice in the Sixteenth and Seventeenth Centuries." In M. Woodmansee and P. Jaszi, eds., *The Construction of Authorship. Textural Appropriation in Law and Literature*, 191–209. Durham, NC: Duke University Press.

———. 1994b. *Publishing, Piracy, and Politics: An Historical Study of Copyright in Britain*. London: Mansell Publishing Limited.

Febvre, Lucien, and Henri-Jean Martin. 1976. *The Coming of the Book. The Impact of Printing 1450–1800*. London: NLB.

Federico, P. J. 1926. "Galileo's Patent." *Journal of the Patent Office Society* 8 (August): 576–581.

———. 1929. "Origin and Early History of Patents." *Journal of the Patent Office Society* 11: 292–305.

Feltes, N. N. 1994. "International Copyright: Structuring 'the Condition of Modernity' in British Publishing." In M. Woodmansee and P. Jaszi, eds., *The Construction of Authorship. Textural Appropriation in Law and Literature*, 271–280. Durham, NC: Duke University Press.

Finger, Michael, and Philip Schuler. 1999. "Implementation of Uruguay Round Commitments: The Development Challenge." Paper presented to the WTO/World Bank Conference on Developing Countries in a Millennium Round, Geneva, 20–21 September.

Fink, Z. S. 1940. "Venice and English Political Thought in the Seventeenth Century." *Modern Philosophy* 38 (November): 155–172.

Finlay, Robert. 1980. *Politics in Renaissance Venice*. New Brunswick, NJ: Rutgers University Press.

Fisher, William W., III. 1999. "The Growth of Intellectual Property: A History of the Ownership of Ideas in the United States." <http://eon.law.harvard.edu/property/history.html> (accessed 26 January 2001).

Fisk, Catherine. 2003. "Authors at Work: The Origins of the Work-for-Hire Doctrine." *Yale Journal of Law and Humanities* 15: 1–69.

Fligstein, Neil. 1996. "Markets as Politics: A Political-Cultural Approach to Market Institutions." *American Sociological Review* 61, no. 4 (August): 656–673.

Friedman, Lawrence M. 2001. "Erewhon: The Coming Global Legal Order." *Stanford Journal of International Law* 37, no. 2: 347–364.

Frost, George E. 1991. "Watt's 31 Year Patent." *Journal of the Patent and Trademark Office Society* 73, no. 2 (February): 136–149.

Frumkin, Maximilian. 1945. "The Origin of Patents." *Journal of the Patent Office Society* 27 (3) (March): 143–149.

———. 1947. "Early History of Patents for Invention." *Transactions of the Newcomen Society* 1947–1949: 47–56.

Gakunu, Peter. 1989. "Intellectual Property: Perspective of the Developing World." Special trade conference issue, *Georgia Journal of International and Competition Law* 19, no. 2: 358–365.

General Agreement on Tariffs and Trade [GATT]. 1990. *News of the Uruguay Round of Multilateral Trade Negotiations* 41 (9 October). Geneva: Information and Media Relations Division of the GATT.

———. 1994. *Final Act Embodying the Results of the Uruguay Round of Multilateral Trade Negotiations.* Geneva: GATT Publication Services.

Genteli, Bruno. 1988. *Poetry and Its Public in Ancient Greece. From Homer to the Fifth Century.* Baltimore: Johns Hopkins University Press.

Gerulaitis, Leonardas Vytautas. 1976. *Printing and Publishing in Fifteenth Century Venice.* London: Mansell Information Publishing/American Library Association.

Gervais, Daniel J. 2002. "The Internationalisation of Intellectual Property: New Challenges from the Very Old and the Very New." *Fordham Intellectual Property Media and Entertainment Journal* 12, no. 4: 929–990.

Ginsburg, Jane C. 2000. "International Copyright: From a 'Bundle' of National Copyright Laws to a Supranational Code?" *Journal of the Copyright Society of the USA* 47: 265–289.

———. 2001. "US Initiatives to Protect Works of Low Authorship." in R. Dreyfuss, D. L. Zimmerman, and H. First, eds., *Expanding the Boundaries of Intellectual Property: Innovation Policy for the Knowledge Society,* 55–77. Oxford: Oxford University Press.

Gleick, James. 2000. "Patently Absurd." *New York Times Magazine,* 12 March.

Goldstein, Paul. 1994. *Copyright's Highway: From Gutenberg to the Celestial Jukebox.* New York: Hill and Wang.

Gonzales, J. Patricio Saiz. 2002. "The Spanish Patent System (1770–1907)." *History of Technology* 24: 45–79.

Gorges, Michael J. 2001. "New Institutionalist Explanations for Institutional Change: A Note of Caution." *Politics* 21, no. 2: 137–145.

Greif, Avner. 1995. "Political Organisations, Social Structure, and Institutional Success: Reflections from Genoa and Venice During the Commercial Revolution." *Journal of Institutional and Theoretical Economics* 15, no. 4: 734–740.

Gutowski, Robert J. 1999. "The Marriage of Intellectual Property and International Trade in the TRIPs Agreement: Strange Bedfellows or a Match Made in Heaven?" *Buffalo Law Review* 47: 713–762.

Halbert, Deborah J. 1999. *Intellectual Property in the Information Age. The Politics of Expanding Ownership Rights.* Westport, CT: Quorum Books.

Halliday, Terence. 2004. "Comment on the Presidential Address: Crossing Oceans, Spanning Continents: Exporting Edelman to Global Lawmaking and Market-Building." *Law and Society Review* 38 (June): 213–219.

Harries, Jill. 1999. *Law and Empire in Late Antiquity.* Cambridge: Cambridge University Press.

Hazan, Victor. 1970. "The Origins of Copyright Law in Ancient Jewish Law." *Bulletin of the Copyright Society of the USA* 18: 23–28.

Hegel, Georg W. F. 1967. *Philosophy of Right.* Oxford: Oxford University Press.

Hesse, Carla. 1990. "Enlightenment Epistemology and the Laws of Authorship in Revolutionary France, 1777–1793." *Representations* 30: 109–137.

———. 2002. "The Rise of Intellectual Property, 700 B.C.–A.D. 2000: An Idea in the Balance." *Daedalus* 131, no. 2 (Spring): 26–45.

Hewish, John. 1987. "From Cromford to Chancery Lane: New Light on the Arkwright Patent Trials." *Technology and Culture* 28: 80–86.

Hilaire-Pérez, Lilianne. 1991. "Invention and the State in 18th-Century France." *Technology and Culture* 32: 911–931.

Hill, Thomas A. 1924. "Origin and Development of Letters Patent for Invention." *Journal of the Patent Office Society* 6: 405–422.

Hirsch, Rudolf. 1967. *Printing, Selling, and Reading 1450–1550.* Wiesbaden, Germany: Otto Harrassowitz.

Hulme, E. Wyndham. 1896. "The History of the Patent System Under the Prerogative and at Common Law." *The Law Quarterly Review* 41 (April): 141–154.

———. 1897. "On the Consideration of the Patent Grant, Past and Present." *Law Quarterly Review* 51 (July): 313–318.

———. 1900. "The History of the Patent System Under the Prerogative and at Common Law. A Sequel." *The Law Quarterly Review* 16 (January): 44–56.

———. 1902. "On the History of Patent Law in the Seventeenth and Eighteenth Centuries." *The Law Quarterly Review* 71 (July): 280–288.

Hunt, Alan. 1993. *Explorations in Law and Society: Towards a Constitutive Theory of Law.* New York: Routledge.

Hunter, David. 1986. "Music Copyright in Britain to 1800." *Music and Letters:* 269–282.

Janis, Mark D. 2002. "Patent Abolitionism." *Berkeley Technology Law Journal* 17: 899–952.

Jaszi, Peter. 1991. "Toward a Theory of Copyright: The Metamorphoses of 'Authorship.'" *Duke Law Journal* (April): 455–502.

Jenkins, Reese V. 2004. "Patents, Market Dominance, Western Union, Edison-GE, and Eastman Kodak." Paper prepared for ESRC Research Seminar Series, "Intellectual Property Rights, Economic Development, and Social Welfare: What Does History Tell Us?" Ironbridge Gorge Museum, Coalbrookdale, UK, 26 April.

Jeremy, David. 2004. "Patents and Technology Transfer Between Nations: 1790–1851: Help, Hindrance, or Irrelevance: Lessons from History." Paper prepared for ESRC Research Seminar Series, "Intellectual Property Rights, Economic Development, and Social Welfare: What Does History Tell Us?" Ironbridge Gorge Museum, Coalbrookdale, UK, 26 April.

Jones, Franklin D. 1926. "Historical Development of the Law of Business Competition." *Yale Law Journal* 35, no. 8 (June): 905–938.

Judge, Cyril Bathurst. [1934] 1968. *Elizabethan Book-Pirates.* New York: Johnson Reprint.

Kastriner, Lawrence. 1991. "The Revival of Confidence in the Patent System." *Journal of The Patent and Trademark Office Society* 73, no. 1 (January): 5–23.

Keating Jeoffrey. [1629] 1854. *History of Ireland.* New York: John O'Mahoney.

Khan, B. Zorina. 2002. *Intellectual Property and Economic Development: Lessons from American and European History.* Commission on Intellectual Property Rights Study Paper 1a. <http://www.ipr.commission.org> (accessed 23 January 2003).

Khor, Martin. 2002. "Rethinking Intellectual Property Rights and TRIPs." In P. Drahos and R. Mayne, eds., *Global Intellectual Property Rights: Knowledge, Access, and Development*, 201–213. Basingstoke, UK: Palgrave Macmillan/Oxfam.

Kim, Selena. 2003. "The Reinforcement of International Copyright for the Digital Age." *Intellectual Property Journal* 16, nos. 1/3: 93–122.

Kingston, William. 1984. *The Political Economy of Innovation*. The Hague: Martinus Nijhoff Publishers.

———. 2004. "Schumpeter and Institutions: Do His 'Business Cycles' Give Enough Weight to Legislation?" Paper prepared for International Joseph A. Schumpeter Society, Tenth ISS Conference, "Innovation, Industrial Dynamics and Structural Transformation: Schumpeterian Legacies," 9–12 June, Universita Boccini, Milan, Italy.

Kirschbaum, Leo. 1946. "Author's Copyright in England Before 1640." *Publications of the Bibliography Society of America* 40: 43–80.

Klitzke, Ramon A. 1959. "Historical Background of the English Patent Law." *Journal of the Patent Office Society* 41, no. 9: 615–650.

Kobak, James, Jr. 1998. "Intellectual Property, Competition Law and Hidden Choice Between Original and Sequential Innovation." *Virginia Journal of Law and Technology* 3: article 6. <http://vjolt.student.virginia.edu/graphics/vol3/home_art6.html> (accessed 17 August 2004).

Kongolo, Tshimnaga. 2000. "The African Intellectual Property Organisations." *Journal of World Intellectual Property* 3, no. 2 (March): 265–288.

Krasner, Stephen. 1985. *Strutural Conflicts: The Third World Against Global Liberation*. Berkeley: University of California Press.

Kronstein, Heinrich, and Irene Till. 1947. "A Reevaluation of the International Patent Convention." *Law and Contemporary Problems* 12, no. 4 (Autumn): 765–781.

Kumar, Nagesh. 2003. "Intellectual Property Rights, Technology and Economic Development." *Economic and Political Weekly* 38, no. 3 (18 January): 209–225. <http://www.epw.org.in/showArticles.php?root=2003&leat=01&filename=5391&filetype=pdf> (accessed 23 January 2003).

Kwakwa, Edward. 2001. "Some Comments on Rulemaking at the World Intellectual Property Organisation." *Duke Journal of Comparative and International Law* 12, no. 1: 179–195.

Ladas, Stephen P. 1975. *Patents, Trademarks, and Related Rights. National and International Protection*. 3 vols. Cambridge, MA: Harvard University Press.

Lametti, David. 2004. "The (Virtue) Ethics of Private Property: A Framework and Implications." in A. Hudson, ed., *New Perspectives on Property Law, Obligations, and Restitution*. London: Cavendish Publications.

Lathrop, H. B. 1922. "The First English Printers and Their Patrons." *The Library*, 4th ser., 3, no. 2 (September): 69–96.

Lemley, Mark A. 2004. "Ex Ante Versus Ex Post Justifications for Intellectual Property." Special issue, Colloquium on Intellectual Property, *University of Chicago Law Review* 71, no. 1 (Winter): 129–149.

Lessig, Lawrence. 2001a. "Copyright's First Amendment." *University of California Los Angeles Law Review* 48, no. 5: 1057–1073.

———. 2001b. *The Future of Ideas: The Fate of the Commons in a Connected World*. New York: Random House.

Lever, J. 1982. "The New Court of Appeals for the Federal Circuit (Part I)." *Journal of the Patent Office Society* 64, no. 3 (March): 178–208.

Litman, Jessica. 1989. "Copyright Legislation and Technological Change." *Oregon Law Review* 68, no. 2: 275–361.

———. 1991. "Copyright as Myth." *University of Pittsburgh Law Review* 53: 235–249.

———. 2001. *Digital Copyright*. Amherst, NY: Prometheus Books.

Locke, John. 1988. *Two Treatises on Government*. Cambridge: Cambridge University Press.

Logan, Oliver. 1972. *Culture and Society in Venice 1470–1790. The Renaissance and Its Heritage*. London: B. T. Batsford.

Long, Pamela O. 1991. "Invention, Authorship, 'Intellectual Property,' and the Origin of Patents: Notes Toward a Conceptual History." *Technology and Culture* 32, no. 4: 846–884.

Love, Harold. 1993. *Scribal Publication in Seventeenth-Century England*. Oxford: Clarendon Press.

Lowry, Martin J. C. 1979. *The World of Aldus Manutius. Business and Scholarship in Renaissance Venice*. Oxford: Basil Blackwell.

Lukes, Steven. 1973. *Individualism*. Oxford: Basil Blackwell.

Macfarlane, Alan. 1978. *The Origins of English Individualism. The Family, Property, and Social Transition*. Oxford: Basil Blackwell.

Machlup, Fritz, and Edith Penrose. 1950. "The Patent Controversy in the Nineteenth Century." *The Journal of Economic History* 10, no. 1 (May):1–29.

Mackenney, Richard. 1987. *Tradesmen and Traders. The World of the Guilds in Venice and Europe, c. 1250– c. 1650*. London: Croom Helm.

———. 1992. "Venice." In R. Porter and M. Teich, eds., *The Renaissance in National Context,* 53–67. Cambridge: Cambridge University Press.

MacLeod, Christine. 1986. "The 1690s Patents Boom: Invention or Stock-Jobbing?" *Economic History Review,* 2nd ser., 39, no. 4: 549–571.

———. 1988. *Inventing the Industrial Revolution. The English Patent System, 1660–1800*. Cambridge: Cambridge University Press.

———. 1991. "The Paradoxes of Patenting: Invention and Its Diffusion in 18th- and 19th-Century Britain, France, and North America." *Technology and Culture* 32, no. 4: 885–910.

———. 1999. "Negotiating the Rewards of Invention: The Shop-floor Inventor in Victorian Britain." *Business History* 41, no. 2 (April): 1–13.

———. 2004. "Would There Have Been No Industrial Revolution Without Patents?" Paper presented at ESRC Research Seminar Series, "Intellectual Property Rights, Economic Development and Social Welfare: What Does History Tell Us?" Ironbridge Gorge Museum, Coalbrookdale, UK, 26 April.

Macpherson, C. B. 1962. *The Political Theory of Possessive Individualism*. Oxford: Oxford University Press.

———, ed. 1978. *Property. Mainstream and Critical Positions*. Oxford: Basil Blackwell.

Mandich, Giulio. 1948. "Venetian Patents (1450–1550)." *Journal of the Patent Office Society* 30, no. 3: 166–224.

March, James G., and Johan P. Olsen. 1989. *Rediscovering Institutions: The Organizational Basis of Politics*. New York: The Free Press.

Marden, Emily. 1999. "The Neem Tree Patent: International Conflict over the Commodification of Life." *Boston College International and Comparative Law Review* 22 (Spring): 272–295.

Marlin-Bennett, Renee. 2004. *Knowledge Power: Intellectual Property, Information, and Privacy*. Boulder, CO: Lynne Rienner Publishers.

Maskus, Keith. 1990. "Normative Concerns in the International Protection of Intellectual Property Rights." *The World Economy* 13 : 387–409.

———. 2000. *Intellectual Property Rights in the Global Economy.* Washington, DC: Institute for International Economics.

Maskus, Keith, and Mohan Penubarti. 1995. "How Trade-Related Are Intellectual Property Rights?" *Journal of International Economics* 39: 227–248.

Maskus, Keith, and Jerome Reichman. 2004. "The Globalization of Private Knowledge Goods and the Privatization of Global Public Goods." *Journal of International Economic Law* 7, no. 2: 279–320.

Masterson, Salathiel C. 1940. "Copyright: History and Development." *California Law Review* 28, no. 5 (July): 620–632.

Matthews, Duncan. 2002. *Globalising Intellectual Property Rights. The TRIPs Agreement.* London: Routledge.

May, Christopher. 2000. *A Global Political Economy of Intellectual Property Rights: The New Enclosures?* London: Routledge.

———. 2002a. *The Information Society: A Sceptical View.* Cambridge: Polity Press.

———. 2002b. "The Venetian Moment: New Technologies, Legal Innovation, and the Institutional Origins of Intellectual Property." *Prometheus* 20, no. 2 (June): 159–179.

———. 2003. "Digital Rights Management and the Breakdown of Social Norms." *First Monday* 8, no. 11 (November 2003). <http://firstmonday.org/issues/issues8_11/may/index.html> (accessed 27 May 2005).

———. 2004. "Capacity Building and the (Re)production of Intellectual Property Rights." *Third World Quarterly* 25, no. 5: 821–837.

McCalman, Phillip. 2001. "Reaping What You Sow: An Empirical Analysis of International Patent Harmonisation." *Journal of International Economics* 55, no. 1: 161–186.

McClure, Daniel M. 1979. "Trademarks and Unfair Competition: A Critical History of Legal Thought." *The Trademark Reporter* 69: 305–356.

Mearsheimer, John. 2002. *The Tragedy of Great Power Politics.* New York: W. W. Norton.

Merges, Robert P. 1995. "The Economic Impact of Intellectual Property Rights: An Overview and a Guide." *Journal of Cultural Economics* 19, no. 2: 103–117.

———. 2000. "One Hundred Years of Solicitude: Intellectual Property Law, 1900–2000." *California Law Review* 88, no. 6 (December): 2187–2240.

Meshbesher, Thomas M. 1996. "The Role of History in Comparative Patent Law." *Journal of the Patent and Trademark Office Society* 78, no. 9: 594–614.

Mgbeoji, Ikechi. 2003. "The Juridical Origins of the International Patent System: Towards a Historiography of the Role of Patents in Industrialisation." *Journal of the History of International Law* 5, no. 2: 403–422.

Michalopoulos, Constantine. 2003. *Special and Differential Treatment of Developing Countries in TRIPs.* TRIPs Issue Papers 2. Geneva: Quaker United Nations Office.

Mill, John Stuart. 1871. *Principles of Political Economy.* 7th ed. 2 vols. London: Longmans, Green, Reader, and Dyer.

Moore, Barrington. 1998. *Moral Aspects of Economic Growth and Other Essays.* Ithaca, NY: Cornell University Press.

Morris, Ian. 1986. "Gift and Commodity in Archaic Greece." *Man* 21: 1–17.

Mossoff, Adam. 2001. "Rethinking the Development of Patents: An Intellectual History 1550–1800." *Hastings Law Journal* 52 (August): 1255–1322.

Mowrey, David, and Nathan Rosenberg. 1998. *Paths of Innovation: Technological*

Change in 20th Century America. Cambridge: Cambridge University Press.

Murumba, Samuel K. 1998. "Globalising Intellectual Property: Linkage and the Challenge of a Justice-Constituency." *University of Pennsylvania Journal of International Economic Law* 19, no. 2: 435–460.

Musungu, Sisule F., and Graham Dutfield. 2003. *Multilateral Agreements and a TRIPs-plus World: The World Intellectual Property Organisation.* TRIPs Issues Papers no. 3. Geneva: Quaker United Nations Office.

Nachbar, Thomas B. 2002. "Constructing Copyright's Mythology." *The Green Bag: An Entertaining Journal of Law* 6, no. 2D (Autumn): 37–46.

Nicoson, William. 1962. "Misuse of the Misuse Doctrine in Infringement Suits." *UCLA Law Review* 9: 74–108.

Nisse, Jason. 2003. "WTO Turned by America into 'Mafia Racket.'" *Independent on Sunday* (Business Section), 4 May, 1.

North, Douglass C. 1981. *Structure and Change in Economic History.* New York: W. W. Norton.

———. 1990. *Institutions, Institutional Change, and Economic Performance.* Cambridge: Cambridge University Press.

Nuvolari, Alessandro. 2001. "Collective Invention During the British Industrial Revolution: The Case of the Cornish Pumping Engine." Eindhoven Centre for Innovation Studies working paper 01.04. Eindhoven, the Netherlands: ECIS/Technische Universitiet Eindohoven.

Ochoa, Tyler T., and Mark Rose. 2002. "The Anti-Monopoly Origins of the Patent and Copyright Clause." *Journal of the Copyright Society of the USA* 49, no. 3: 675–706.

Oddi, A. Samuel. 1996. "TRIPS—Natural Rights and a 'Polite Form of Economic Imperialism.'" *Vanderbilt Journal of Transnational Law* 29: 415–470.

Okediji, Ruth. 1995. "Has Creativity Died in the Third World? Some Implications of the Internationalisation of Intellectual Property." *Denver Journal of International Law and Policy* 24, no. 1: 109–144.

———. 1996. "The Myth of Development, the Progress of Rights: Human Rights to Intellectual Property and Development." *Law and Policy* 18, nos. 3 and 4 (July/October): 315–354.

———. 1999. "Copyright and Public Welfare in Global Perspective." *Indiana Journal of Global Legal Studies* 7, no. 11: 117–189.

———. 2000. "Towards an International Fair Use Doctrine." *Columbia Journal of Transnational Law* 39: 75–175.

———. 2003. "Public Welfare and the Role of the WTO: Reconsidering the TRIPs Agreement." *Emory International Law Review* 17, no. 2 (Summer): 819–918.

Ostergard, Robert. 1999. "The Political Economy of the South African–United States Patent Dispute." *Journal of World Intellectual Property* 2, no. 6: 875–888.

Parsons, Ian. 1974. "Copyright and Society." In A. Briggs, ed., *Essays in the History of Publishing, in Celebration of the 250th Anniversary of the House of Longman,* 31–60. London: Longman.

Paster, Benjamin G. 1969. "Trademarks—Their Early History." *The Trademark Reporter* 59: 551–572.

Patterson, Lyman Ray. 1968. *Copyright in Historical Perspective.* Nashville, TN: Vanderbilt University Press.

———. 2001. "Copyright in the New Millennium: Resolving the Conflict Between Property Rights and Political Rights." *Ohio State Law Journal* 62, no. 20: 703–732.

Patterson, Ray, and Craig Joyce. 2003. "Copyright in 1791: An Essay Concerning the Founders' View of the Copyright Power Granted to Congress in Article I, Section 8, Clause 8 of the U.S. Constitution." *Emory Law Journal* 52, no. 3 (Spring): 909–952.

Pauwelyn, Joost. 2001. "The Role of Public International Law in the WTO: How Far Can We Go?" *American Journal of International Law* 95, no. 3 (July): 535–578.

Penrose, Edith T. 1951. *The Economics of the International Patent System.* Baltimore: Johns Hopkins University Press.

Perelman, Michael. 2002. *Steal This Idea: Intellectual Property Rights and the Corporate Confiscation of Creativity.* New York: Palgrave.

Petherbridge, Lee. 2001. "Intelligent TRIPs Implementation: A Strategy for Countries on the Cusp of Development." *University of Pennsylvania Journal of International Economic Law* 22, no. 4: 1029–1066.

Pforzheimer, Walter L. 1964 [1972]. "Historical Perspective on Copyright Law and Fair Use." In G. P. Bush, ed., *Technology and Copyright: Annotated Bibliography and Source Materials.* Mt. Airy, MD: Lamond Systems.

Phillips, Jeremy. 1982. "The English Patent as a Reward for Invention: The Importation of an Idea." *Journal of Legal History* 3, no. 1 (May): 71–79.

Picciotto, Sol. 2002. "Defending the Public Interest in TRIPs and the WTO." In P. Drahos and R. Mayne, eds., *Global Intellectual Property Rights: Knowledge, Access, and Development,* 224–243. Basingstoke, UK: Palgrave Macmillan/Oxfam.

Picciotto, Sol, and David Campbell. 2003. "Whose Molecule Is It Anyway? Private and Social Perspectives on Intellectual Property." In A. Hudson, ed., *New Perspectives on Property Law, Obligations, and Restitution,* 279–303. London: Cavendish.

Plant, Arnold. 1934. "The Economic Theory Concerning Patents for Inventions." *Economica* 1 (February): 30–51.

Ploman, Edward W., and L. Clark Hamilton. 1980. *Copyright. Intellectual Property in the Information Age.* London: Routledge and Kegan Paul.

Pohlmann, Hansjoerg. 1961. "The Inventor's Right in Early German Law." *Journal of the Patent Office Society* 43, no. 2: 121–139.

Polanyi, Karl. [1944] 1957. *The Great Transformation. The Political and Economic Origins of Our Time.* Boston: Beacon Press.

Pollard, Graham. 1937. "The Company of Stationers Before 1557." *The Library,* 4th ser., 18, no. 1 (June): 1–38.

Popplow, Marcus. 1998. "Protection and Promotion: Privileges for Inventions and Books of Machines in the Early Modern Period." *History of Technology* 20: 103–124.

Porter, Tony. 1999. "Hegemony and the Private Governance of International Industries." In C. Cutler, V. Haufler, and T. Porter, eds., *Private Authority and International Affairs,* 257–282. Albany: State University of New York Press.

Posner, Richard A. 2002. "The Law and Economics of Intellectual Property." *Daedalus* 131, no. 2 (Spring): 5–12.

Prager, Frank D. 1944. "A History of Intellectual Property from 1545 to 1787." *Journal of the Patent Office Society* 26, no. 11 (November): 711–760.

———. 1952. "The Early Growth and Influence of Intellectual Property." *Journal of the Patent Office Society* 34, no. 2: 106–140.

———. 1964. "Examination of Inventions from the Middle Ages to 1836." *Journal of the Patent Office Society* 56, no. 4: 268–291.

Prescott, Peter. 1989. "The Origins of Copyright: A Debunking View." *European Intellectual Property Review* 1989, no. 12: 453–455.

Primo Braga, Carlos A. 1989. "The Economics of Intellectual Property Rights and the GATT: A View from the South." *Vanderbilt Journal of Transnational Law* 22: 243–264.

Rai, Arti, and Rebecca Eisenberg. 2003. "The Public Domain: Bayh-Dole Reform and the Progress of Biomedicine." *Law and Contemporary Problems* 66, nos. 1 and 2: 289–314.

Ramesh, Randeep. 2004. "Monsanto's Chapati Patent Raises Indian Ire." *The Guardian,* 31 January, 19.

Rangnekar, Dwijen. 2003. "Implementing the *Sui Generis* Option in the TRIPs Agreement: A Framework for Analysis." In H. Katrak and R. Strange, eds., *The WTO and Developing Countries,* 87–111. Basingstoke, UK: Palgrave Macmillan.

Ravetz, Jerome R. 1973. *Scientific Knowledge and its Social Problems.* Harmondsworth, UK: Penguin.

Reich, Arie. 2004. "The WTO as a Law-Harmonising Institution." *University of Pennsylvania Journal of International Economic Law* 25, no. 1: 321–382.

Reichman, Jerome. 1997. "From Free Riders to Fair Followers: Global Competition Under the TRIPs Agreement." *New York University Journal of International Law and Politics* 29: 11–93.

———. 2000. "The TRIPs Agreement Comes of Age: Conflict or Cooperation with the Developing Countries." *Case Western Reserve Journal of International Law* 32: 441–470.

———. 2002. "Database Protection in a Global Economy." *Revue Internationale de Droit Economique* 2–3: 455–504.

Reichman, Jerome H., and Catherine Hasenzahl. 2002. *Non-Voluntary Licensing of Patented Inventions.* Geneva: UN Conference on Trade and Development/ International Centre for Trade and Sustainable Development.

Reichman, Jerome, and Paul Uhlir. 2003. "A Contractually Reconstructed Research Commons for Scientific Data in a Highly Protectionist Intellectual Property Environment." *Law and Contemporary Problems* 66, nos. 1 and 2: 315–462.

Reitz, John C. 2001. "Political Economy as a Major Architectural Principle of Public Law." *Tulane Law Review* 75, no. 4 (March): 1121–1157.

Renouard, A. C. [1844] 1987. *Traite des Brevets d'invention.* Paris: Conservatoire National des Arts et Metiers.

Resnick, Stephen, and Richard Wolff. 2003. "Exploitation, Consumption, and the Uniqueness of US Capitalism." *Historical Materialism* 11, no. 4: 209–226.

Richards, Donald G. 2002. "The Ideology of Intellectual Property Rights in the International Economy." *Review of Social Economy* 60, no. 4 (December): 521–541.

Ricketson, Sam. 1987. *The Berne Convention for the Protection of Literary and Artistic Works: 1886–1986.* London: Kluwer/Centre for Commercial Law Studies.

Ritter, Dominique S. 2004. "Switzerland's Patent Law History." *Fordham Intellectual Property Media and Entertainment Law Journal* 14, no. 2: 463–496.

Robinson, A. J. K. 1991. "The Evolution of Copyright, 1476–1776." *The Cambrian Law Review* 22: 55–77.

Robinson, Eric. 1972. "James Watt and the Law of Patents." *Technology and Culture* 13: 115–139.

Rogers, E. S. 1910. "Some Historical Matter Concerning Trademarks." *University of Michigan Law Review* 9: 29–43.

Root, Robert K. 1913. "Publication Before Printing." *Publications of the Modern Language Association* 28: 417–431.

Rose, Mark. 1993. *Authors and Owners. The Invention of Copyright.* Cambridge, MA: Harvard University Press.

———. 2002. "Copyright and Its Metaphors." *University of California Los Angeles Law Review* 50, no. 1: 1–15.

Rosenberg, Tina, 2001. "Look at Brazil." *New York Times* (Sunday magazine), 28 January. <http://www.nytimes.com/library/magazine/home/20010128mag .aids.html> (accessed 4 September 2004).

Ruggie, John Gerard. 1998. *Constructing the World Polity. Essays on International Institutionalization.* London: Routledge.

Ruston, Gerald. 1955. "On the Origin of Trademarks." *The Trade-Mark Reporter* 45: 127–144.

Sahai, Suman. 2003. "Indigenous Knowledge and Its Protection in India." In C. Bellmann, G. Dutfield, and R. Meléndez-Ortiz, eds., *Trading in Knowledge: Development Perspectives on TRIPS, Trade and Sustainability,* 166–174. London: Earthscan.

Salgar, Ana Maria. 2003. "Traditional Knowledge and the Biotrade: The Colombian Experience." In C. Bellmann, G. Dutfield, and R. Meléndez-Ortiz, eds., *Trading in Knowledge: Development Perspectives on TRIPS, Trade and Sustainability,* 184–189. London: Earthscan.

Samuelson, Pamela. 1997. "The U.S. Digital Agenda at WIPO." *Virginia Journal of International Law* 17: 369–439.

Saunders, David. 1993. "Purposes or Principle? Early Copyright and the Court of Chancery." *European Intellectual Property Review* (December): 452–456.

———. 1994. "Dropping the Subject: An Argument for a Positive History of Authorship and the Law of Copyright." In B. Sherman and A. Strowel, eds., *Of Authors and Origins: Essays in Copyright Law,* 93–110. Oxford: Clarendon Press.

Schiff, Eric. 1971. *Industrialisation Without National Patents: The Netherlands, 1869–1912; Switzerland, 1850–1907.* Princeton, NJ: Princeton University Press.

Scott, Brendan. 2001. "Copyright in a Frictionless World: Toward a Rhetoric of Responsibility." *First Monday* 6, no. 9 (September). <http://firstmonday.org/ issues/issues6_9/scott/index.html> (accessed 30 September 2001).

Sell, Susan K. 1996. "North-South Environmental Bargaining: Ozone, Climate Change, and Biodiversity." *Global Governance* 2, no. 1 (February): 93–116.

———. 1998. *Power and Ideas. North-South Politics of Intellectual Property and Antitrust.* Albany: State University of New York Press.

———. 2003. *Private Power, Public Law. The Globalisation of Intellectual Property Rights.* Cambridge: Cambridge University Press.

Sell, Susan, and Aseem Prakash. 2004. "Using Ideas Strategically: The Contest Between Business and NGO Networks in Intellectual Property." *International Studies Quarterly* 48: 143–175.

Sen, Gautam. 2003. "The United States and the GATT/WTO System." In R. Foot, S. N. MacFarlane, and M. Mastanduno, eds., *US Hegemony and International Organisations,* 115–139. Oxford: Oxford University Press.

Shanker, Daya. 2003. "Legitimacy and the TRIPs Agreement." *Journal of World Intellectual Property* 6, no. 1: 155–189.

Sherman, Brad. 1995. "Remembering and Forgetting: The Birth of Modern Copyright Law." *Intellectual Property Journal* 10 (December): 1–34.

Shiffrin, Seana Valentine. 2001. "Lockean Arguments for Private Intellectual Property." In S. R. Mumzer, ed., *New Essays in the Legal and Political Theory of Property,* 138–167. Cambridge: Cambridge University Press.

Shiva, Vandana. 1997. *Biopiracy: The Plunder of Nature and Knowledge.* Cambridge, MA: South End Press.

———. 2001. *Protect or Plunder? Understanding Intellectual Property Rights.* London: Zed Books.

Silverstein, David. 1991. "Patents, Science, and Innovation: Historical Linkages and Implications for Global Competitiveness." *Rutgers Computer and Technology Journal* 17, no. 2: 261–319.

Smith, Adam. [1776] 1993. *An Inquiry into the Nature and Causes of the Wealth of Nations.* World Classics ed. Oxford: Oxford University Press.

Smith, Pamela. 2001. "How Do Foreign Patent Rights Affect U.S. Exports, Affiliate Sales, and Licenses?" *Journal of International Economics* 55: 411–440.

Stearns, Laurie. 1992. "Copy Wrong: Plagiarism, Process, Property, and the Law." *California Law Review* 80, no. 2: 513–553.

Steinberg, Richard H. 2002. "In the Shadow of Law or Power? Consensus-Based Bargaining in the GATT/WTO." *International Organisation* 56, no. 2 (Spring): 339–374.

Stewart, S. 1977. "Two Hundred Years of English Copyright Law." In *Two Hundred Years of English and American Patent, Trademark, and Copyright Law.* Papers delivered at the Bicentennial Symposium of the Section of Patent, Trademark, and Copyright Law, Annual Meeting, Atlanta, Georgia, 9 August 1976. Chicago: American Bar Association/American Bar Centre.

Stewart, Terence P. 1993. *The GATT Uruguay Round. A Negotiating History (1986–1992).* Deventer, the Netherlands: Kluwer Law and Taxation Publishers.

Streibich, Harold C. 1975. "The Moral Right of Ownership to Intellectual Property: Part 1—From the Beginning to the Age of Printing." *Memphis State University Law Review* 6, no. 1: 1–35.

Suchman, Mark C. 1989. "Invention and Ritual: Notes on the Interrelation of Magic and Intellectual Property in Preliterate Societies." *Columbia Law Review* 89, no. 5 (June): 1264–1294.

Sullivan, Richard J. 1989. "England's 'Age of Invention': The Acceleration of Patents and Patentable Invention During the Industrial Revolution." *Explorations in Economic History* 26, no. 4 (October): 424–452.

Swinburne, James. 1886. "The Edison Filament Case." *The Telegraphic Journal and Electrical Review* 6 (August): 129–132.

Sykes, Katie. 2003. "Towards a Public Justification of Copyright." *University of Toronto Faculty of Law Review* 61, no. 1 (Winter): 1–38.

Thomas, Marcel. 1976. "Manuscripts." In L. Febvre and H-J. Martin. *The Coming of the Book. The Impact of Printing 1450–1800,* 15–26. London: NLB.

Thompson, James Westfall, ed. [1911] 1968. *The Frankfort Book Fair: The Francofordiense Emporium of Henri Estiemme.* With historical introduction. New York: Burt Franklin.

Thrupp, Sylvia L. 1963. "The Gilds." In M. M. Postan, E. E. Rich, and E. Miller, eds., *Economic Organisation and Policies in the Middle Ages.* Vol. 3 of *The Cambridge Economic History of Europe,* 230–280. Cambridge: Cambridge University Press.

Tooze, Roger, and Christopher May. 2002. *Authority and Markets: Susan Strange's*

Writings on International Political Economy. Basingstoke, UK: PalgraveMacmillan.

Tschmuck, Peter. 2002. "Creativity Without Copyright: Music Production in Vienna in the Late Eighteenth Century." In R. Towse, ed., *Copyright in the Cultural Industries,* 210–220. London: Edward Elgar.

Tyler, Tom R. 1997. "Compliance with Intellectual Property Laws: A Psychological Perspective." *New York University Journal of International Law and Policy* 29: 219–235.

Uhlendorf, B. A. 1932. "The Invention of Printing and Its Spread till 1470, with Special Reference to Social and Economic Factors." *The Library Quarterly* 2, no. 3: 179–231.

Utkarsh, Ghate. 2003. "Documentation of Traditional Knowledge: People's Biodiversity Registers." In C. Bellmann, G. Dutfield, and R. Meléndez-Ortiz, eds., *Trading in Knowledge: Development Perspectives on TRIPS, Trade, and Sustainability,* 190–195. London: Earthscan.

Vaidhyanathan, Siva. 2001. *Copyrights and Copywrongs: The Rise of Intellectual Property and How It Threatens Creativity.* New York: New York University Press.

Vaitsos, Constantine. 1972. "Patents Revisited: Their Function in Developing Countries." Special issue: Science and Technology Development, *Journal of Development Studies* 9, no. 1 (October): 71–97.

Vaver, David. 2001. "Recreating a Fair Intellectual Property System for the 21st Century." *Intellectual Property Journal* 15, no. 2: 123–141.

Verma, S. K. 1996. "TRIPs—Development and Technological Transfer." *International Review of Industrial Property and Copyright Law* 27, no. 3: 331–364.

VerSteeg, Russ. 2000. "The Roman Law Roots of Copyright." *Maryland Law Review* 59: 522–552.

Vukmir, Mladen. 1992. "The Roots of Anglo-American Intellectual Property Law in Roman Law." *IDEA—The Journal of Law and Technology* 32, no. 2: 123–154.

Wade, Robert Hunter. 2003. "What Strategies Are Viable for Developing Countries Today? The World Trade Organisation and the Shrinking of 'Development Space.'" *Review of International Political Economy* 10, no. 4 (November): 621–644.

Waldron, Jeremy. 1993. "From Authors to Copiers: Individual Rights and Social Values in Intellectual Property." *Chicago-Kent Law Review* 68: 841–887.

Walterscheid, Edward C. 1994a. "The Early Evolution of the United States Patent Law: Antecedents (Part 1)." *Journal of the Patent and Trademark Office Society* 76 (February): 77–107.

———. 1994b. "The Early Evolution of the United States Patent Law: Antecedents (Part 2)." *Journal of the Patent and Trademark Office Society* 76 (September): 697–715.

———. 1995a. "The Early Evolution of the United States Patent Law: Antecedents (Part 3:1)." *Journal of the Patent and Trademark Office Society* 77 (October): 771–802.

———. 1995b. "The Early Evolution of the United States Patent Law: Antecedents (Part 3:2)." *Journal of the Patent and Trademark Office Society* 77 (November): 847–857.

———. 1996. "The Early Evolution of the United States Patent Law: Antecedents (Part 4)." *Journal of the Patent and Trademark Office Society* 78 (February): 77–107.

Waltz, Kenneth. 1979. *Theory of International Politics.* Reading, MA: Addison-Wesley.

Warner, Julian. 1999. "Information Society or Cash Nexus? A Study of the United States as a Copyright Haven." *Journal of the American Society for Information Science* 50, no. 5 (April): 461–470.

Warner, Mark. 2002. "Global Intellectual Property Rights: Boundaries of Access and Enforcement: Panel I: AIDS Drugs and the Developing World: The Role of Patents in the Access of Medicines." *Fordham Intellectual Property, Media, and Entertainment Law Journal* 12 (Spring): 675–751.

Watal, Jayashree. 2003. *Intellectual Property Rights in the WTO and Developing Countries.* New Delhi: Oxford India Paperbacks.

Weeraworawit, Weerawit. 2003. "International Legal Protection for Genetic Resources, Traditional Knowledge, and Folklore: Challenges for the Intellectual Property System." In C. Bellmann, G. Dutfield, and R. Meléndez-Ortiz, eds., *Trading in Knowledge: Development Perspectives on TRIPS, Trade, and Sustainability,* 157–165. London: Earthscan.

Wegner, Harold C. 1993. *Patent Harmonisation.* London: Sweet and Maxwell.

Weiler, Joseph H. H. 2000. *The Rule of Lawyers and the Ethos of Diplomats: Reflections on the Internal and External Legitimacy of WTO Dispute Settlement.* Harvard Jean Monnet Working Paper 9/00. Cambridge, MA: Harvard Law School.

Wilkins, Mira. 1992. "The Neglected Intangible Asset: The Influence of the Trade Mark on the Rise of the Modern Corporation." *Business History* 34, no. 1 (January): 66–95.

Williston, Samuel. 1909. "The History of the Law of Business Corporations Before 1800." In *Select Essays in Anglo-American Legal History,* vol. 3. Cambridge: Cambridge University Press.

Wilson, Nigel. 1977. "The Book Trade in Venice ca 1400–1515." In H. G. Beck, M. Manoussacas, and A. Pertusi, eds., *Venzia. Centro di Mediazione fra Oriente e Occidente (secoli XV–XVI): Aspekti e Problemi,* 381–397. Vol. 2. Florence: Leo. S. Olschki.

Woodbury, L. 1968. "Pindar and the Mercenary Muse: *ISTHM.* 2.1–13." *Transactions and Proceedings of the American Philological Association* 99: 527–542.

Woodmansee, Martha. 1984. "The Genius and the Copyright: Economic and Legal Conditions of the Emergence of the 'Author.'" *Eighteenth Century Studies* 17: 425–448.

Woodmansee, Martha, and Peter Jaszi. 2004. "Copyright in Transition." Paper presented at Queen Mary/ESRC Research Seminar, "Intellectual Property Rights, Economic Development, and Social Welfare: What Does History Tell Us?" Edinburgh, 9 July.

———, eds. 1994. *The Construction of Authorship. Textual Appropriation in Law and Literature.* Durham, NC: Duke University Press.

World Bank. 2002. *Global Economic Prospects and the Developing Countries.* Washington, DC: International Bank for Reconstruction and Development.

World Intellectual Property Organisation [WIPO]. 1988. *Background Reading Material on Intellectual Property.* WIPO Publication 40. Geneva: WIPO.

———. 2002. *WIPO Patent Agenda: Options for Development of the International Patent System.* Document A/37/6. Geneva: WIPO.

Yu, Peter. 2004. "The Escalating Copyright Wars." *Hofstra Law Review* 32 (Spring): 907–951.

Zoundjihekpon, Jeanne. 2003. "The Revised Bangui Agreement and Plant Variety Protection in OAPI Countries." In C. Bellmann, G. Dutfield, and R. Meléndez-Ortiz, eds., *Trading in Knowledge: Development Perspectives on TRIPs, Trade, and Sustainability,* 109–116. London: Earthscan Publications.

Index

About the Book

WITH INTELLECTUAL property widely acknowledged today as a key component of economic development, those accused of stealing knowledge and information are also charged with undermining industrial innovation, artistic creativity, and the availability of information itself. How valid are these claims? Has the Trade Related Aspects of Intellectual Property Rights (TRIPs) Agreement ushered in a new, better era? Christopher May and Susan Sell trace the history of social conflict and political machinations surrounding the making of property out of knowledge.

Ranging from ancient commerce in Greek poems to present-day controversies about online piracy and the availability of AIDS drugs in the poorest countries, May and Sell present intellectual property law as a continuing process in which particular conceptions of rights and duties are institutionalized; each settlement prompts new disputes, policy shifts, and new disputes again. They also examine the post-TRIPs era in the context of this process. Their account of two thousand years of technological advances, legal innovation, and philosophical arguments about the character of knowledge production suggests that the future of intellectual property law will be as contested as its past.

Christopher May is professor of political economy at Lancaster University. His recent publications include *The Information Society: A Sceptical View* and *A Global Political Economy of Intellectual Property Rights: The New Enclosures?* **Susan K. Sell** is associate professor of political science at George Washington University. She is author of *Private Power, Public Law: The Globalization of Intellectual Property Rights* and *Power and Ideas: North-South Politics of Intellectual Property and Antitrust.*